LEGENDARY LOCALS OF RAWLINS WYOMING

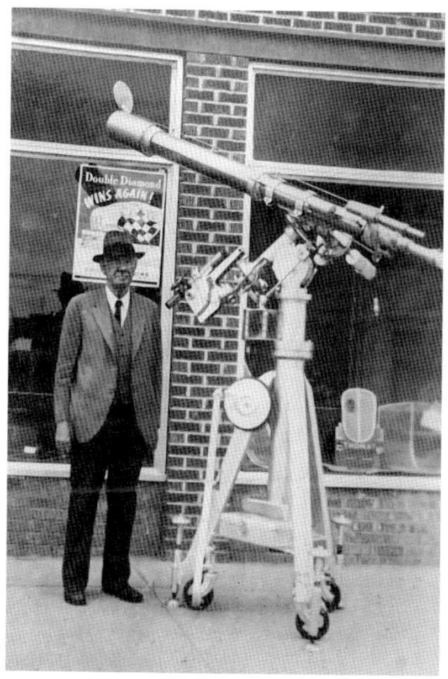

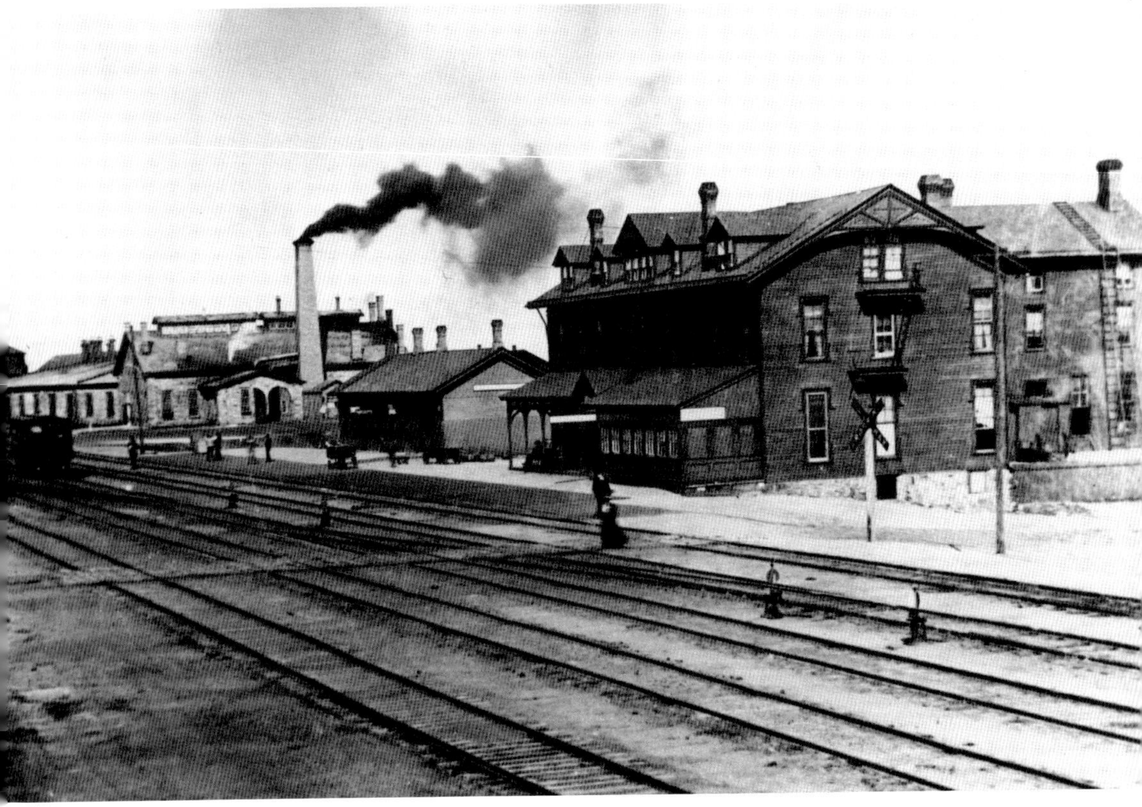

Old Railroad Depot
The Union Pacific Railroad's tracks reached Cheyenne in 1867 and entered Carbon County in the spring of 1868. Just a few months later, Rawlins was born. This photograph was taken around 1880 and shows the old railroad depot. (Courtesy Carbon County Museum.)

Page 1: Stargazer
Early Rawlins resident D.C. Kinnaman is seen in front of his shop with one of his homemade telescopes. See page 41 for his story. (Courtesy Daniel L. Kinnaman.)

LEGENDARY LOCALS

OF

RAWLINS

WYOMING

HAN CHEUNG

LEGENDARY LOCALS

ISBN 978-1-4671-0175-2

Legendary Locals is an imprint of Arcadia Publishing
Charleston, South Carolina

Printed in the United States of America

Library of Congress Control Number: 2014936975

For all general information, please contact Arcadia Publishing:
Telephone 843-853-2070
Fax 843-853-0044
E-mail sales@arcadiapublishing.com
For customer service and orders:
Toll-Free 1-888-313-2665

Visit us on the Internet at www.arcadiapublishing.com

Dedication
To Mom and Dad, who fostered in me a thirst for knowledge and showed me what dedication means. I hope this book makes you proud.

On the Cover: Clockwise from top left:
Valerie Nelson, first female railroad engineer in Wyoming (courtesy Valerie Nelson; see page 51), Charles W. Jeffrey, doctor and philanthropist (courtesy *Rawlins Daily Times*; see page 69), Bud Ford, World War II veteran (photograph by Han Cheung; see page 80), Lillian Heath, first female doctor in Wyoming (courtesy Carbon County Museum; see page 26), Isaac Miller, first Rawlins mayor (courtesy Rawlins National Bank; see page 44), Clare Espy, early cowboy (courtesy Carbon County Museum; see page 10), Jesse Garcia, Hollywood actor (courtesy El Rey Network; see page 101); Bill Williams, longtime high school art teacher (photograph by Jerry Raehal, courtesy *Rawlins Daily Times*; see page 95), and Big Nose George, infamous outlaw (courtesy Carbon County Museum; see page 24).

On the Back Cover: From left to right:
Bootleggers during the Prohibition era (courtesy Carbon County Museum; see page 39) and Rawlins SummerFest (photograph by Han Cheung, courtesy *Rawlins Daily Times*; see page 115).

CONTENTS

ACKNOWLEDGMENTS

I had never heard of Rawlins until I was offered a job here in 2012. After about four months as city reporter, I was assigned to start a weekly historical column for the paper.

Having no idea what to write about, I visited the Carbon County Museum. I still remember how warmly I was received and how the staff members provided me with so many story ideas I didn't know where to start.

Thus began a partnership that has been going strong for almost two years. I would like to thank the museum staff for making research at the museum so easy. I would not have learned this much about the area without you.

Of course, this book would not have happened without the support of the *Rawlins Daily Times*. I would like to thank Holly Dabb and Gavin Elliott for encouraging my ever-growing interest in historical writing. I would like to thank Holly Dabb again for allowing me to use materials belonging to the *Daily Times* for this book.

I would like to thank historians Dan Kinnaman, Rans Baker, Dan Meschter, and Lori Van Pelt for researching and writing about Rawlins before I did so I would have excellent reference materials.

I would like to thank Kelly Ferris for reading over my text every time I finished one entry or sometimes even one paragraph.

Finally, I would like to thank the people of Rawlins for welcoming me with open arms and believing in my efforts. You are what make this book—and this book is for you.

INTRODUCTION

Like most southern Wyoming towns, Rawlins owes its existence to the Union Pacific Railroad. In 1860, the company began a vigorous westward expansion of what would eventually become the first transcontinental railroad. Its tracks entered the boundaries of today's Wyoming in 1867. The same year, Union Pacific chief engineer Grenville Dodge set out to cross the Laramie Mountains on a surveying trip. With him was Gen. John A. Rawlins, a Civil War veteran who was suffering from a respiratory ailment. Rawlins was hoping the drier air of the West would help his condition.

The party ran out of water somewhere in present-day Carbon County. Growing desperate, Dodge discovered a spring near where the town of Rawlins now stands.

General Rawlins proclaimed it to be the most refreshing water he had ever tasted. He also proclaimed that if anything would ever be named after him, he would want it to be a spring of water.

"We will name this Rawlins Springs," Dodge responded immediately.

The next year, a railroad town sprang up near Rawlins Springs and took the name of the lifesaving water source. In the early days, official documents from Cheyenne would frequently misspell the town's name as "Rawling's Springs." Soon, it became known simply as "Rawlins."

Many "hell on wheels" towns along the railroad disappeared as quickly as they sprang up. Rawlins, however, was a permanent settlement because the Union Pacific designated it as a division point and a transportation hub.

When Benton—11 miles to the east—vanished without a trace in the summer of 1868 after only existing for a few months, many of its former residents moved to Rawlins.

By 1880, more than 1,000 people were living north of the train tracks.

Rawlins went through its Wild West days when shootings were an everyday occurrence and lynchings were common. Probably the most famous outlaw of all time, Butch Cassidy, had a hideout near Baggs, just 45 miles south of Rawlins.

Law and order started to come to Rawlins after it became incorporated in 1890. The first mayor formed a police force to combat vigilante behavior. The town soon prospered as a booming sheep center.

Because of the boom-and-bust nature of the area, many families have come and gone. A prime example is the early 1980s, when scores flocked to Rawlins riding a mineral boom. The bottom fell out three years later, people left, and businesses collapsed.

There have been Spanish surnames in town since the early days, but it wasn't until the 1940s that Latino families from the American Southwest started coming to Rawlins, drawn by railroad jobs that became available when the Japanese workers were sent to internment camps during World War II.

Mexican immigrants didn't start coming in until the 1960s and 1970s. Latinos are now an integral part of the town, constituting about 25 percent of the population.

As the town has no university, Rawlins High School sports, arts, and music are a source of pride and entertainment for many residents. Residents can often be spotted in town wearing red, black, and white Outlaw (the school mascot) apparel.

Today, Rawlins is home to the Wyoming State Penitentiary and is an anchor point for the nearby oil, gas, and uranium industries. Many residents work at the nearby Sinclair Wyoming Oil Refinery. With several energy projects on the horizon, locals have been waiting eagerly for the next boom, which may or may not happen in the next few years.

To most travelers, Rawlins is just a blip on the Overland Trail, the Lincoln Highway, the Continental Divide Trail, and Interstate 80. Those who decide to stop and look around, however, will find a place rich with history and a home to many legendary people with legendary stories.

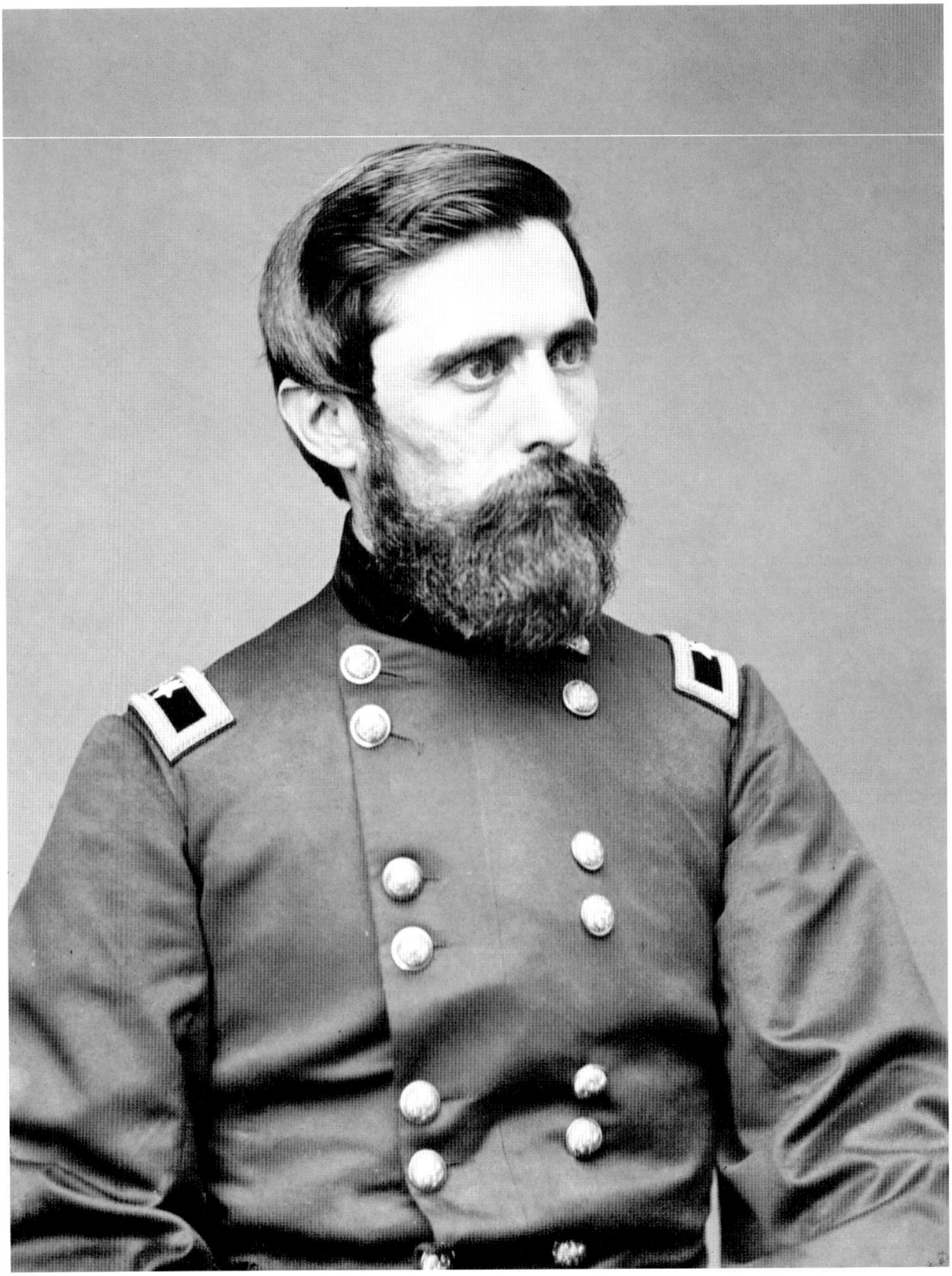

John A. Rawlins

Rawlins is named after Gen. John A. Rawlins, a Civil War veteran who accompanied Union Pacific chief engineer Grenville Dodge on a westward expedition out of Laramie in hopes that the dry plains air would help his tuberculosis. The party ran out of water and discovered a spring near present-day Rawlins. The life-saving water source was dubbed "Rawlins Springs," and the town that sprang up near the springs in turn took on the general's name. (Courtesy Library of Congress.)

CHAPTER ONE

Cowboys and Outlaws

When people decided to "go west" to find their fortunes in the 19th century, they would often end up in Rawlins.

It was a hardscrabble town, but it was also a place of opportunity. Aside from investing in mining operations, the best way to get rich was to file a homestead, acquire livestock, and become a cowboy.

There were no fences back then, and cowboys had to gather their cattle on the open range. "You just had to get out in the morning and ride until you found what you were looking for," Clare Espy explained in a newspaper article published shortly before his death. "You ride, make a circle, get your stuff in and brand up yours, get mine, and take them home."

Cattle roundup operations could become massive. George Glass remembered a force of 300 from the Powder, Sweetwater, and Platte Rivers that worked together for 10 days dividing cattle.

Then there were the outlaws. Former Wyoming governor Fenimore Chatterton described the town as a place where "the bark of the forty-five gun and the whiz of a leaden missile in the night was a constant reminder that one would do better to stay indoors." Former county coroner C.W. Jeffrey once said, "If there was a week went by without a killing we would wonder what was wrong."

In the early days, before there was a regular police force, the sheriff would round up his posse, and the group would set out on horseback searching for criminals. One of the more notable arrests in the area was that of William Carlisle, also known as the "White-Masked Bandit." Rubie Rivera, the sheriff who caught the outlaw, once said that while Carlisle was the most famous outlaw he dealt with, he wasn't the scariest.

This chapter also tells the stories of homesteaders clashing against wealthy land barons, a courageous rescue ride, and a wild stallion that could not be captured.

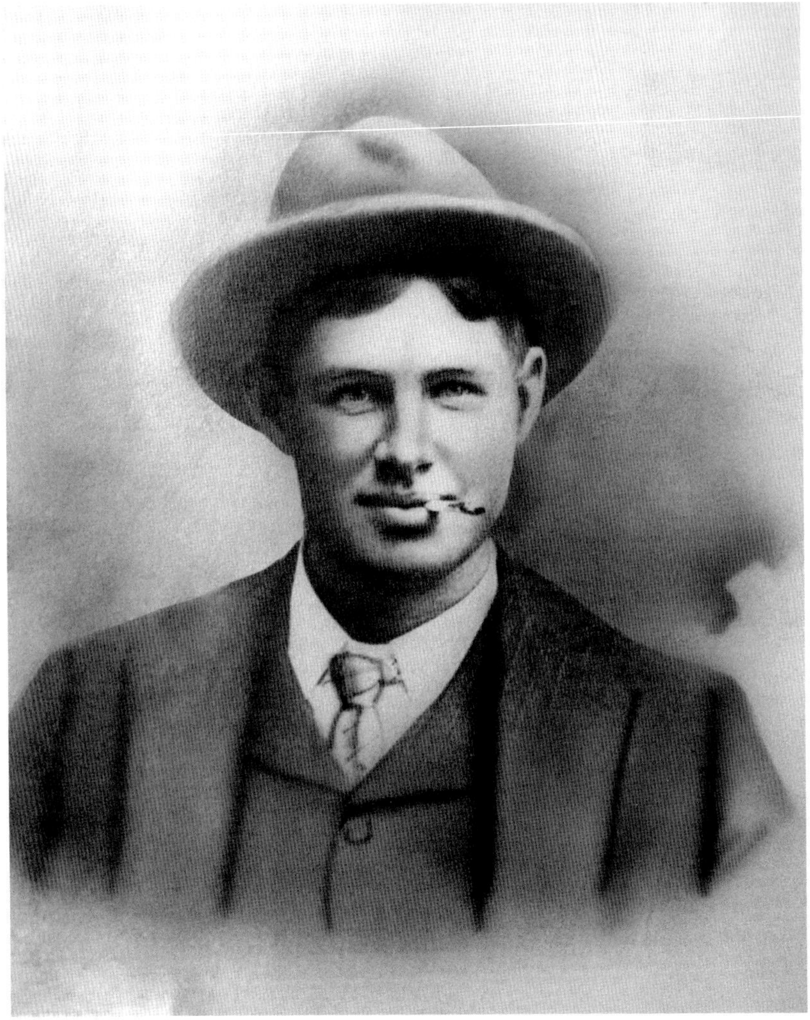

Clare Espy

Clare Espy was 12 years old when he set out from Nebraska in 1895 by himself. His destination: Rawlins.

Espy was one of many adventurers who arrived in Wyoming in the late 19th century hoping to make names for themselves on the open range. Despite stopping to pick up a hitchhiker and having to fix a broken wheel, Espy completed the trip in 10 days. He brought with him six horses and two wagons.

How does a young boy with a dirty shirt find a job in the Wild West? "I was sitting in front of Murphy's Corner on Fifth Street—there were big steps back then—and a fellow named Ben Casey came along and wanted to know if I wanted a job," Espy recalled years later.

He worked as a dishwasher for about six weeks and then headed to the popular outlaw hangout area of the Snake River, where he called himself a "renegade." When asked if he met any notorious outlaws, he replied, "They were all wild, I'm telling you. All the crooks held out at Snake River."

Espy said the lawmen in the area pretty much just let the outlaws be. "They would shoot up the town, have a lot of fun and away they would go," he recalled.

Espy found work at his uncle Mose Doze's sheep outfit and later became a "cowpuncher"—another term for ranch hand.

By 1922, Espy owned a ranch south of Rawlins with 100 cattle and horses. The Espys are still prominent ranchers in the area. (Courtesy Carbon County Museum.)

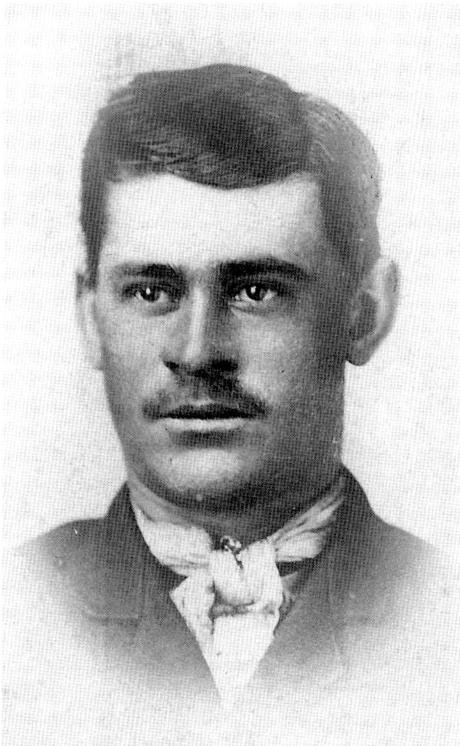

George Glass
Glass also left home at a young age to find his fortune. Born in 1861 in California, he took a job shipping 600 head of cattle to Nevada when he was 14 years old. Glass later took part in driving 12,000 cattle from Oregon to the Rawlins area. "I was determined to take the first train back to California, and I'm still here," he told the *Rawlins Republican* in 1938. He chose his line of work because it was exciting for a young man and because it was an opportunity to see the country. (Courtesy Carbon County Museum.)

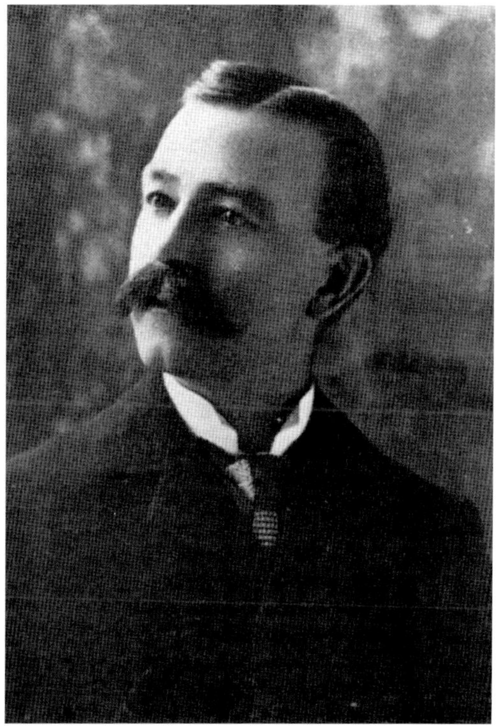

George Wren, Carbon County Museum
A barber in New York, Wren spent all his savings on a train ticket that brought him as far as Rawlins. He continued his barber trade in town until he had enough money to buy a few head of cattle and start ranching. After Wren's herd was wiped out in a bad winter, he returned to town and managed the Ferris Hotel and also worked as the county clerk. (Courtesy Carbon County Museum.)

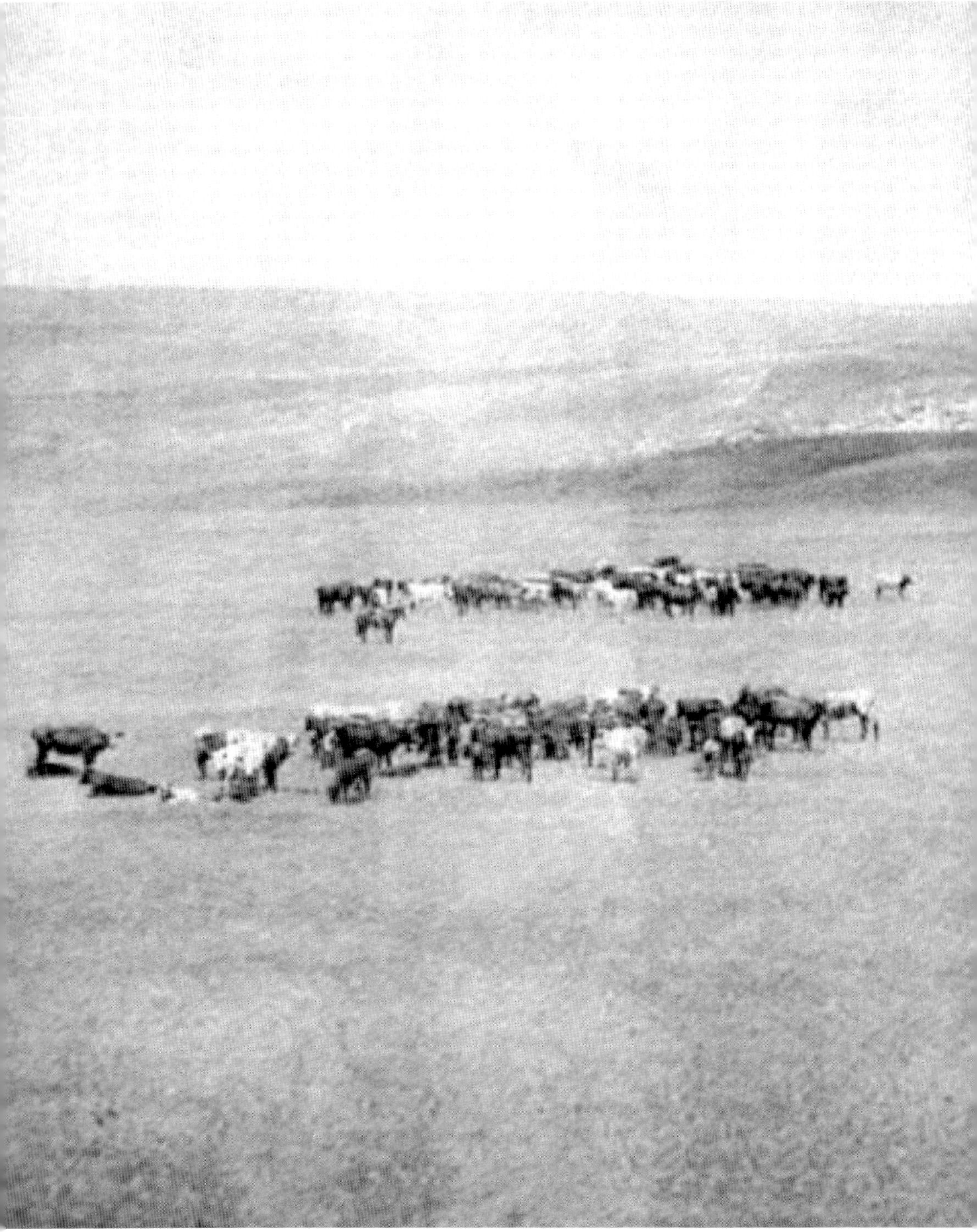

Cowboy Roundup

George Glass recalled a roundup force of 300 from the Powder, Sweetwater, and Platte Rivers that worked together for 10 days dividing cattle into separate roundups. This photograph shows a different

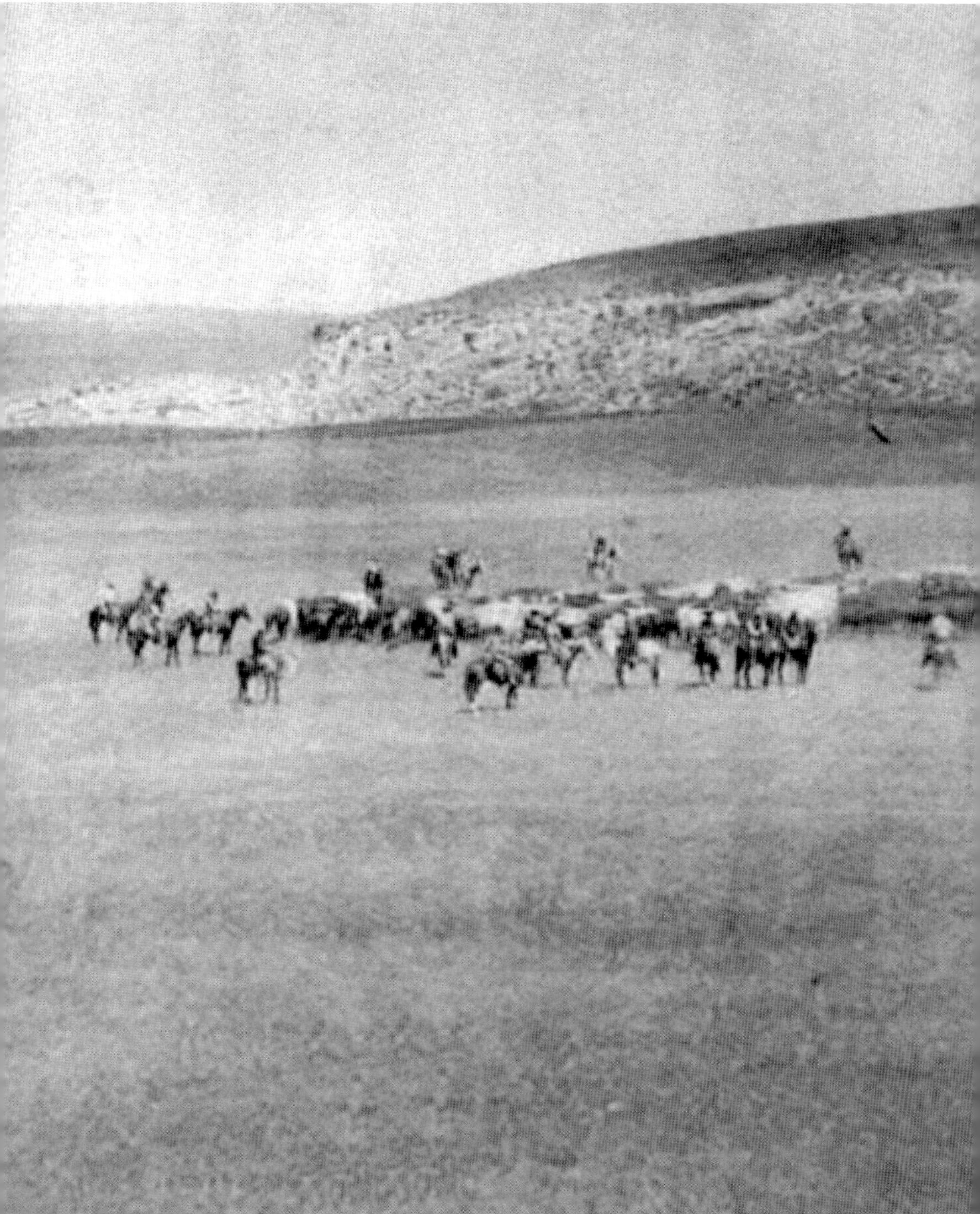

roundup that was similar in nature. (Courtesy Carbon County Museum.)

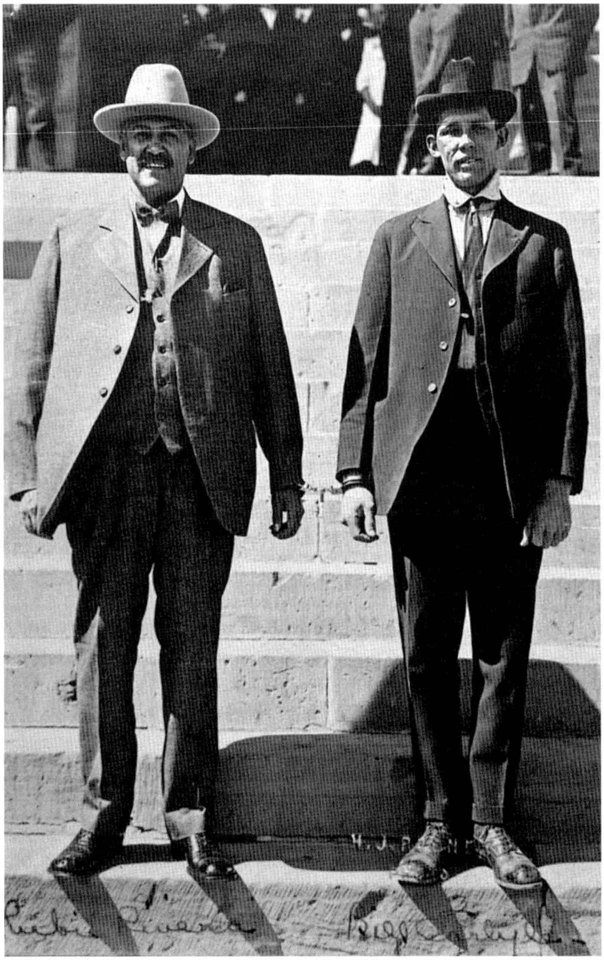

Rubie Rivera and William Carlisle

In the spring of 1916, the train robber known as the "White-Masked Bandit" struck for the third time in two months—this time, it was near Walcott, about 20 miles from Rawlins.

As usual, William Carlisle covered his face with a white bandana, robbed only men, and apologized to women and children when he disturbed them.

The Carbon County sheriff at that time was Rubie Rivera, a member of an old Spanish ranching family in Los Angeles. Rivera came to Wyoming in 1882 on a massive sheep and cattle drive from California during which he was in charge of 3,000 sheep. In Wyoming, Rivera had a reputation for being a daredevil and gambler. Many times, he lost all his earnings playing poker until he quit for good in 1889.

Shortly after the Walcott robbery, Rivera gathered a posse and set out from Rawlins. He followed the tracks all night and was joined by lawmen from Laramie and Cheyenne in the morning. Around 3:00 p.m., a posse member found Carlisle at a river bottom. The outlaw surrendered on the spot and was taken to Rawlins.

Rivera and his posse claimed the Union Pacific Railroad's $6,500 reward for the outlaw. The next day, Rivera and Carlisle, linked by handcuffs, had their photograph taken in front of the Rawlins courthouse. The photographs were reportedly sold on the street for 50¢ each.

Rivera went after Carlisle again when the bandit escaped from the state penitentiary and robbed another train three years later. But this time someone else prevailed, and Carlisle was taken back to Rawlins, where he was incarcerated until his parole in 1936. (Courtesy Carbon County Museum.)

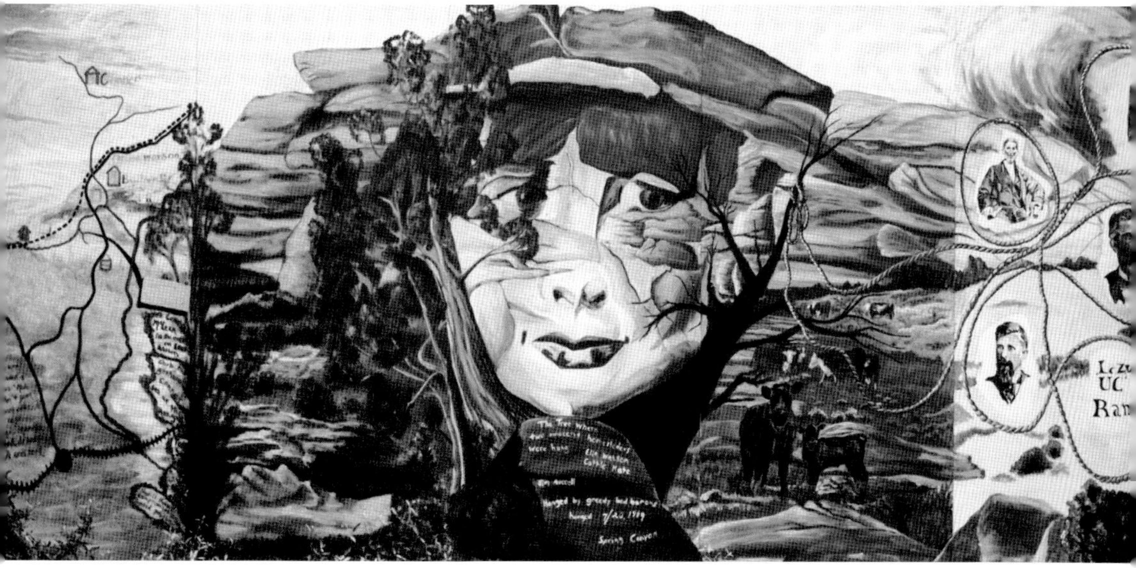

Cattle Kate Mural

A mural by Dianne Johansson hangs outside the *Rawlins Daily Times* building with the words "Two innocent homesteaders hanged here. Hanged by greedy land barons, 7/20/1889" on the bottom.

Most Rawlinsites can tell you the story: Six prominent cattle barons abducted homesteaders Ella Watson and James Averell, accused them of cattle rustling, and hanged them near the northern border of Carbon County. Watson was the only woman ever known to be lynched in Wyoming. The perpetrators were apprehended but never went to trial.

The press played a significant part in justifying the perpetrators' actions. Many of the newspapers were mouthpieces for the powerful Stock Grower's Association, and they slandered the victims while painting the barons in a positive light.

The Cheyenne papers called the pair "cattle rustlers" and incorrectly (and perhaps purposely) identified Watson as a prostitute named "Cattle Kate" who traded sex for calves. It was a blatant smear campaign. The journalists probably got the name "Kate" from Kate Maxwell, a prostitute and alleged murderer who lived about 20 miles away.

Today, the mural on the newspaper building serves as a reminder for the journalists working inside to stay honest and fair. (Photograph by Han Cheung, mural by Dianne Johansson.)

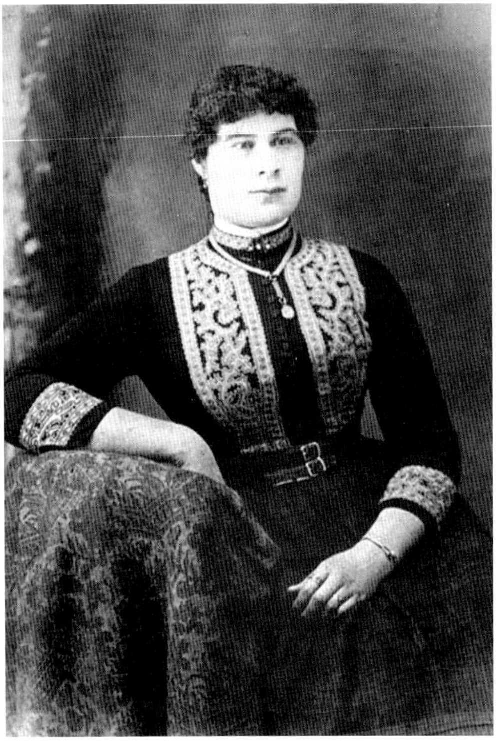

Cattle Kate
The legend of Cattle Kate stuck until the 1970s, when George Hufsmith unearthed a completely different version of events while doing research for his opera about the incident. Who was the real Ella Watson? It is known that she was a Canadian immigrant. She left an abusive marriage in Kansas and eventually drifted to Wyoming in a time when few women traveled alone. She found work in Rawlins as a cook and waitress before meeting widower James Averell. (Courtesy Carbon County Museum.)

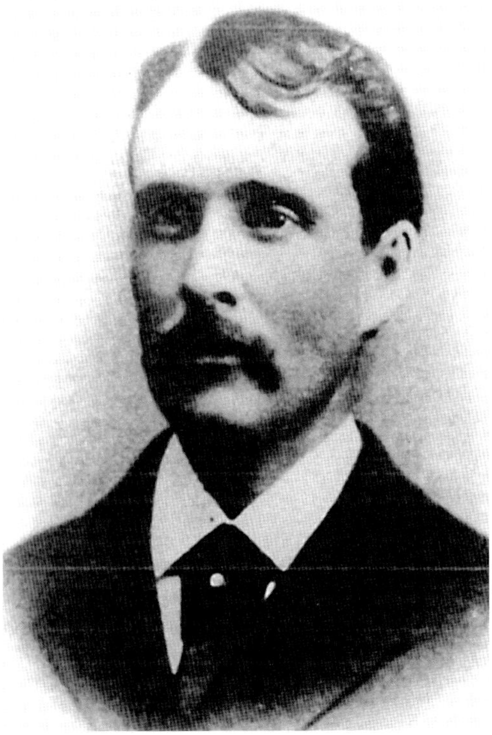

James Averell
Like Watson, Averell was also Canadian. In 1886, he established a homestead about 50 miles north of Rawlins. Shortly after meeting Watson, he hired her as a cook. Watson would later file her own homestead on land adjacent to Averell's. The two were reportedly married but kept it a secret because only single women could file homestead claims at the time.

According to historian Daniel Meschter, the cattle barons wanted Averell's and Watson's land, but the pair refused to sell. Averell angered the barons further by writing letters to local newspapers criticizing them.

"The lynching was simply an attempt to run Jim and Ella out of the country that got out of hand," Meschter wrote. (Courtesy Carbon County Museum.)

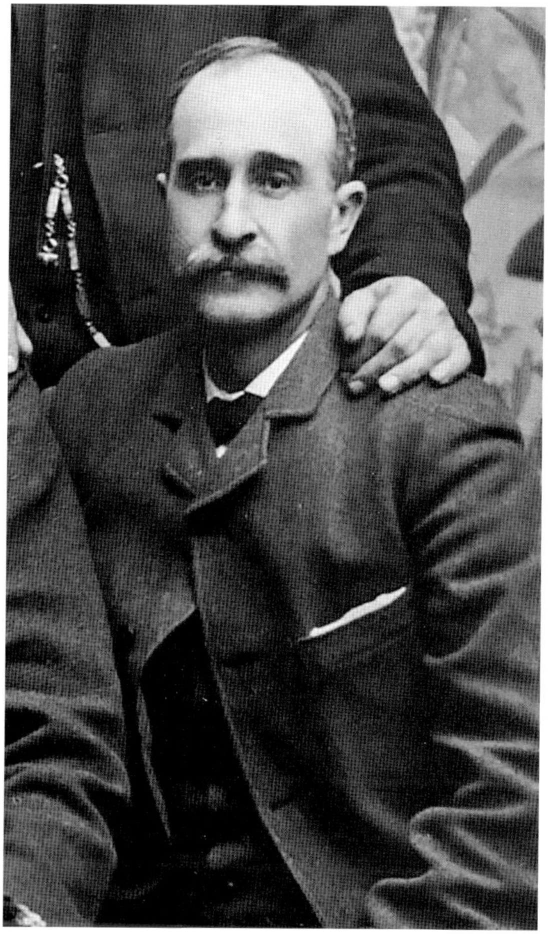

Joe Rankin's Ride

In the late 1800s, seven members of the Rankin clan left Pennsylvania and came to Carbon County in search of a better life.

The family became well known in Rawlins, the most famous of them probably being Joseph. As an Army scout, he made a remarkable 165-mile rescue ride from Colorado to Rawlins in a little over 27 hours.

In 1879, Rankin was accompanying Maj. T.T. Thornburgh on a 160-man expedition from Rawlins to the White River Ute Agency in Colorado. The party was ambushed by an army of Utes about 25 miles north of the agency, and Thornburgh was killed in the attack. The party fell under siege, and Rankin volunteered to ride back to Rawlins to seek help.

Rankin and four other soldiers set out in the dark. They successfully evaded the enemies, and Rankin continued alone. The trip usually would have taken two days, but Rankin made it in about half the time, arriving on Front Street in the early morning of October 1.

Rankin was said to have stopped by the Foote Saloon for a drink before heading to the telegraph office. The telegram reached Gen. George Crook in Chicago, and Gen. Wesley Merritt mobilized a rescue force from Fort Russell near Cheyenne.

Rankin was enlisted as a guide again. The rescue team left Rawlins on the morning of October 2 and reached the besieged party in 72 hours, ending the six-day siege.

Rankin's job was over, and he headed back to Rawlins—this time, at his own leisurely pace. (Courtesy Carbon County Museum.)

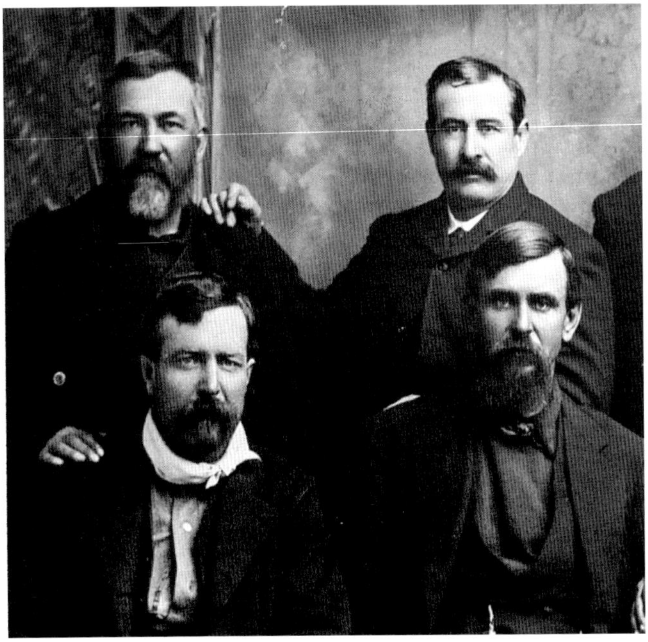

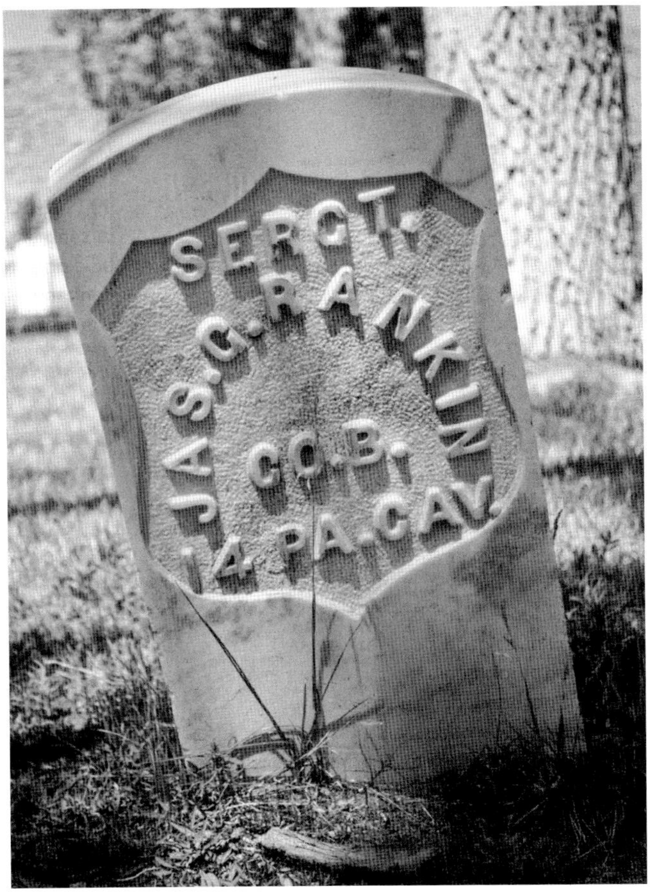

James Rankin

The lives of brothers James and Joseph Rankin diverged soon after they arrived in Rawlins. James Rankin established himself as a lawman early on as a frequent member of then-sheriff Bill Hawley's posse, which would ride out to fight Native Americans and accost criminals.

Rankin ran a livery stable in town and became undersheriff in 1876. He made a good name for himself, apprehending the culprits of the Percy Train Robbery and killing Frank Murray right after Murray shot a man in a bar dispute.

As sheriff in 1880, Rankin traveled to Montana to arrest Big Nose George. His later accomplishments include running the Rawlins-Saratoga stage line and taking part in organizing the town of Grand Encampment. He is the only Rankin buried in Rawlins. He is pictured at top in the back row at left. (Top, courtesy Carbon County Museum; bottom, photograph by Han Cheung.)

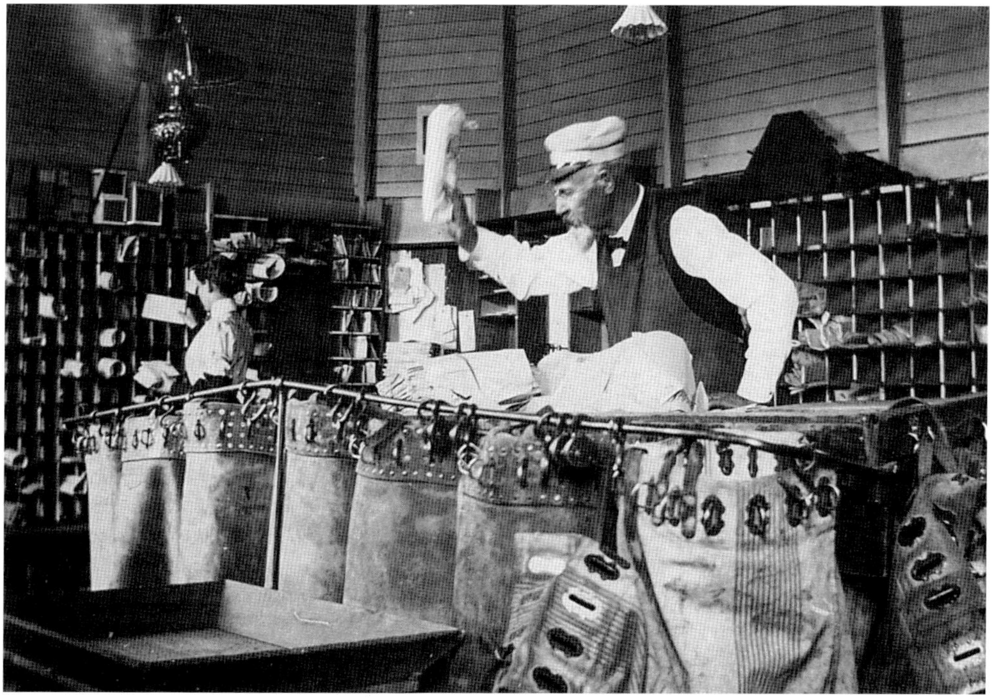

Perry Smith

Perry Smith was James Rankin's brother-in-law. He ran a butcher shop in town and employed local men as hunters. It is said that in the winter of 1870–1871, he shipped 1,500 antelope and deer to San Francisco.

Smith was one of the first three Carbon County commissioners in 1869. He later served as county clerk and postmaster and was on the territorial legislature. He was the one to introduce the bill for the construction of the original Carbon County courthouse. (Both courtesy Carbon County Museum.)

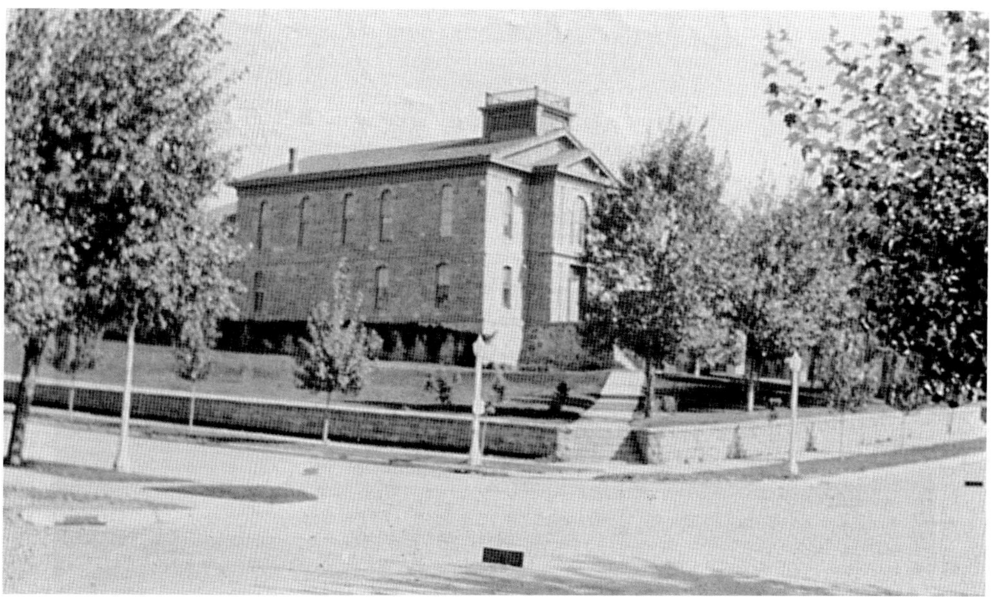

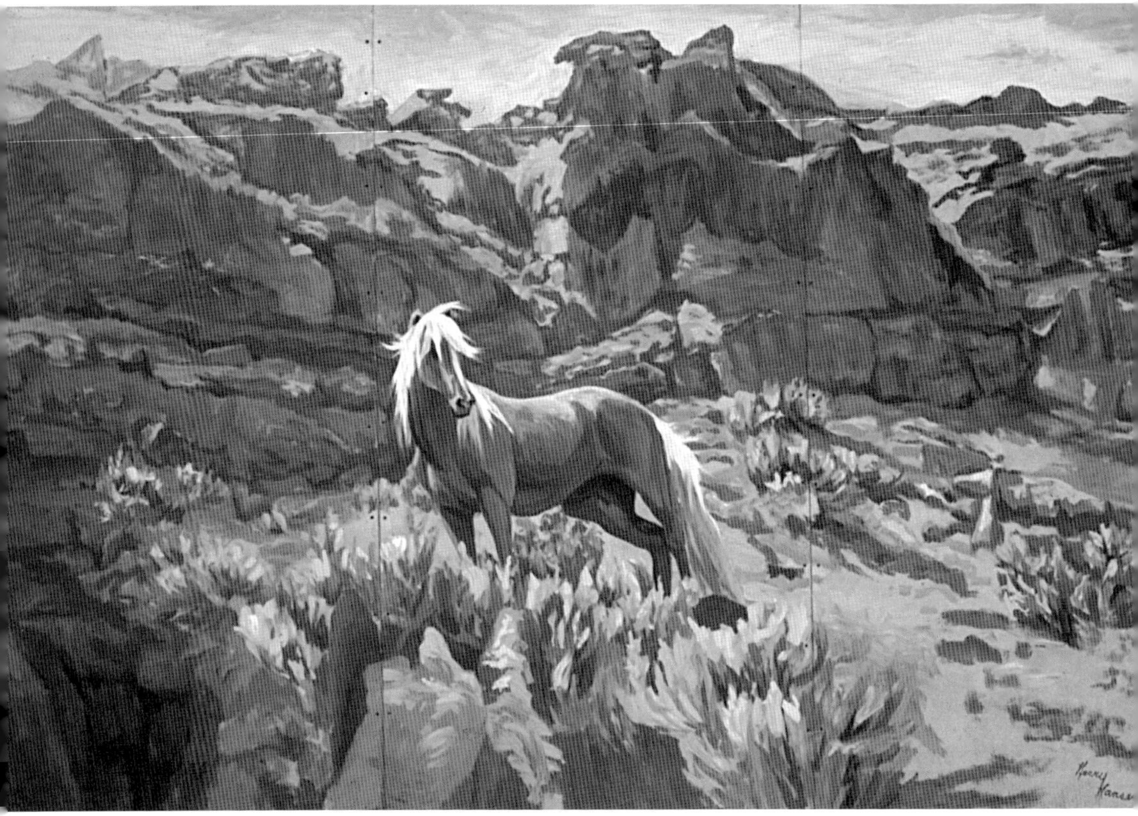

The Dust Never Settles

They called him Desert Dust for his ability to disappear into the Red Desert. He was a wild palomino stallion that reportedly weighed 1,200 pounds and led a band of 18 mares and 15 colts.

This was before the passage of the Wild and Free Roaming Horse and Burro Act of 1971, and people were allowed to help themselves to unbranded horses on federal lands. The captured horses would often be sent to slaughterhouses in the East.

Many tried to capture Desert Dust in the late 1930s and early 1940s, but nobody succeeded until the day a rancher and a photographer took on the task. (Photograph by Han Cheung; mural by Kerry Hanson.)

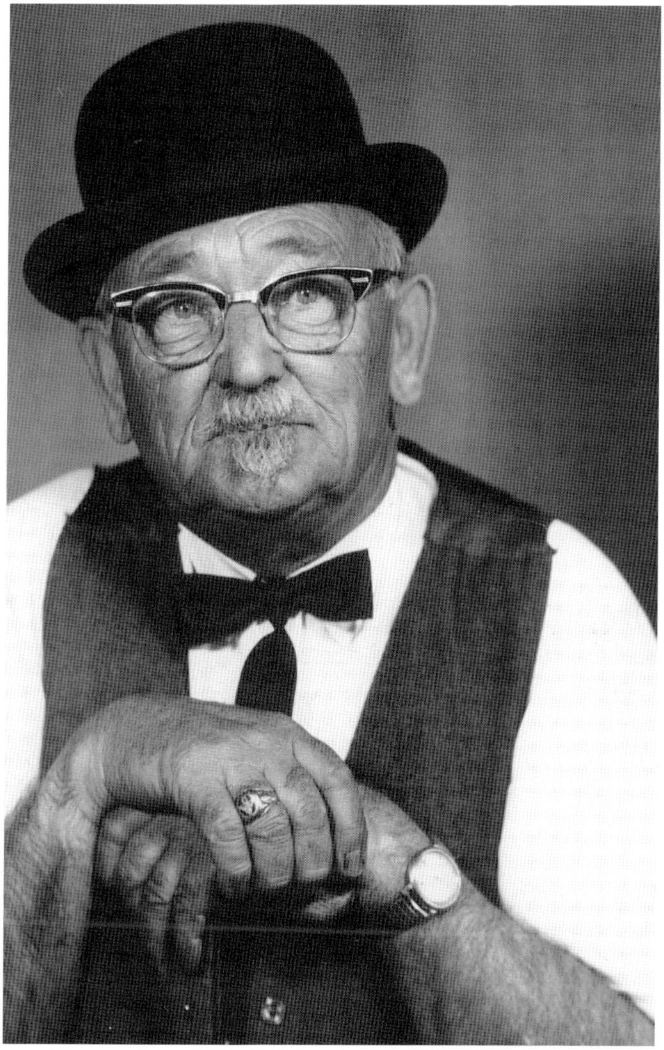

Vern Wood

In July 1945, Glenrock rancher Frank Robbins arrived in the Red Desert area to round up wild horses. With him was Rawlins photographer Vern Wood.

Wood had run into Desert Dust before and was hoping to meet the horse again to snap his picture. Robbins employed an airplane to chase the horses while men on horseback drove them into an enclosure. On July 12, they managed to drive Desert Dust into a box canyon.

"There was no way out except where I was, fortunately," Wood told the *Denver Post*. "He had turned toward me," and Wood pressed down on the shutter.

The *Denver Post* published the photograph that December, and it ended up appearing in *National Geographic*, *Readers Digest*, and other prestigious magazines. Wood later recalled receiving orders for the photograph from at least 15 foreign countries.

Robbins decided to spare Desert Dust the fate of the slaughterhouse and kept him on his ranch for breeding and showing. Unfortunately, the magnificent animal was shot to death in 1952 in what the Converse County sheriff called "an act of vandalism."

Wood died in 1979 and left behind a book of poetry and photographs titled *Desert Dust*. (Courtesy *Rawlins Daily Times*.)

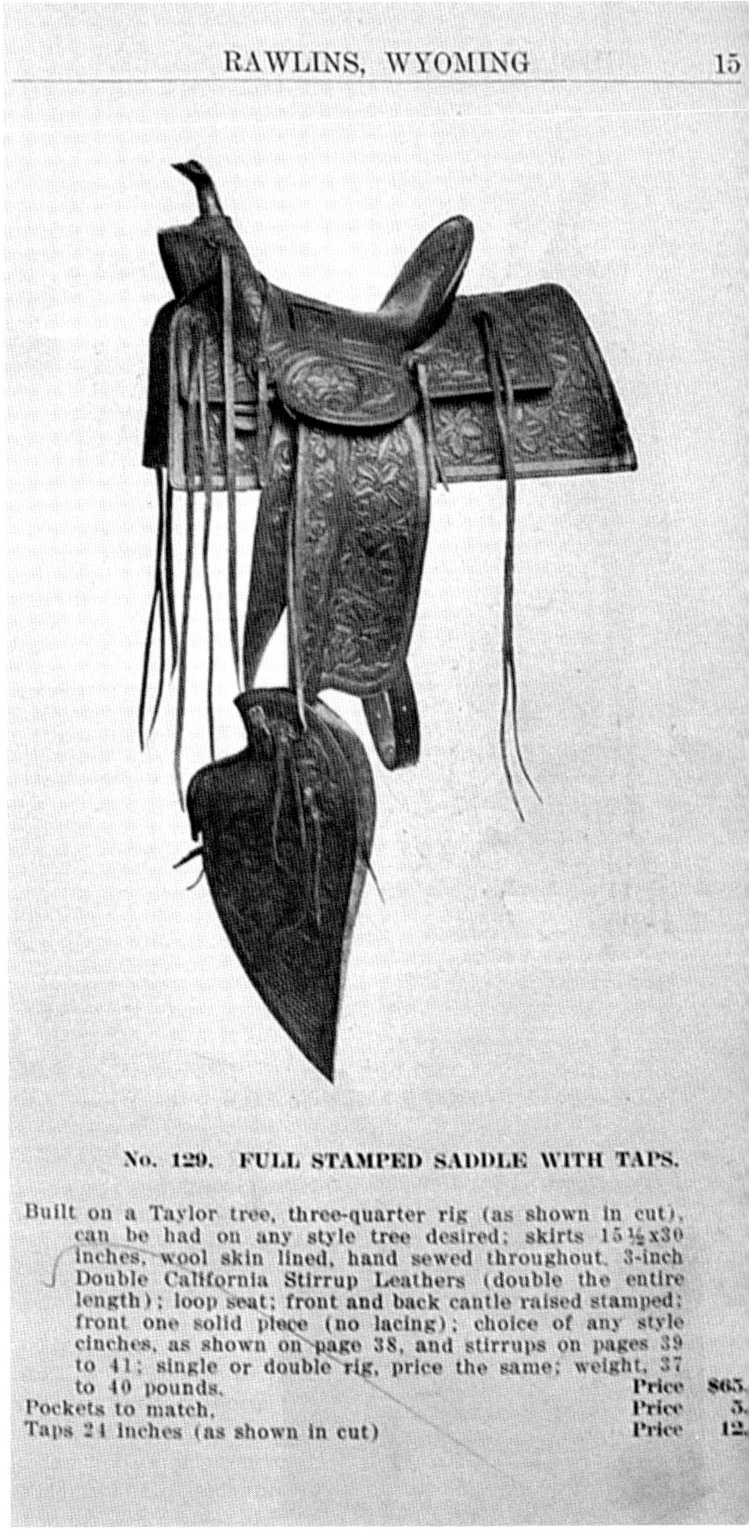

RAWLINS, WYOMING 15

No. 129. FULL STAMPED SADDLE WITH TAPS.

Built on a Taylor tree, three-quarter rig (as shown in cut), can be had on any style tree desired; skirts 15½x30 inches, wool skin lined, hand sewed throughout, 3-inch Double California Stirrup Leathers (double the entire length); loop seat; front and back cantle raised stamped; front one solid piece (no lacing); choice of any style cinches, as shown on page 38, and stirrups on pages 39 to 41; single or double rig, price the same; weight, 37 to 40 pounds. Price $65.

Pockets to match. Price 5.

Taps 24 inches (as shown in cut) Price 12.

The Last Great Saddlemakers

Knox & Tanner Co. of Rawlins was one of the best-known saddle manufacturers in the West at the beginning of the 20th century.

In 1883, R.B. Knox was put in charge of John Foote's saddlery and harness house. By 1901, Knox and George A. Tanner owned the business and gave it its legendary name.

Emil Krueger, a journeyman saddlemaker from Denver, took over the shop after Knox's death in 1904. Business boomed, and within three years, the modest storefront made way for a two-story stone building.

One of the company's highest-profile orders was a saddle for the 1908 National Democratic Convention in Denver, which was the first convention of any major political party ever held in a western state.

The company's fortunes fell with the advent of automobiles. In March 1920, a car accessory and supply business replaced the saddlery in the building. (Courtesy Carbon County Museum.)

CHAPTER TWO

The Big Nose George Connection

On August 16, 1878, "Big Nose" George Parrott, who apparently had a large proboscis, was waiting with his cohorts in the bushes near Medicine Bow for the train to arrive.

George and his gang had a simple plan: rob a train by derailing it. Unfortunately, crewmen discovered the tampered rail and fixed it, leaving the outlaws no choice but to retreat. Word of the crime made it to Rawlins, and a posse was formed to track down the criminals. George's gang encountered two of the lawmen in Elk Mountain and killed both in a shootout.

Now wanted for murder, the outlaws split up. "Dutch Charley" Burris was the first one to be caught. When the train transporting him passed by the town of Carbon, a mob stopped the train, dragged Burris out, and lynched him.

Big Nose George eluded captivity for two years, but he couldn't keep his mouth shut. He got drunk in a saloon in Miles City, Montana, and boasted of his crimes. A telegraph was sent to Rawlins, and in July 1880, Carbon County sheriff James Rankin traveled to Montana to bring George to prison in Rawlins. When the train passed by Carbon again, the same mob tried to lynch George. The crowd let him go after he pleaded for his life and promised to tell all he knew about the crimes.

George was found guilty and sentenced to death. One night, he managed to obtain a knife and sawed his leg shackles off. He then allegedly hit jailor Robert Rankin (the sheriff's brother) on the head several times and tried to escape. A wounded Robert called for his wife, Rosa, to bring him his pistol. Rosa did so and also shut and locked the door so Parrott couldn't get away.

After the news of the escape spread, a mob from town stormed the jail, dragged George out, and, after several attempts, hanged him on a telegraph pole on Front Street.

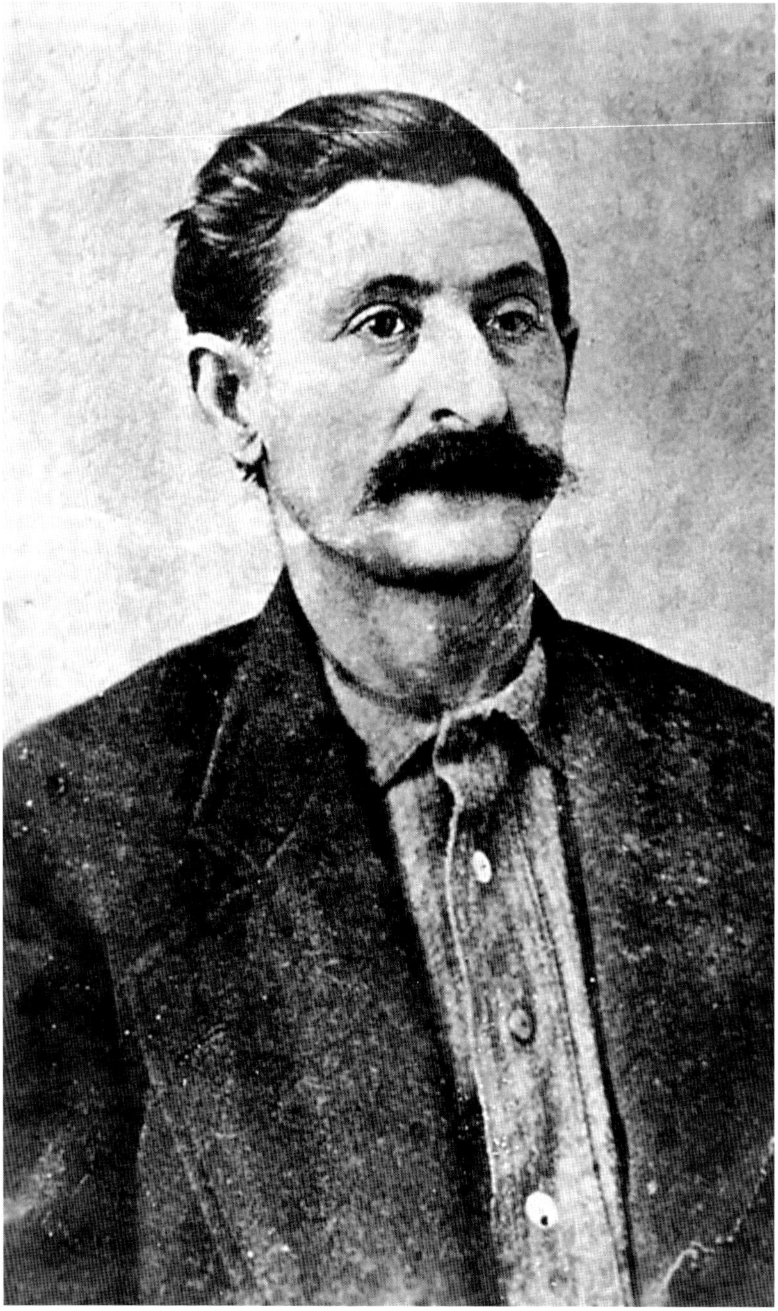

Big Nose George

Who was Big Nose George? Not much is known about his early life. Some said he was from France, but there are no reports of him speaking with an accent. He was reputedly part of a gang of highwaymen, cattle rustlers, and horse thieves.

George was most likely a run-of-the-mill outlaw, as it wasn't his crime but his fate that made him so memorable. What some local doctors did with George's body after he was lynched is a truly a tale of the bizarre. (Courtesy Carbon County Museum.)

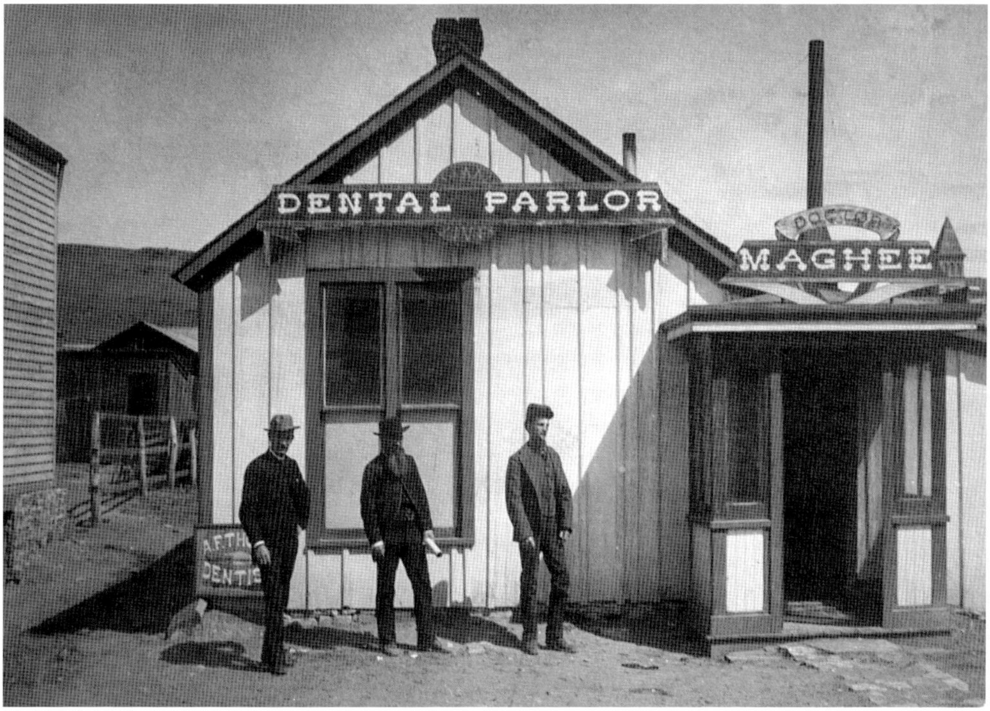

Thomas Maghee

After the lynching, Drs. Thomas Maghee and John Osborne took possession of the body and dissected George's brain to see if it was any different from that of a "good" person. Working as an assistant for Dr. Maghee was 15-year-old Lillian Heath.

After the dissection of the brain, Dr. Osborne removed the skin from George's thighs and chest and had a pair of shoes made out of it. The top half of George's skullcap was given to Heath. She would later recall that she kept the skull as a memento of her training days. (Courtesy Carbon County Museum.)

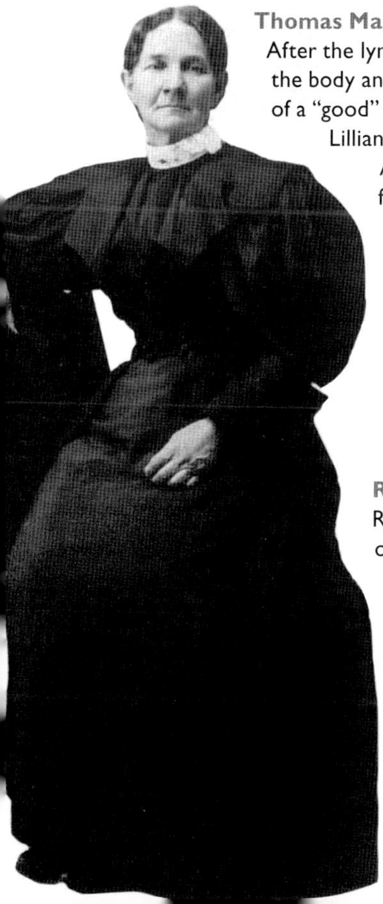

Rosa Rankin

Robert Rankin was never the same after Big Nose George hit him on the head. According to historian Daniel Meschter, "Robert suffered a serious concussion and gradual impairment of mental facilities."

While Robert was the one who was hurt, it was Rosa who was recognized as the heroine and respected for the rest of her life. She received an inscribed gold watch from county officials for her efforts. (Courtesy Carbon County Museum.)

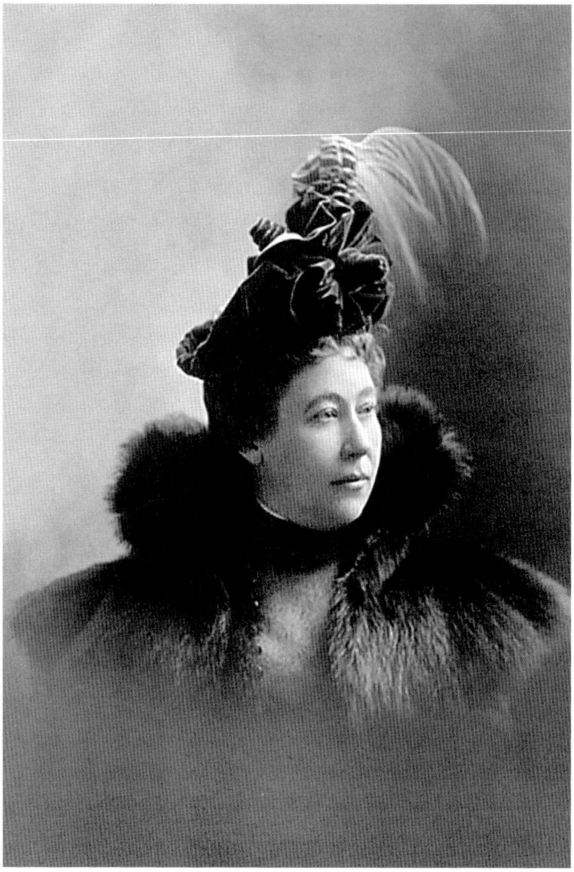

Lillian Heath

Lillian Heath became Dr. Maghee's assistant through her father, William, who himself enjoyed assisting Maghee with patients.

Heath trained for five years under Maghee and helped the doctor deliver babies, treat bullet wounds, and amputate limbs. Before plastic surgery was even called plastic surgery, Heath and Maghee performed more than 30 operations to reconstruct a sheepherder's face after a failed suicide attempt.

The facial reconstruction made Maghee somewhat of a national celebrity in medical circles. In 1907, the *Cheyenne Leader* reported, "No name in his profession is more widely or more favorably known in Wyoming than that of Dr. Maghee."

Heath graduated from Rawlins High School in 1888, and with the encouragement of her father and Maghee, she attended the College of Physicians and Surgeons in Keokuk, Iowa, to specialize in obstetrics. There were only two other women in the 22-person program.

Heath began her medical practice in 1893 in her parents' home in Rawlins. For safety, she would dress in boys' clothing and carry a pistol when she went out on calls at night. Interestingly, when she was not treating patients, she modeled female clothing for a department store.

According to historian Lori Van Pelt, men were generally cordial to Heath, but women were "as catty as they could be." One woman refused to pay because the doctor was female.

Heath practiced medicine for about 15 years before moving to Colorado to run a hotel with her husband, Louis J. Nelson, in 1909. They returned to Rawlins in 1911.

Though Heath was no longer a doctor, she kept "an unfailing interest in medical matters," her obituary stated. This continued even at the age of 90, when she flew to Denver to take a tour of some hospitals. (Courtesy Carbon County Museum.)

John Osborne

While the speculation that Osborne wore the shoes made out of Big Nose George's skin to his inauguration ceremony as governor of Wyoming is legendary enough, he is also well known for serving in the US Congress and being first assistant to the US secretary of state.

But the most fascinating episode in Osborne's life is probably his trip around the world in 1926. Throughout the trip, he kept a manuscript with detailed observations and recordings of the population, industry, economy, and history of his stops.

Osborne set out with his family on the *Laconia* from New York on January 20 and headed toward the Caribbean. He wrote about cemetery practices in Cuba and marveled at the workings of the Panama Canal. Hawaiian natives greeted him with music and leis.

When the *Laconia* crossed the international date line, Osborne mourned his lost day. "Oh where oh where has my rest day gone," he wrote. "A meridian line had been drawn long ago way out in the briny deep. When crossing this line a whole day is lost while we were down in our bunks fast asleep." (Courtesy City of Rawlins.)

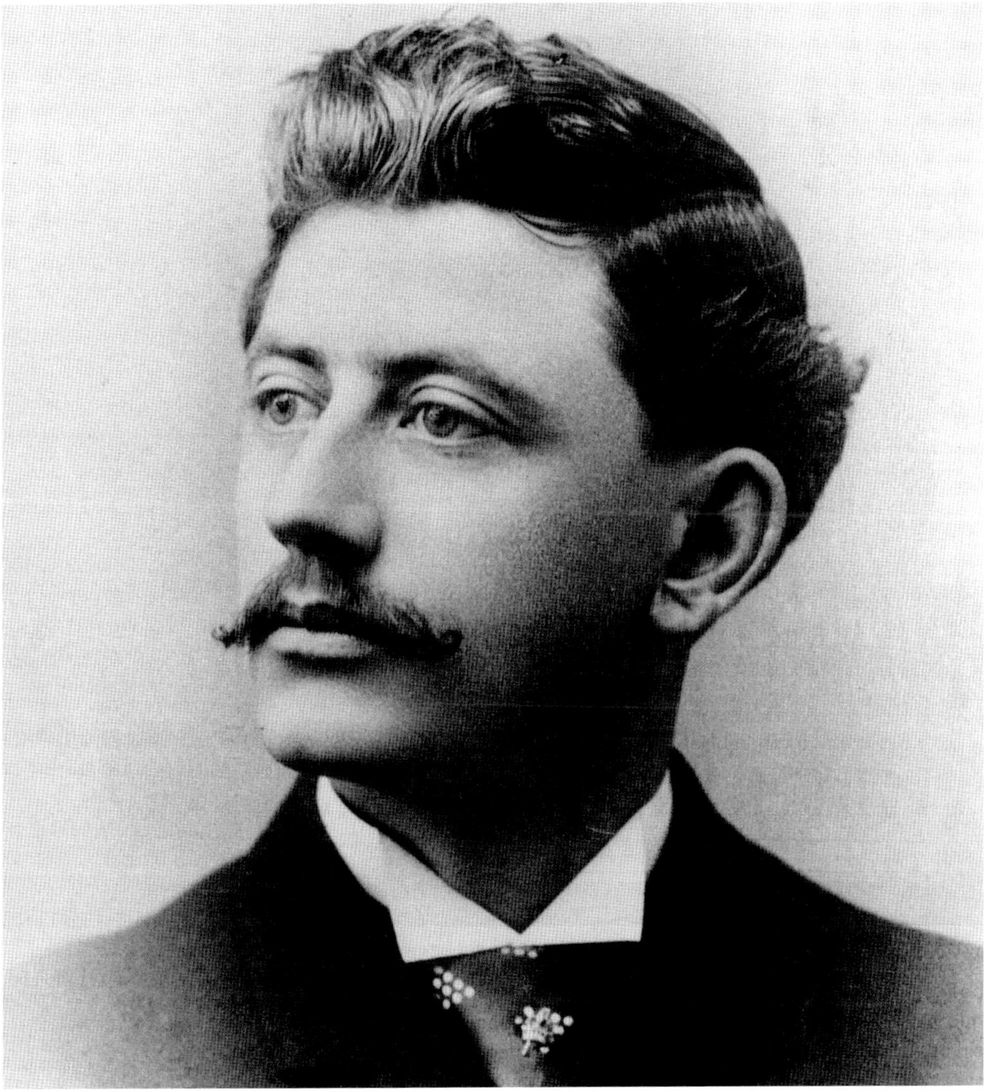

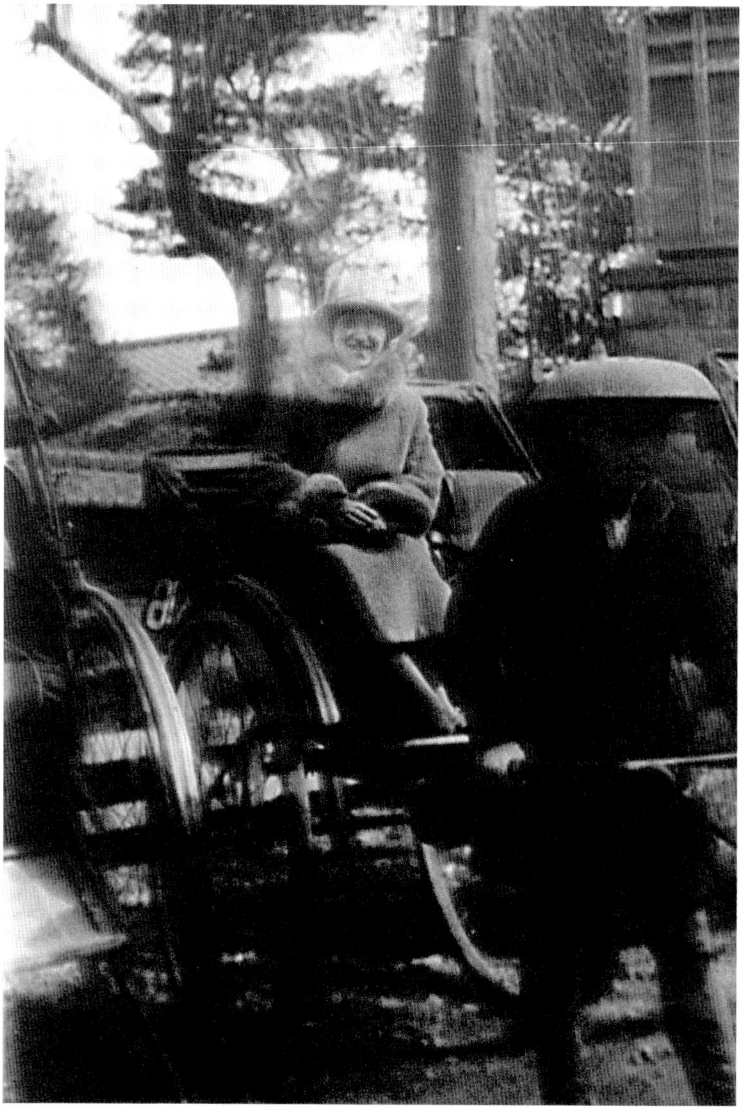

Osborne's Daughter on a Rickshaw in Japan

The Osbornes arrived in Yokohama, Japan, about a month into the trip. The city was still in ruins from the earthquake that had occurred a few years before. The family experienced a rickshaw ride in Tokyo and also visited the ancient Japanese capitals of Kyoto and Nara.

On Osborne's way to Korea, he compared the color of the Yellow Sea to the "color of the Platte River in spring." In the Philippines, which was under US rule at that time, Osborne met with Gov. Gen. Leonard Wood and discussed the prospect of Philippine independence over lunch.

Via Indonesia, Burma, and India, the family found themselves in Cairo on May 4. There, Osborne encountered archaeologists excavating an ancient Roman city and picked up a human foot among the discarded debris that he brought back to Wyoming.

The Osbornes ended the trip with a tour through Europe, making stops in Greece, Italy, Monaco, and Paris, arriving full circle in New York on May 28.

Osborne continued to mourn his lost day and concluded that if he were to do it again, he would sail eastward. (Courtesy Carbon County Museum.)

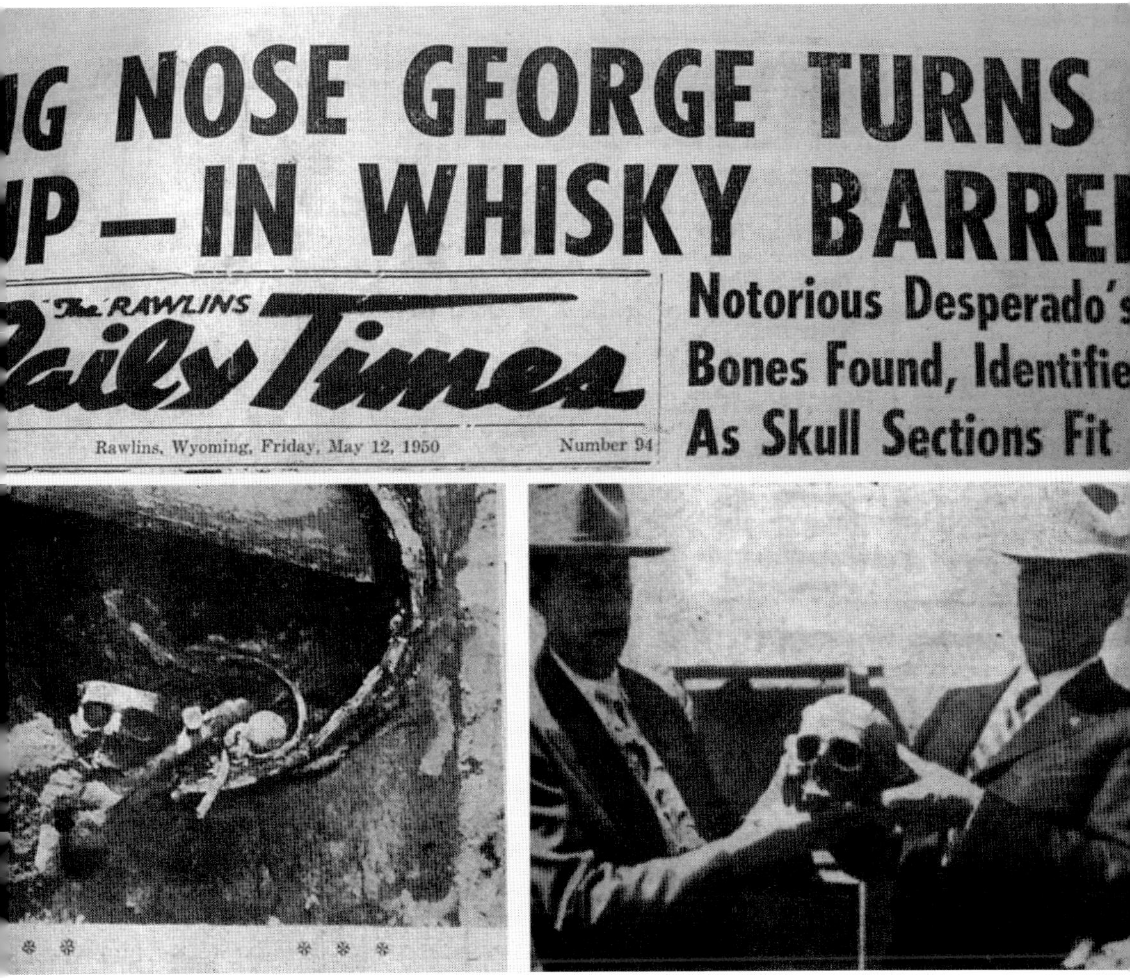

Big Nose George Resurfaces, Literally

More than 60 years after his death, Big Nose George made headlines again in 1950. On May 11, construction workers excavated a whiskey barrel in the alley between Fourth and Fifth Streets north of West Cedar Street.

The barrel had several bones in it, including a skull with the top sawed off. A resident who remembered Big Nose George's fate suggested calling Lillian Heath, who was then 85 years old. Heath's husband, Lou Nelson, arrived on the scene with the top half of the skull—which fit perfectly with the bottom half found in the barrel.

Heath told the newspapers she was "positive" that it was Big Nose George's bones.

This brief reunion of George's skull did not last long. After Heath's death, the top of the skull was gifted to the Union Pacific Railroad Museum in Council Bluffs, Iowa, while the bottom half remains in Rawlins with the Carbon County Museum. (Courtesy *Rawlins Daily Times*.)

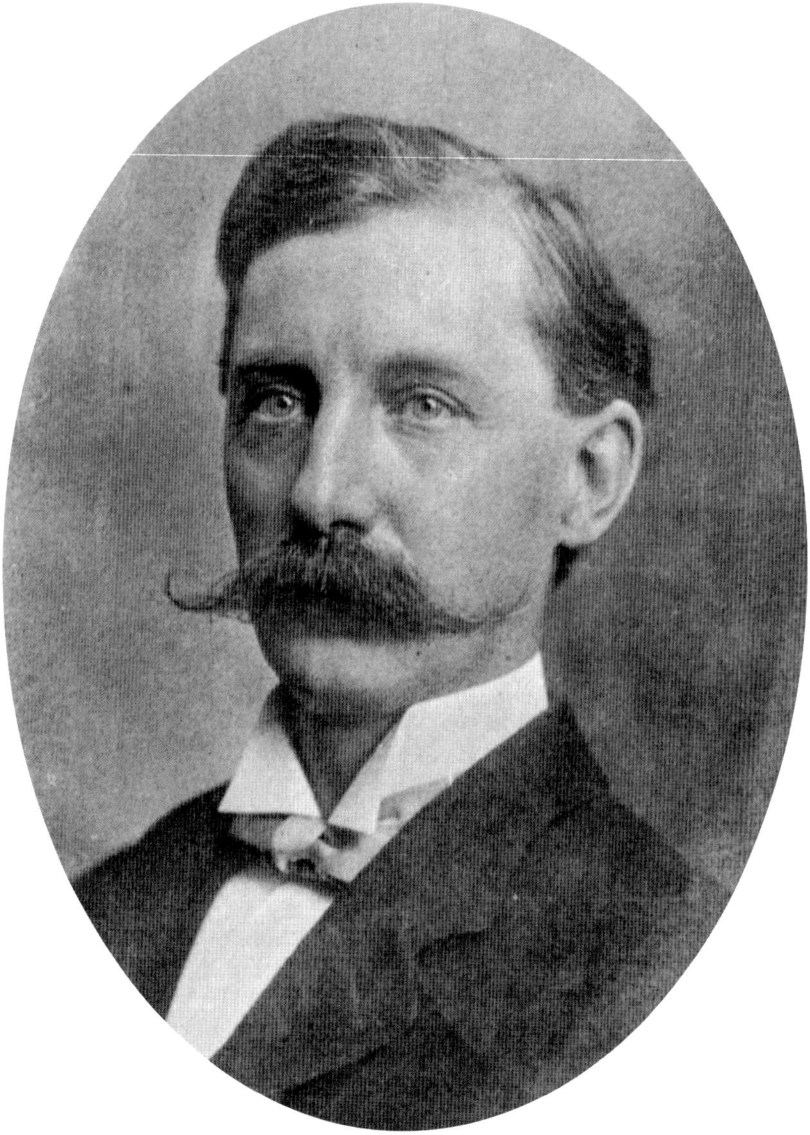

Fenimore Chatterton
The day after Big Nose George's train derailing attempt, a young and broke Fenimore Chatterton was riding on the same line to his new job at Fort Steele. When the train passed by the point where the crime almost happened, the conductor told Chatterton and other passengers of the deed.

"This was my introduction to the West," Chatterton wrote in a memoir. "I little dreamed that in the years ahead, I would, as an official, have to cope with desperate characters."

Chatterton worked as a bookkeeper for what was then the flagship J.W. Hugus store, which will be discussed in the next chapter.

Chatterton moved to Rawlins in 1888 after he was elected probate judge and county treasurer. It is said he managed to collect over $160,000 in delinquent taxes within one year. In 1892, Chatterton achieved his lifelong dream of obtaining a law degree and served as Carbon County attorney until 1898, when he was appointed secretary of state. When Gov. DeForest Richards died in 1903, Chatterton succeeded him, reaching the highest political position in the state. (Courtesy Carbon County Museum.)

CHAPTER THREE

Early Inventors

A mural of Thomas Edison adorns the exterior wall of The Keg saloon in Rawlins.

Indeed, the famous inventor did spend time in Rawlins, arriving in July 1878 as part of Henry Draper's scientific expedition to view a total eclipse of the sun. The party chose a site 13 miles west of Rawlins to view the event. Edison brought with him a "tasimeter" to test if the sun's corona emitted heat and to what extent. The experiment reportedly failed.

Two weeks later, Edison returned to Rawlins to hunt and fish in the Battle Lake area, about 70 miles south of town. Legend has it that Edison invented the light bulb while on this trip, and there is a historical marker on the highway near Battle Lake that details the story. Edison supposedly arrived at the idea of using bamboo for the bulb's filament after seeing the pieces of his broken bamboo fishing pole glow in the campfire.

Whether the account is true or not is up to the reader's discretion. But this chapter is not about Edison. It's about Rawlins locals who, like Edison, invented and built fantastic things.

Perhaps it was the magic of Edison's visit that propelled early residents to start tinkering away on their own contraptions, but as residents of an isolated town with few resources, they most likely were driven by simple necessity.

The most well-known creation to come out of Rawlins was probably the sheepwagon, conceived by a local blacksmith and used all over the West for almost a century.

There was an automatic gun that fired blanks throughout the night to scare away coyotes, an accurate toy gun that was used around the world, and at least two attempts at building an airplane. The first one failed, but the second was a success.

The last story tells of a mechanical genius who, in his spare time, built a telescope to look at the heavens.

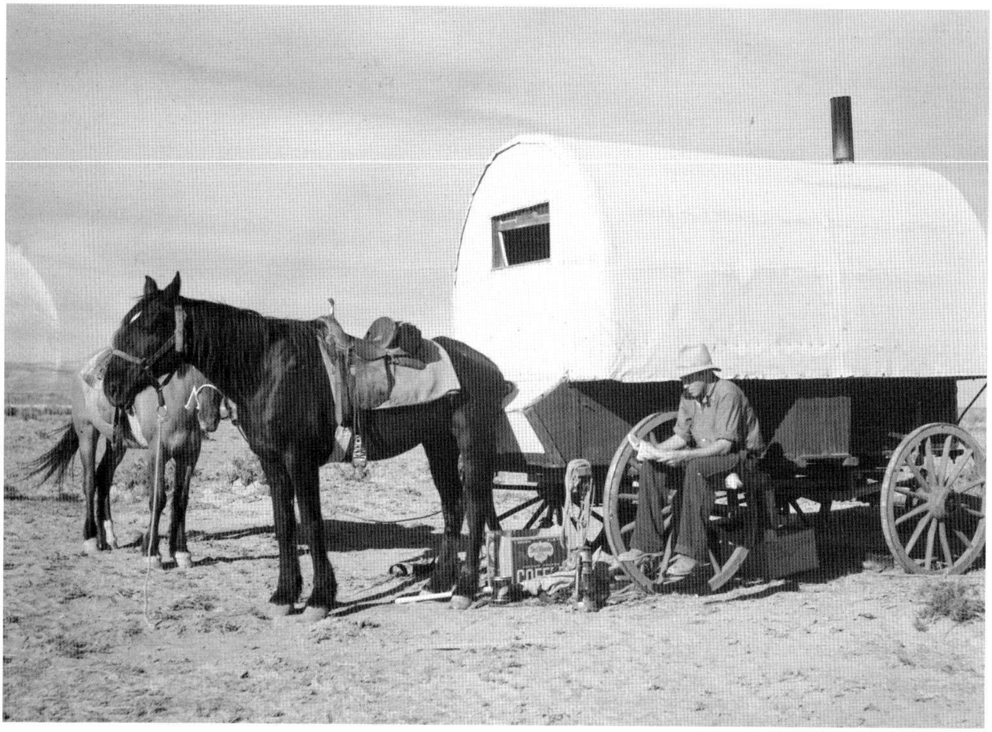

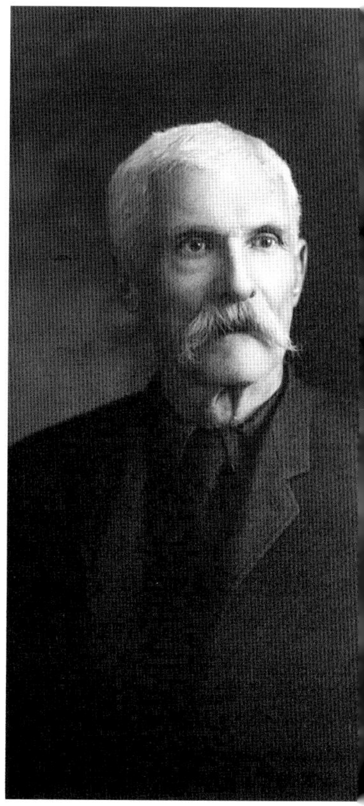

James Candlish

Herding sheep wasn't easy in the 19th century, especially in Wyoming. Sheepherders faced severe weather, which made it difficult to set up camp. They also had to travel long distances because of open-range grazing practices. Thus arose a need for accessible, comfortable shelter.

In 1884, Rawlins blacksmith James Candlish made a model of the first authenticated "sheepwagon" as it is known today. Drawn by two horses, it was basically a mobile home for sheepherders.

The most popular version of events is that Candlish listened to the needs of many sheepherders and created the wagon in the back of his shop.

Others say that George Ferris, also of Rawlins, was the one who designed the wagon. He started the construction, but because he lacked the proper tools, he asked Candlish to finish it for him.

Whoever the inventor was, Candlish was the one recognized by the Wyoming Woolgrower's Association. In 1909, the association presented him with a commemorative watch fob consisting of three discs: one with a sheep's head, one with a plaque of Candlish, and one with a tiny picture of the sheepwagon.

This Rawlins invention was used all over the West for over a century until the practice of herding sheep declined in the 1990s. Sheepwagons are still made today but are mostly used as guesthouses on ranches or for recreational purposes. (Above, photograph by Arthur Rothstein, courtesy Library of Congress; right, courtesy Carbon County Museum.)

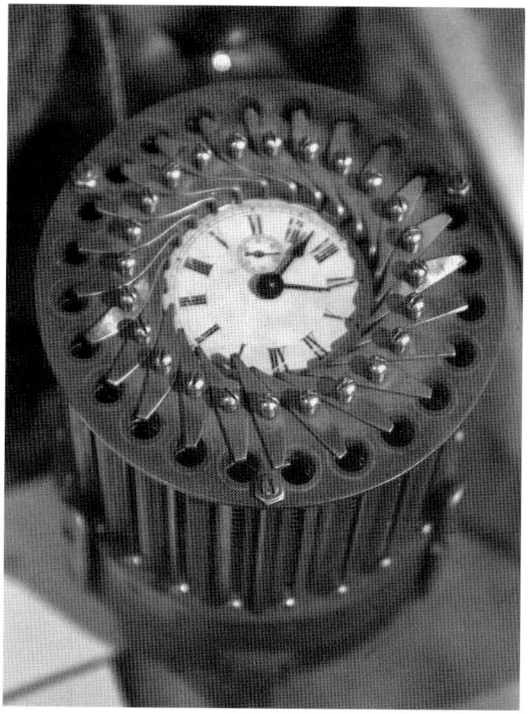

The Night Herder

Another bother about herding sheep in the early 1900s was that you had to get up several times throughout the night and fire shots into the air to keep coyotes away.

In 1901, sheepherder Jim Weed came up with a solution: an automatic gun that would fire rounds at regular intervals throughout the night to scare predators away. The cylindrical contraption could fire .44-caliber blanks every hour for up to 12 hours unattended. It was dubbed the "Night Herder."

Weed came to Rawlins looking for investors and found one in photographer A.A. Brown. They set up shop in the basement of Brown's photography studio.

Shortly after the invention hit the market in 1902, it appeared that Weed had been pushed out of the partnership, as his name no longer appeared in company documents. A few months later, Brown relocated to Salt Lake City, returning to Rawlins only to transport the machinery to his new home.

In Utah, Brown took full credit for the invention. In 1903, an article appeared in the *Salt Lake Telegram* describing the gun. The inventor? "A.A. Brown, a Salt Laker."

No information could be found on what happened afterward. (Above, courtesy Carbon County Museum; below, courtesy Utah Digital Newspapers.)

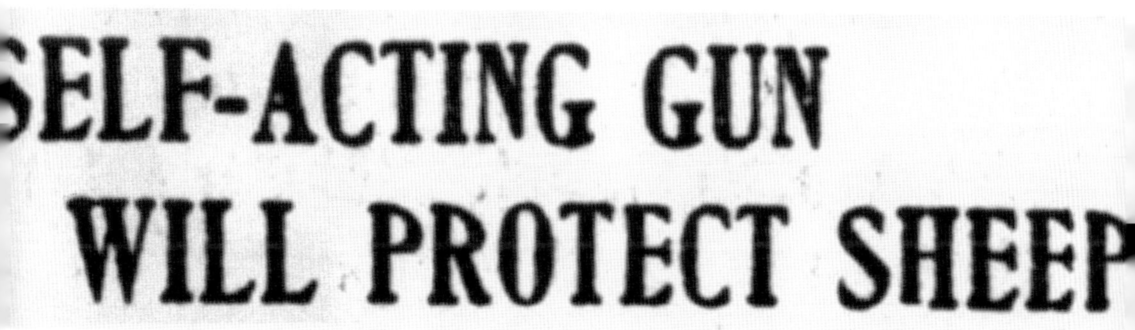

SELF-ACTING GUN

WILL PROTECT SHEEP

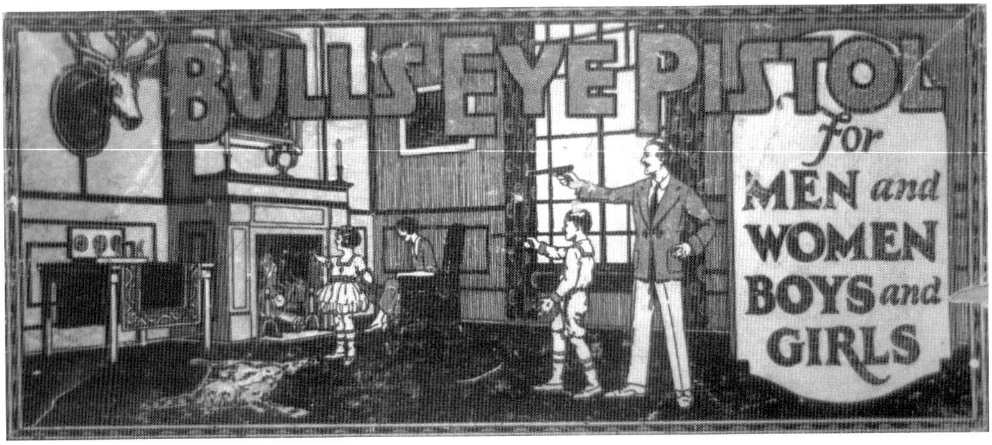

The Shot Heard Around the World

It may be a rare auction item now, but at one point, a Rawlins-conceived toy pistol was sold all over the world. The Bulls Eye Pistol was invented in 1924 by former Rawlins dentist C.L. Bunten, who once said he enjoyed "tinkering for fun."

The invention hit the shelves in 1925 at $2. It was reputed to be extremely accurate: Bunten reportedly knocked two No. 6 BBs off a sheet of paper at a distance of 10 feet during a demonstration in his dentist office.

Bunten was the inventor, but his partner and fellow dentist, E.G. Peterson, had the business brains. Peterson's marketing strategies included hiring a 1920 USA Olympic rifle team member as a salesperson.

Between 50,000 and 70,000 guns were sold while Bunten held the patent. Military personnel, gun experts, and the sporting press deemed the gun "excellent for training and practice."

The US Army supplied some troops in the Pacific with the pistol during World War II for recreational purposes, but the German army reportedly bought "piles" of them to actually train soldiers. (Both photographs by Han Cheung, artifacts courtesy Carbon County Museum.)

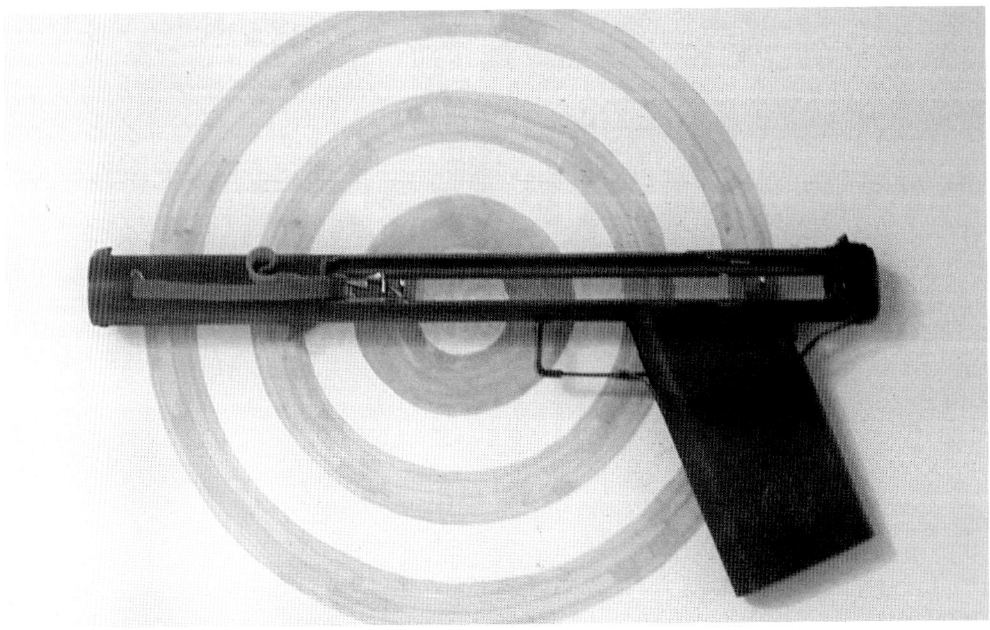

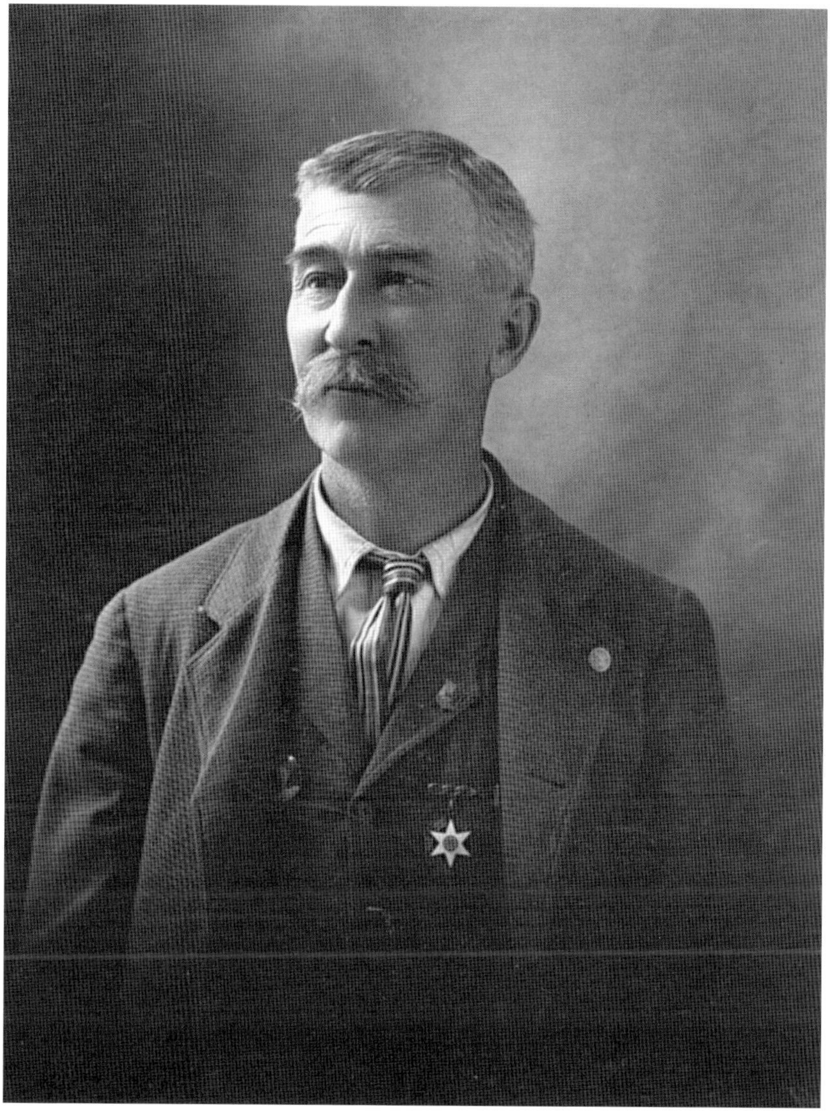

William Heath and His "Flying Machines"
At the same time the Wright brothers were tinkering away at their "Flyer," one man in Rawlins also had dreams of taking to the skies.

In January 1901, the local papers reported that William Heath had invented a "flying machine." The articles described Heath's model, which was made of "muslin, a few sticks, some few pieces of wire and equipped with old clockworks." While on a much smaller scale, the model did fly a significant distance.

Heath told the newspaper that the actual machine would be made out of aluminum and the "finest of steel" and that it would be able to carry up to two tons of weight. It would be powered by liquid or hot air and could run from 20 to over 100 miles per hour.

Heath was able to raise enough money to have a sample built in Chicago. There was no follow-up report, and the machine probably failed.

Even though the Wright brothers beat Heath to the chase in 1903, he kept trying until at least 1906. The last reported model was powered by a spring from a music box and relied on the flapping of its wings instead of a propeller. (Courtesy Carbon County Museum.)

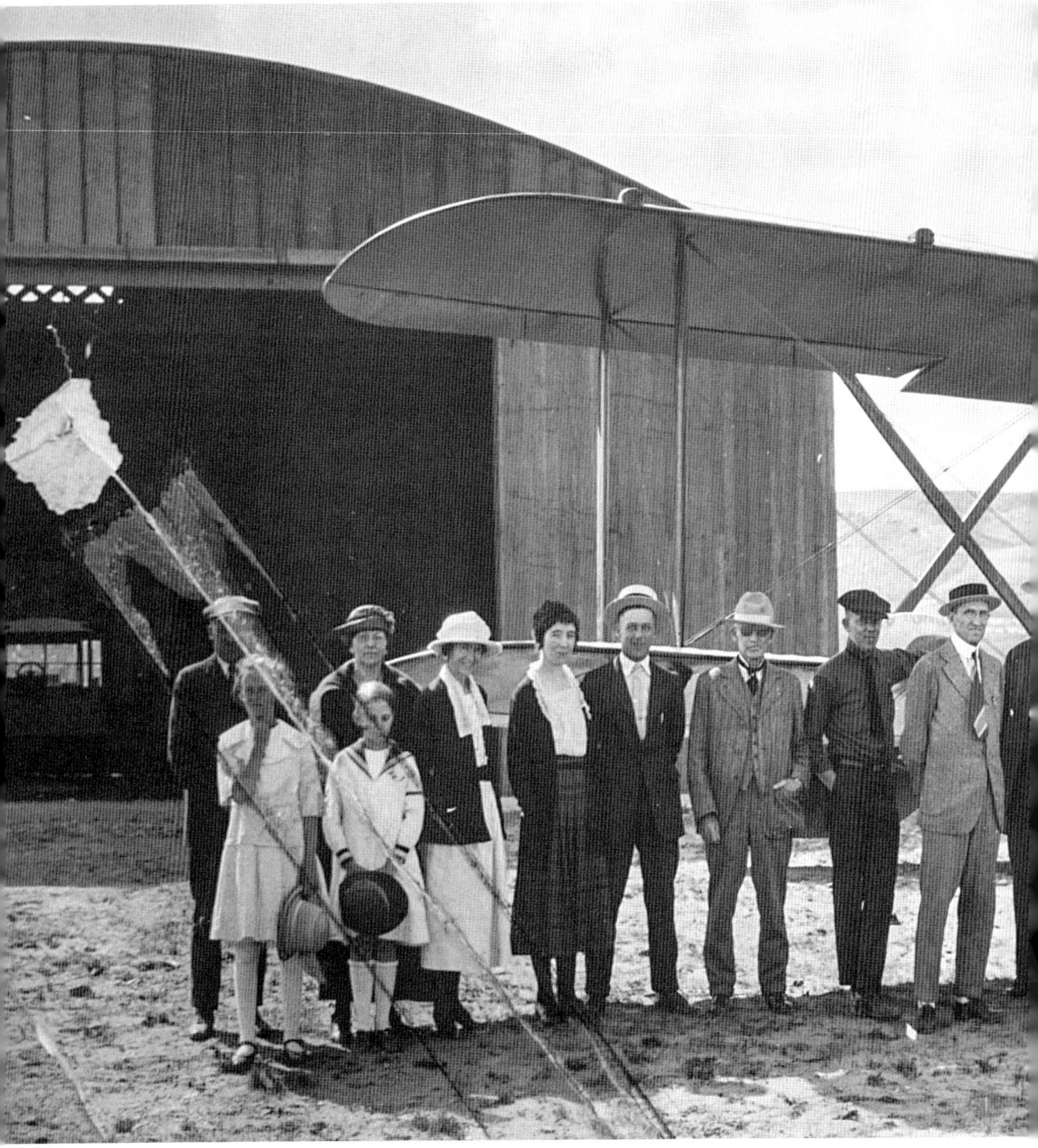

First Airmail

By 1919, the airplane had become a fixture in Rawlins. At first, planes would land and take off at the fairgrounds, but frequent accidents led to the construction of an airfield. A large crowd gathered to

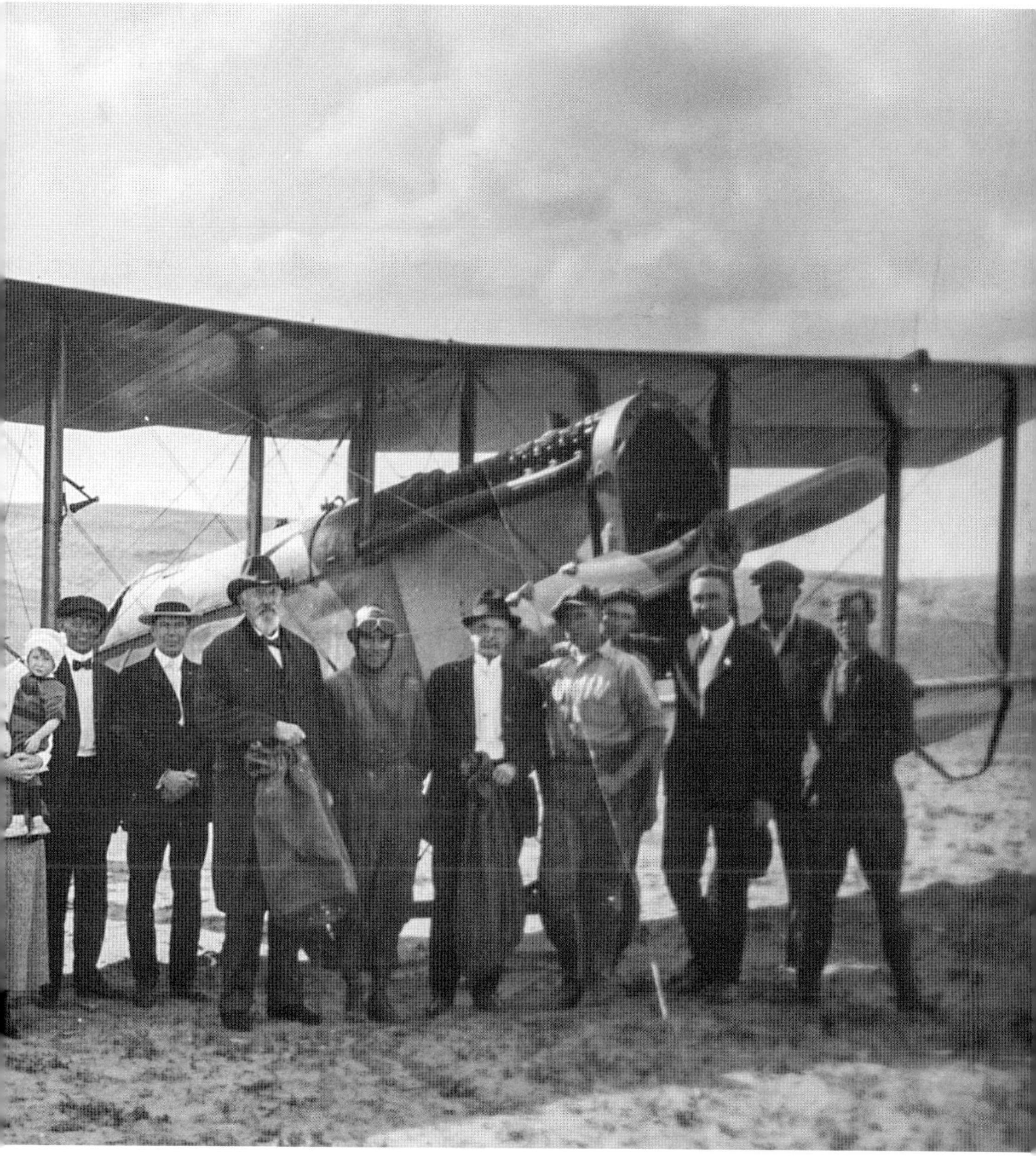

watch when the first airmail arrived on August 9, 1921. (Courtesy Carbon County Museum.)

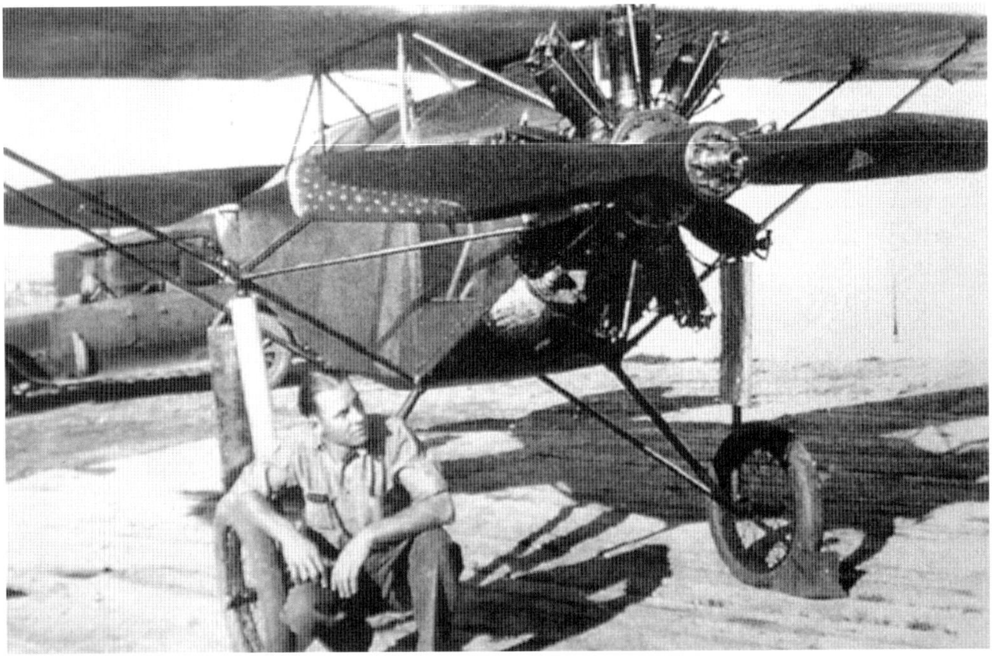

Holman Brothers' Homemade Plane

There is no record of anyone in Rawlins trying to build a homemade flying machine again until 1928, when brothers C.T. and C.B. Holman began designing and constructing their own airplane in town.

According to C.T.'s son, his father and uncle built the machine so they could shoot mountain lions for reward money.

The *Rawlins Republican* reported on the project that September: "The plane is of unusually rugged construction throughout, yet is lighter than the average three place commercial job and has exceptionally trim lines."

The first public test flight in 1930 failed. But the brothers didn't give up, and the townspeople rooted them on. They had always been skeptical about Heath's ventures, but they believed that the Holman plane would work.

Four months later, the Holmans were ready for another public trial. Having no actual flying experience, they hired a professional pilot, Fred Wahl, to do the job. Wahl was able to stay in the air for 20 minutes and commented that the plane "handled nicely." Locals celebrated the success with a two-foot-long cake decorated with a frosting airplane.

Several weeks later—still without any flying experience or instruction—C.B. decided to try the plane himself. He could fly it, all right. The problem was he didn't know how to land. On his second attempt, the plane tipped to one side, and the propeller broke.

C.T.'s son said his father never got around to shooting mountain lions because C.B. broke the plane, and he was probably referring to this incident.

The rest of C.T.'s life still revolved around airplanes. In 1934, he made headlines for inventing an efficient propeller that eliminated noise. Three years later, he moved to California to take a job as the regional director of the Civil Aeronautics Authority, which later became the Federal Aviation Administration. At one point, he was a consultant to aviation mogul Howard Hughes. (Courtesy Carbon County Museum, gift of the Holman family.)

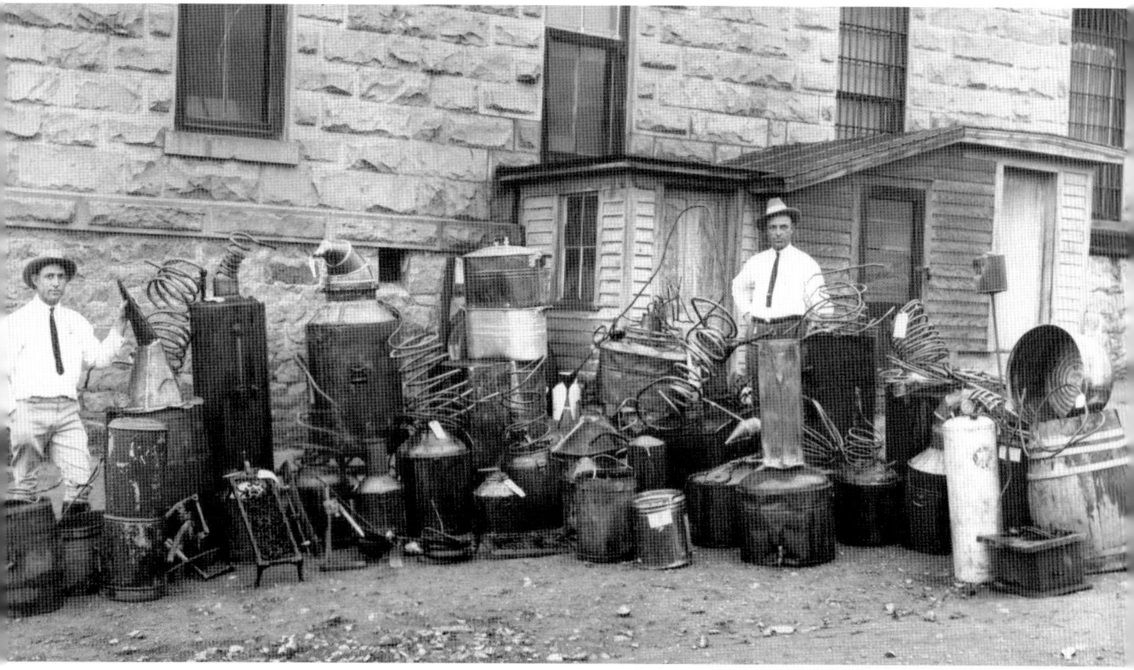

Bootleggers and Moonshiners
Speaking of inventing out of necessity, the Prohibition era brought out the creativity of thirsty Rawlinsites, who devised any method they could to evade the law and keep themselves intoxicated.

Records show the Rawlins police force started a "crusade" against bootleggers in late 1920, but by 1921, city officials seemed to realize they couldn't stop the illegal production of alcohol. (Courtesy Carbon County Museum.)

billiards

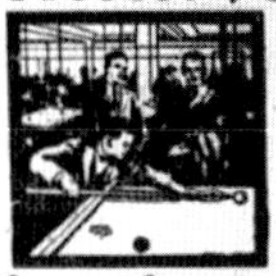

a fine after-meal exercise

As a mild form of exercise after lunch or after dinner, billiards cannot be excelled. Billiards brings into play practically every muscle of the body. The bending, twisting, leaning and stooping required to make various shots is a wonderful aid to digestion.

Equipped with Brunswick tables and accessories—the world's finest billiard equipment—our recreation room offers excellent opportunities for the enjoyment of

THE BEST ICE CREAM

Ice cream to deserve the caption "BEST" must meet many requirements. It must be made from pure ingredients, made under sanitary conditions, and it must be full flavored and smoothly frozen. OUR CHEYENNE CREAMERY ICE CREAM will meet every test.

SPECIAL PRICES SATURDAYS AND SUNDAYS

THE BEST POCKET AND BILLIARD TABLES IN TOWN

LICHENSTEIN HIDE & FUR HEADQUARTERS
at Ferris Fountain Room.
Phone 479

THE SANITARY SOFT DRINK PARLOR

FERRIS HOTEL A. R. LICHENSTEIN, Prop.

Soft Drink Parlor

Many speakeasies masqueraded as restaurants or "soft drink parlors." The Wyoming Bar in Rawlins indeed changed its name to the Wyoming Soft Drink Parlor during Prohibition. This "Sanitary Soft Drink Parlor" may or may not have sold alcohol clandestinely. (Courtesy *Rawlins Daily Times.*)

MOONSHINERS PLEASE BE CAREFUL

Those persons who are making moonshine are respectfully requested by the City Officials to be careful and not dump mash into the sewers.

During the past few months the city has been put to much expense because of the necessity of tearing up sewer mains and cleaning out mash that has been dumped into the sewer and that has clogged it up.

On Monday last over a barrel of this mash was taken from the sewer in the east end of the city.

Moonshiners should be more careful in disposing of their mash as the city can ill afford to spend the money necessary to continually tear up and clean out sewer mains.

Any Moonshiner caught can rest assurred that if his case is tried before the Police Judge the maximum penalty will be given to him.

City's Plea to Bootleggers

The illegal production of booze had created a different problem by 1921: the leftover mash from alcohol production was clogging up the city's sewers. Instead of telling the bootleggers to stop, this article appeared in the *Rawlins Republican* on November 10, 1921. On December 5, 1933, the 21st Amendment was ratified, effectively repealing the 18th Amendment and ending Prohibition. (Courtesy *Rawlins Daily Times.*)

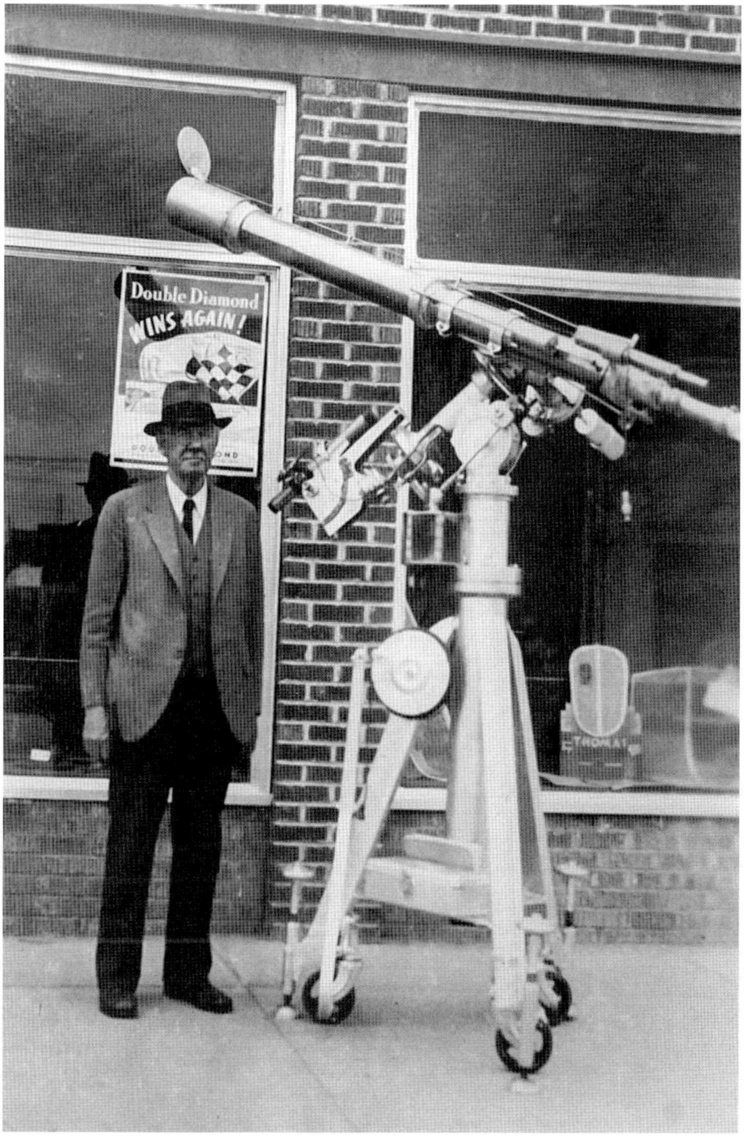

Stargazer

Daniel C. Kinnaman, who moved to Rawlins in 1901, was a smart man. Although his formal education stopped at the eighth grade, he was known as an architect, engineer, inventor, scientist, and astronomer. He was also a successful businessman, but that will be covered in a later chapter.

In 1896, Kinnaman worked for the Union Pacific's hydraulic engineering department, and his logarithmic diagram for the flow of water in open channels was published by the University of Wyoming in 1906.

At age 75, Kinnaman decided to start building telescopes in his spare time. He could often be seen in front of his shop observing the moons of Jupiter and the rings of Saturn with his eight-inch reflecting telescope.

It was remarkable how precise Kinnaman was with his construction. He ground the glass himself to "two millionth of an inch to one twentieth of a light wave," according to an article in the *Snake River Press*. When he sent the glass to Chicago to be silvered, the professionals proclaimed that none of the experts could have ground it any better. (Courtesy Daniel L. Kinnaman.)

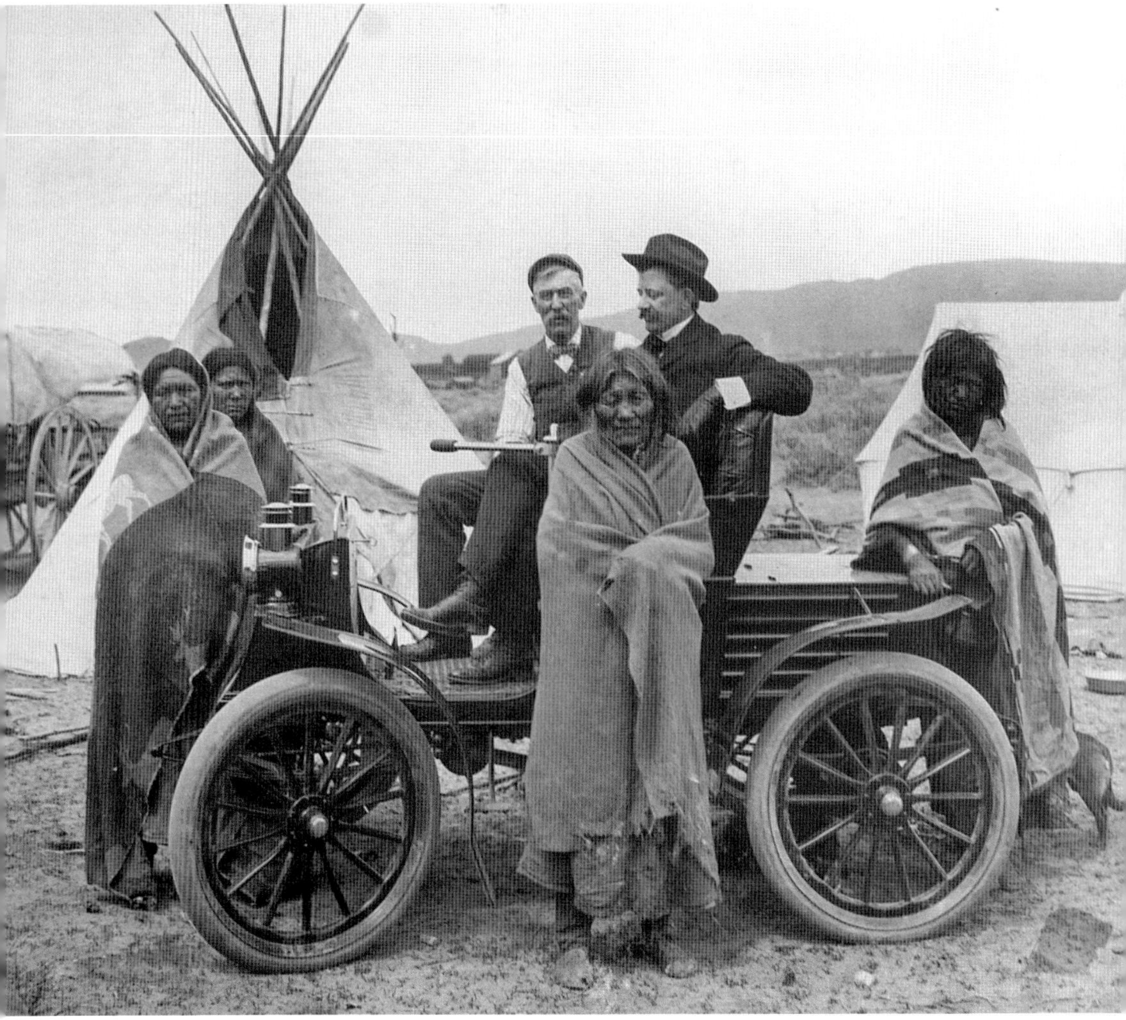

First Automobile in Rawlins
When John Osborne became the first automobile owner in Rawlins in 1901, Kinnaman was reportedly the only person who knew how to work it. He would crank the single cylinder and start the car every time before Osborne drove it. In this image, Osborne is pictured with William Heath and, for reasons unknown, several Native Americans. (Courtesy Carbon County Museum.)

CHAPTER FOUR

Land of Opportunity

Take a walk down Cedar Street, the main drag in Rawlins.

You'll see a Mexican café, a Thai restaurant, and an Asian grocery store. As isolated as Rawlins is, immigrants have always found their way here and, for the most part, have been able to prosper.

In the late 19th century, the Wild West was where people came to find their fortune. It may not have been highlighted in the history books, but many early pioneers were born in other countries.

There were enough Danish people in Rawlins in the early days to form a Danish Brotherhood. Three of the first six mayors were born in Denmark, and the first mayor wasn't even a US citizen when he was elected. There were also Irish, Swedes, Germans, and sporadic accounts of "Chinamen" running businesses in town here and there.

The most common way for immigrants to become prominent citizens was through ranching. One of the largest landowners in the area had humble beginnings as a poor Russian immigrant who spoke no English when he first arrived.

A few Chinese immigrants came later to open restaurants. Their children grew up in Rawlins, and their families were well respected in the community.

Latino families started coming to Rawlins mostly in the 1930s and 1940s. It is important to note that these weren't immigrants—they were Spanish-Americans who mostly came from southern Colorado and northern New Mexico. They did, however, bring a distinct culture and added to the city's diversity. These families mostly kept to themselves in the south side of town in the beginning, but they are now an integral part of the community. Still, that didn't happen overnight. In the 1970s, a young Latino who grew up in Rawlins challenged a large corporation for denying him the opportunity to move up the ladder.

While prospering in the "land of opportunity" was a common theme for immigrants, it wasn't always the case for racial minorities and women. Wyoming was the first state to give women the right to vote, but gender equality still came slowly. In 1963, the Equal Pay Act was established, and in 1964, Title VII of the Civil Rights Act passed, prohibiting employment discrimination.

"I was involved in the various laws, many [of] which hadn't been acted up in the state of Wyoming or on the Union Pacific Railroad," wrote Valerie Nelson. She later became the first female railroad engineer in the country, though not without suffering her share of discrimination.

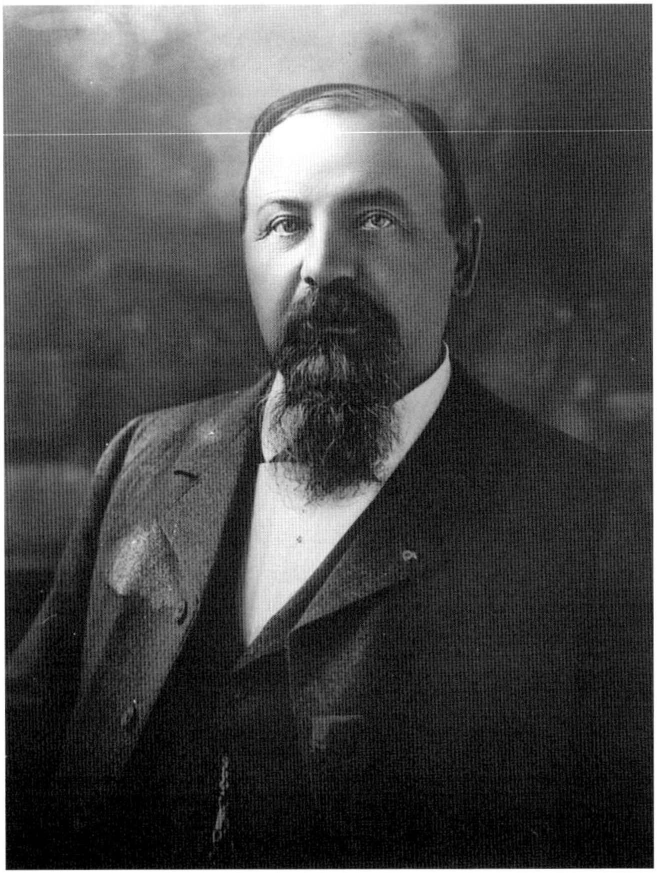

Isaac C. Miller

"I came from Denmark with almost no money, and built just exactly what I wanted."

This is what Isaac Miller, the first mayor of Rawlins, told his daughter shortly before his death in 1912. The tale of this Danishman, who landed in New York with just 35¢ in his pocket, is one of an American dream come true.

In 1864, a 20-year-old Miller left his homeland and sailed toward America in hope of a better life. Like many fortune-seekers, Miller headed west after disembarking on the East Coast and landed in Rawlins in 1870.

At first, he ran a saloon and wholesale retail business. He later partnered with Joel J. Hurt to become one of the leading sheep operators in Carbon County. Miller was instrumental in organizing the Wyoming Stock Growers Association and became the president of the Rocky Mountain Wool Growers Association. Miller was also involved in organizing the Rawlins National Bank, which is still in operation today.

In 1880, Miller defeated James Rankin and became Carbon County sheriff. He was away on business during Big Nose George's prison break and subsequent lynching, but after yet another lynching took place, he decided to crack down on vigilante behavior.

Miller oversaw the first legal execution in Rawlins and formed a police force to combat vigilantes. He also used prisoners for public works projects, which improved the local views on the penal system.

When Rawlins was incorporated in 1886, residents elected Miller as their first mayor. He served for one year, laying down the groundwork for the city's bylaws and government structure.

It is said that Miller was not yet a US citizen when he was elected. Indeed, his great-grandson Mark E. Miller's family research shows that Miller did not obtain his citizenship until 1887. (Courtesy Rawlins National Bank.)

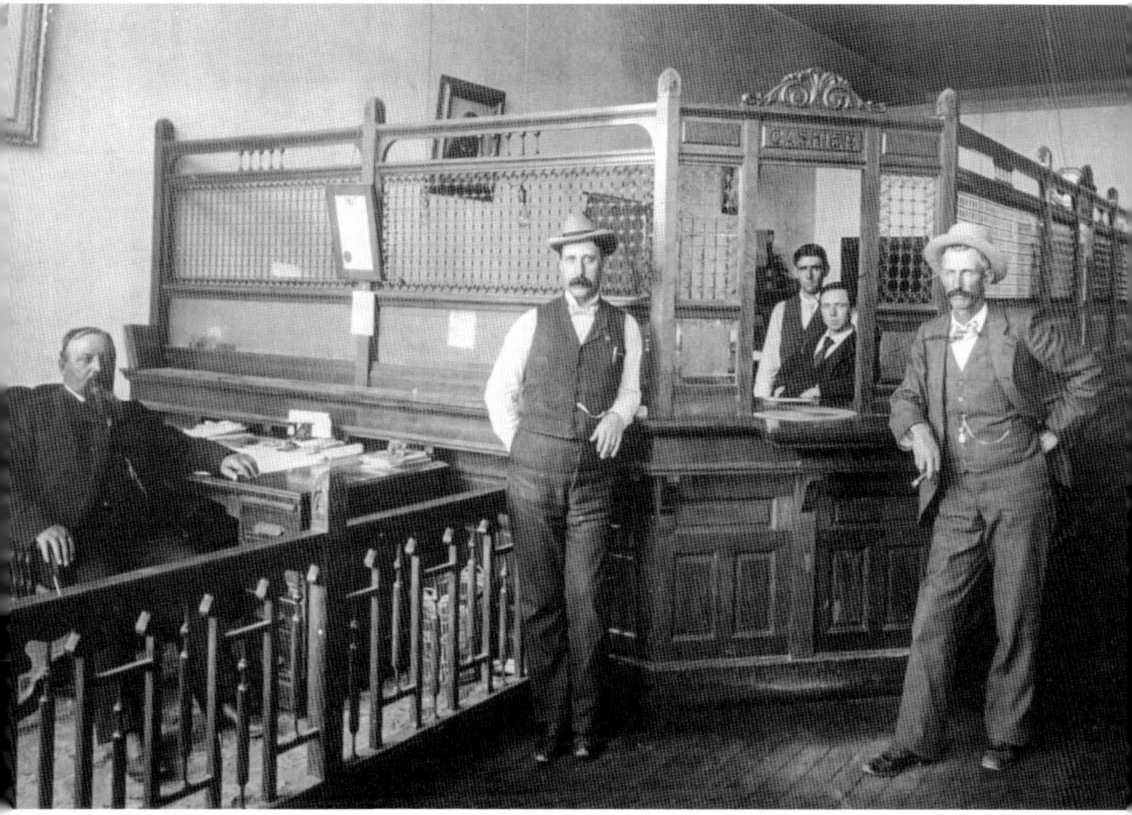

Rawlins National Bank

One of Miller's lasting legacies in town is the Rawlins National Bank. Miller and a group of associates organized the Rawlins State Bank in 1899 with Miller as president.

Early pictures of the bank's interior show pistols behind the counters and spittoons in the corners. The bank was granted a national charter in 1900 and adopted its current name. Its directors made headlines in 1904 for electing a woman, Julia Ferris, to the bank board, which was a very progressive move at the time.

"Heretofore these offices have always been given to the men, and the selection of Mrs. Ferris is a deserved recognition of a woman of rare business capacity as well as a large stockholder in the bank," the *Rawlins Republican* reported. (Courtesy Rawlins National Bank.)

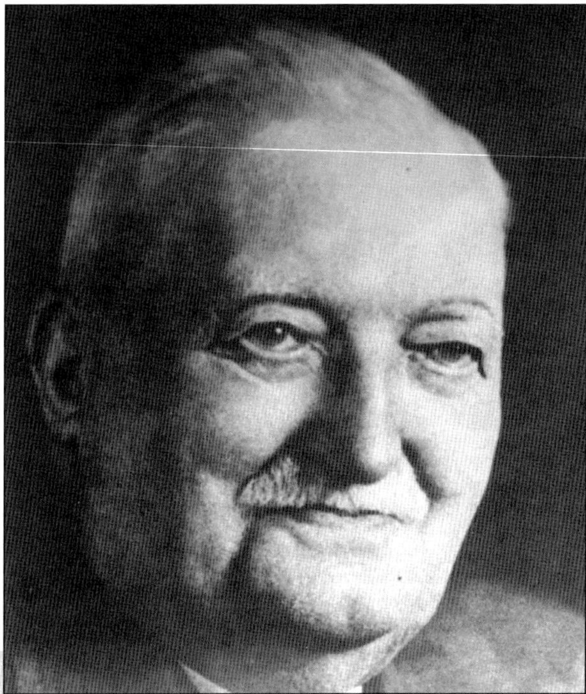

Hans Larsen

Isaac Miller wasn't the only Danish-born mayor of Rawlins. There was also Hans Larsen, who took office in 1895.

Larsen came to America when he was 20 years old. He moved to Rawlins and became a prominent lumber and paint dealer in town. He also owned a coal mine, a stone quarry, an oil company, a hardware store, and a concrete brick plant.

Through his contracting business, Larsen reportedly built 337 homes between 1891 and 1937. (Right, courtesy City of Rawlins; below, courtesy Carbon County Museum.)

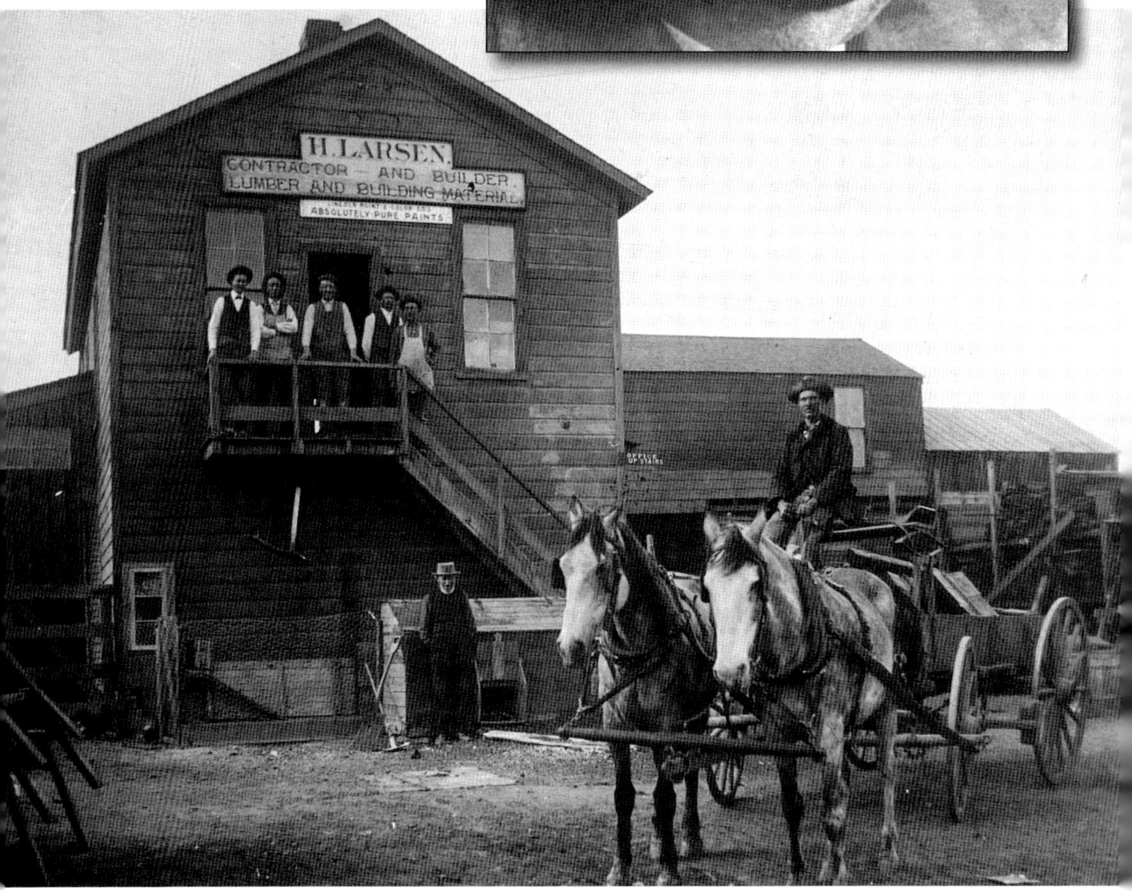

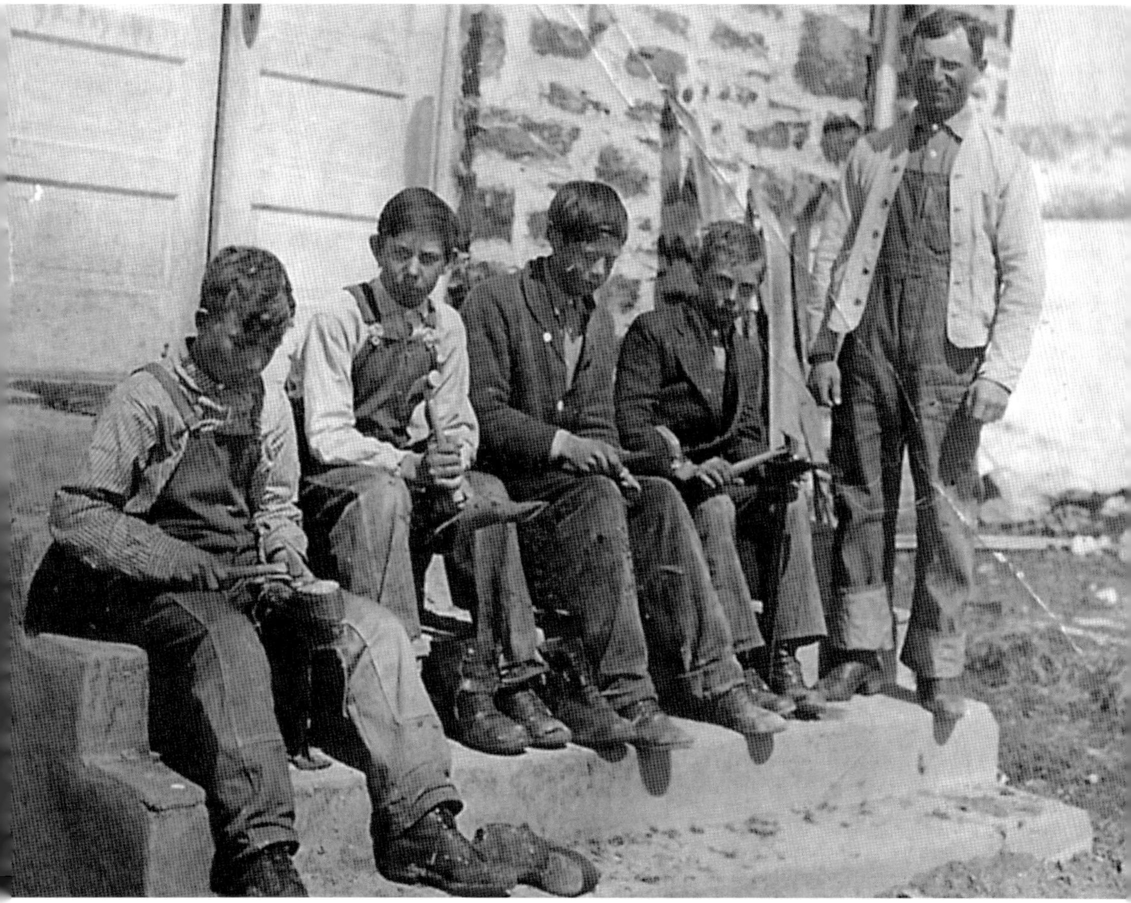

Isadore Bolten

"There was nothing for me in Russia—absolutely nothing. I had the whole world to move about in, but some kind of destiny pulled me toward America," said Isadore Bolten.

Bolten landed in New York in 1905, penniless and not knowing a word of English. He worked as a shoemaker in Chicago, and it is said that is where he learned to read. He eventually read about homesteading in the Wild West and headed toward Colorado.

About 18 miles north of Hayden, he found a piece of land he thought was ideal to settle on. This homestead eventually grew to 25,000 acres. After losing his cattle, Bolten decided to buy sheep, which was unheard of in cattle country at that time. This drew him into the Routt County sheep wars between cattlemen and sheepherders, which didn't end until the Colorado militia was called.

Bolten later partnered with Roblin Davis to form the Bolten and Davis Land and Livestock Company, which brought him into the Rawlins area. At its peak, the company owned more than 20,000 head of sheep, 2,000 cattle, and a herd of buffalo.

Bolten eventually bought out the interest held by the Davis family and became the company's president and sole proprietor.

"I would be grateful to America even if she had given me nothing, but she's been kind to me beyond my wildest dreams," he once told the *Rawlins Daily Times*.

After achieving his American dream, Bolten decided to give back. He paid for and built Bolten Park on the south side of Rawlins because the youth there didn't have a proper playground. The City of Rawlins still makes use of money generated from Bolten's trust fund to upgrade and maintain the park. (Courtesy Hayden Heritage Center.)

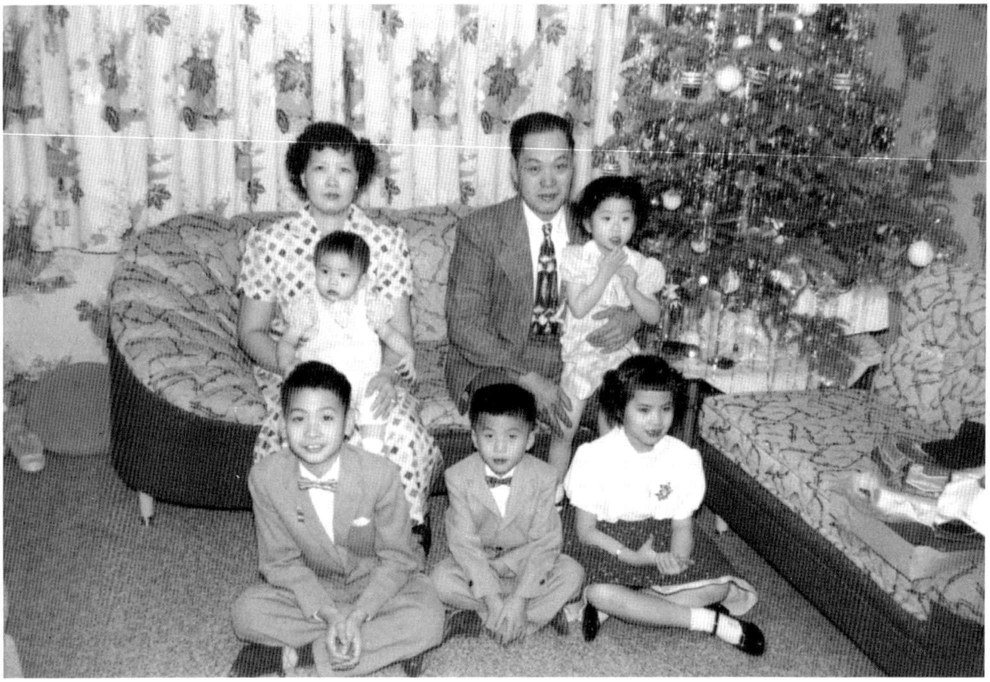

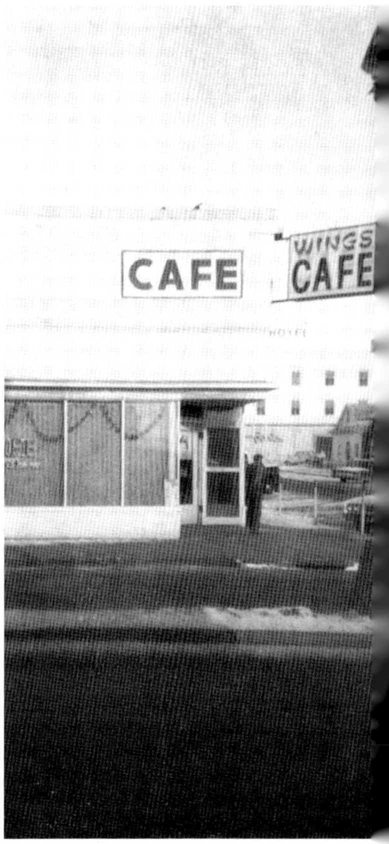

Wing Family

The Wings, along with the Lews, were the only two Chinese families in town for many years. Liu Ban Kwong first came to Rawlins from China in the 1930s and opened King Fong restaurant on Front Street to serve the railroad workers. His son Moy Kong "Charlie" Wing worked at the restaurant and later partnered with Lew Jow to establish the Willow Inn in the 1950s.

"We were always business people," said Charlie's son, Moy—the only member of the family who still lives in Rawlins. Charlie established Wing's Café in downtown Rawlins in 1963. The restaurant burned down in the 1970s, and the Wings built what is now the Days Inn on the east side of town. It contained the Ming Tree restaurant and Images bar. "It was a ripping bar at that time," Moy recalled. "Gary Lewis and the Playboys played there."

The family was well known and respected in town. Charlie's wife, Chin, was affectionately known as "Mama Wing" by her friends and customers. Five Wing children graduated from Rawlins High School: Moy in 1966, Mee in 1969, Gene in 1971, Toa in 1973, and Quong in 1976. All five worked at the restaurant, and the family was especially close with longtime waitress Delcy Moulder. When Charlie died in 1987, his pallbearers all consisted of prominent community members and businessmen.

When asked how it was growing up as one of the few Chinese kids in town, Moy said, "I don't remember anything bad. Everybody knew us, and there was no prejudice."

"Rawlins was a great town to grow up in," Mee said. (Both courtesy Wing family.)

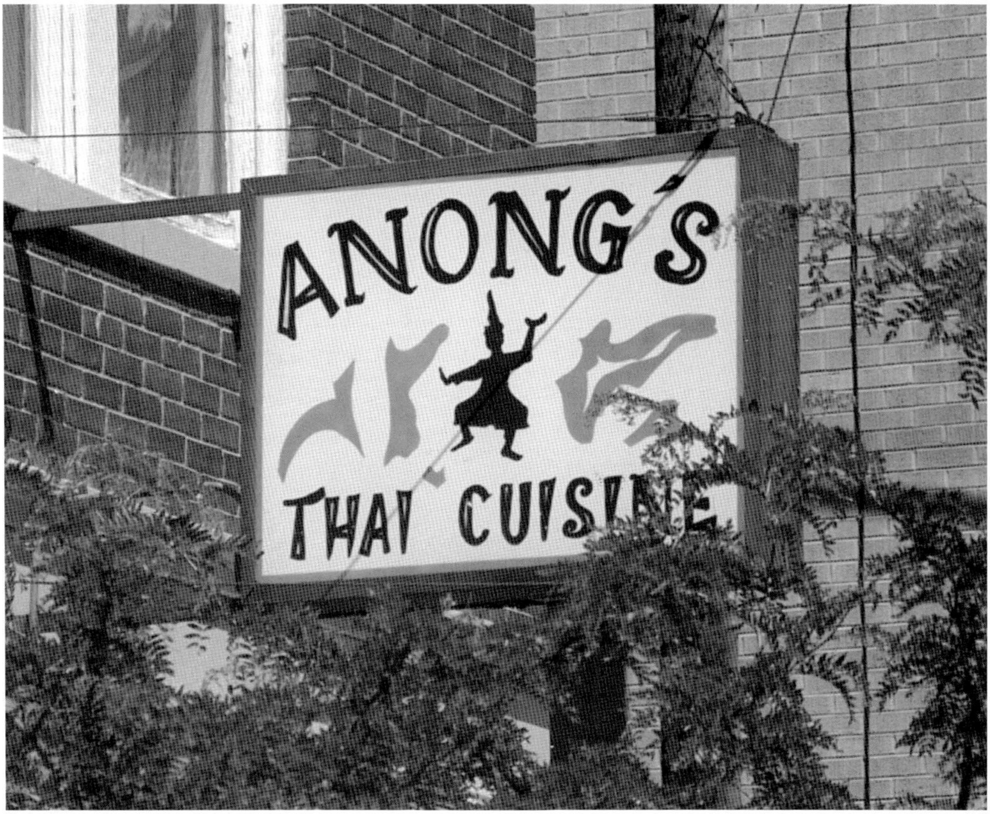

Anong Larsen

Rawlins is not exactly the place people come to pursue the American dream nowadays, and it probably wasn't Anong Larsen's intention to achieve it here.

In 1990, Larsen was sewing T-shirts in a Los Angeles factory. She had just come to the United States from a small village in Thailand.

Fast-forward to 2013. Larsen is celebrating the grand opening of Anong's Thai Cuisine in Cheyenne—her third restaurant in Wyoming.

It all started here in Rawlins, though. After a few years in the United States, Anong decided to turn to restaurant work, which eventually brought her to Lander, Wyoming. In Lander, she met her husband, Brett, who is a Rawlins native and a descendant of Hans Larsen.

In 2002, the couple moved back to Rawlins, where Larsen decided to do something about the "lack of Thai flavor in the local dining community."

She assembled a staff of family and close friends from Thailand and launched the restaurant in downtown Rawlins, and it became a smash hit. It expanded to Laramie in 2008. Larsen said she didn't plan on her latest expansion; she was persuaded by popular request. (Both photographs by Han Cheung.)

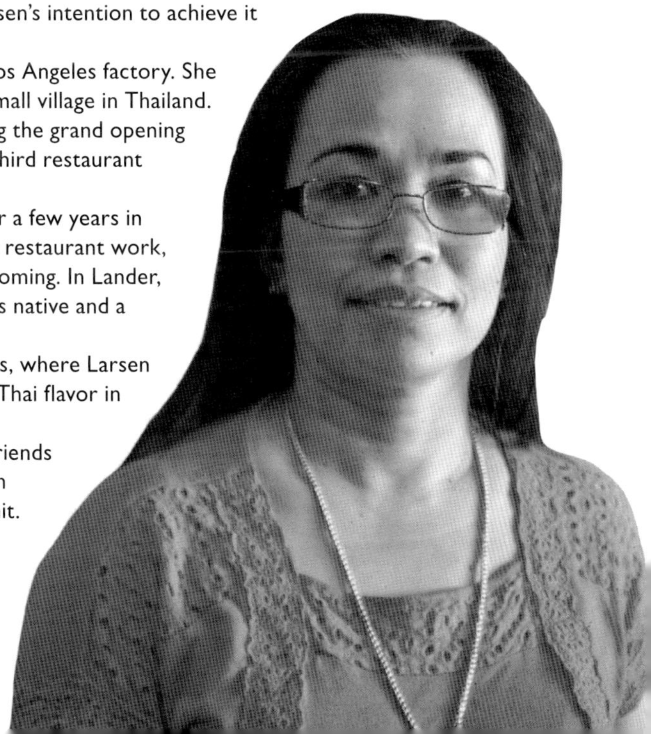

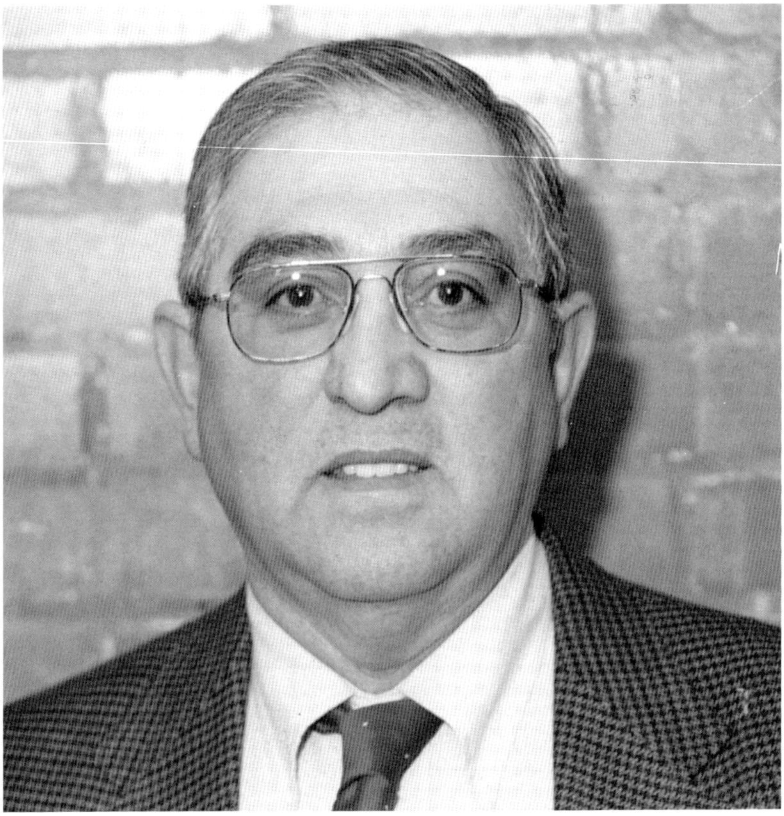

DeBari Martinez

Martinez is known in town as the longest-tenured former city council member (36 years) and a former mayor—but a notable chapter of his life dealt with battling discrimination.

Martinez's family settled in Rawlins in the 1930s. He fondly remembers growing up on a block where there were 40 kids in four houses.

There was an unspoken social divide with the folks on the north side, at least in the beginning. "But we all attended the same school and started to intermingle a little bit," he said. "Later on we started buying in different parts of town."

Martinez's father had faced discrimination on the railroad. "They never put Latinos in engine service," he said. "My dad had a cousin get in, but his last name was Branch. Most were fuelers—my dad shoveled coal."

In the 1970s, a 23-year-old Martinez started working at the Sinclair Wyoming Oil Refinery. "Back then, there were only five Latinos in operations," he said. "The rest were all in labor, driving trucks and such."

Martinez was interested in an operations job, but he said the refinery took measures to make sure it wouldn't happen. "They would work me for 44 days, lay me off and hire me again so I couldn't gain seniority," he said.

When Martinez complained about his situation, he said his boss told him to go back to digging ditches.

"I got a hold of the federal government, and they told me, 'You have to challenge the union and company,' " he said. "A black man told me, 'You will win this—but everyone will be mad at you.' "

Martinez won the case and was put in operations. When asked if people were indeed mad, he said, "It never did feel like they were."

Martinez eventually worked his way up to shift supervisor and held that position for 17 years until he retired. (Courtesy City of Rawlins.)

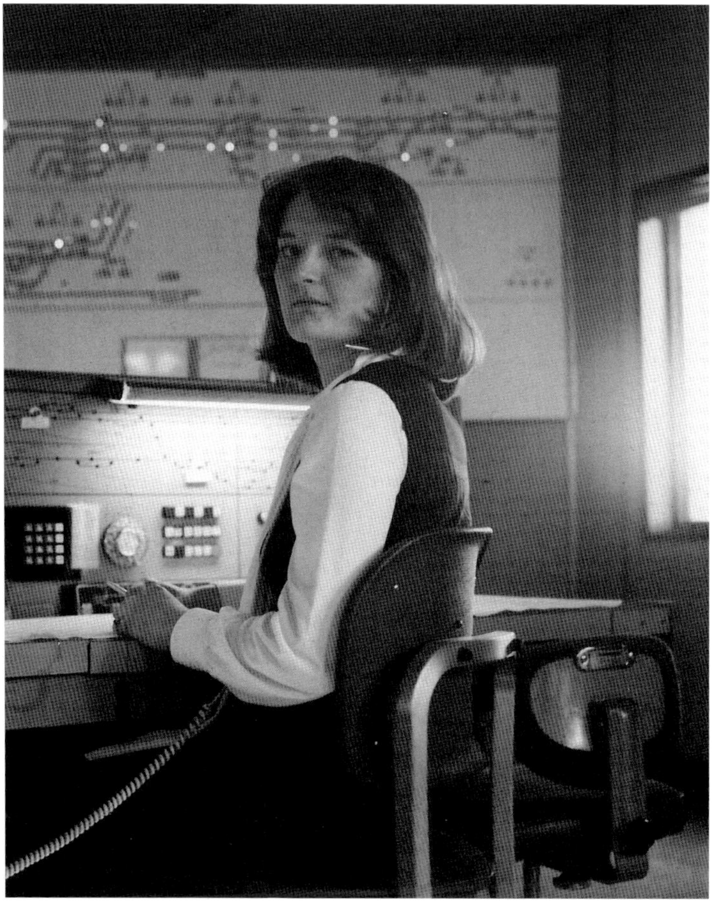

Valerie Nelson

When Valerie Nelson first joined the Union Pacific Railroad in 1974, the railroad's operating rules stated, "Women, children, intoxicated persons or persons otherwise incapable of caring for livestock or other freight must not be permitted to act as attendants for such freight."

However, Nelson not only became Wyoming's first female train dispatcher but also took it a step further and became the state's first train engineer.

Nelson grew up in Rawlins, where her father was also a locomotive engineer. Married at 19 and divorced at 22, she found herself having to fend for herself and her daughter, Tara, for the first time.

Nelson's $2-an-hour job as a bookkeeper wasn't going to cut it, and when a railroad crew caller and janitor position for $5 an hour opened up, she "literally begged for the job."

Thus began Nelson's 24-year career on the railroad. "It was really fun to be the crew caller, or 'call girl,' " she said. "I got to drive around in a taxi and call people to go to work."

At Nelson's father's encouragement, she put in an application for engineer in 1975. This raised some eyebrows, but Nelson became Wyoming's first female train dispatcher that November.

Nelson broke into her job quickly and enjoyed the work, which reminded her of a large chess game. But even after performing at a high level for two years, she said some engineers still wouldn't answer the radios or would argue with her. One even said, "I'll be damned if a woman is going to tell me what to do."

Nelson was also often bypassed for job bids, even when she held seniority. Her coworkers and even the assistant superintendent of UP Wyoming told her to file a discrimination suit, but she never did. (Courtesy Valerie Nelson.)

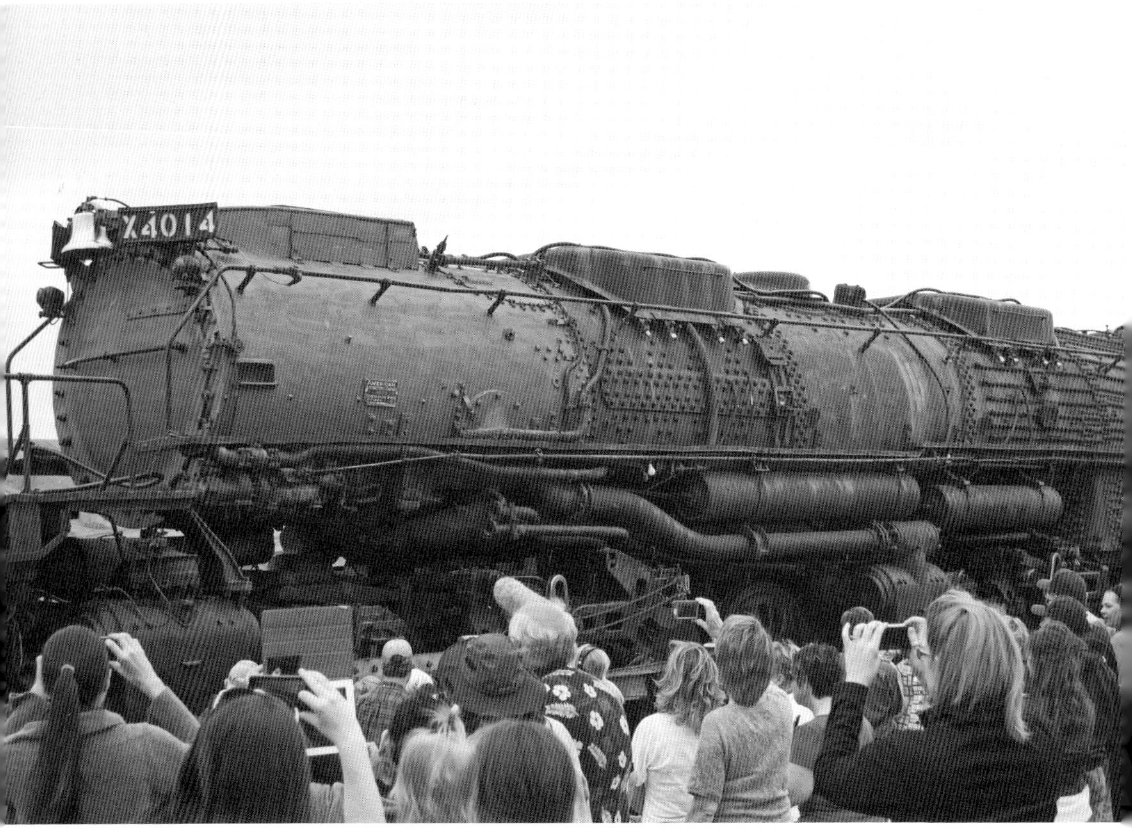

Old Locomotive Engine
In 1978, Valerie Nelson was called in for an interview for locomotive engineer. After seeing her engineer brother's paycheck, she decided to go for the job. "He didn't tell me he worked *all* the time," she laughed.

In August 1979, Nelson completed her training and became the first female engineer in Wyoming.

She continued to face all kinds of sexual discrimination over the years, including having demeaning slurs directed toward her painted in tar on overpasses.

There were also many attempts to get her in trouble, and Nelson said the main reason she survived was because she learned to document "any and all questionable situations."

By 1992, Nelson was able to use her seniority to obtain a more comfortable route. But in 1996, her career ended when a new Rawlins trainmaster squeezed her hand so hard when introducing himself that he broke parts of it, which she had originally injured when she was young.

"After all that, I'm kind of sad [about] the way it ended," she said. (Photograph by Han Cheung.)

CHAPTER FIVE

Family Names

As a boom-and-bust community, Rawlins has seen many families come and go. The Rankins have moved on and the Holman descendants now live in Oregon.

But a few other families have been here since the beginning and have stayed relevant for more than a century. James France was one of the first residents and first bankers in town, and to this day, the France family is still in the banking business.

The O'Melias started out as railroad workers, but the name is associated in modern times with a respected journalist and two dedicated educators.

Though no longer owned by the Rasmusson family, when Rasmusson Furniture was sold to the Penlands, it was the oldest family-owned business in town. Now it is owned by second-generation Penlands who are also active in community affairs.

Three generations of Kinnamans have lived in the same neighborhood for over 100 years. They all tried their hands at politics, with varying degrees of success.

Residents won't find a Jeffrey in town, but they automatically recognize the last name because it is immortalized on a sign in front of the town's community hall, the Jeffrey Memorial Center.

Many of Rawlins's streets were named after early residents who no longer have kin in town. A local could drive on Daley Street every day but have no idea who William Daley was. As the city expanded to the east, some later residents were able to have their names incorporated into Rawlins street lore.

Facilities that carry names of former residents include a community center, a golf course, and a luxurious bed-and-breakfast.

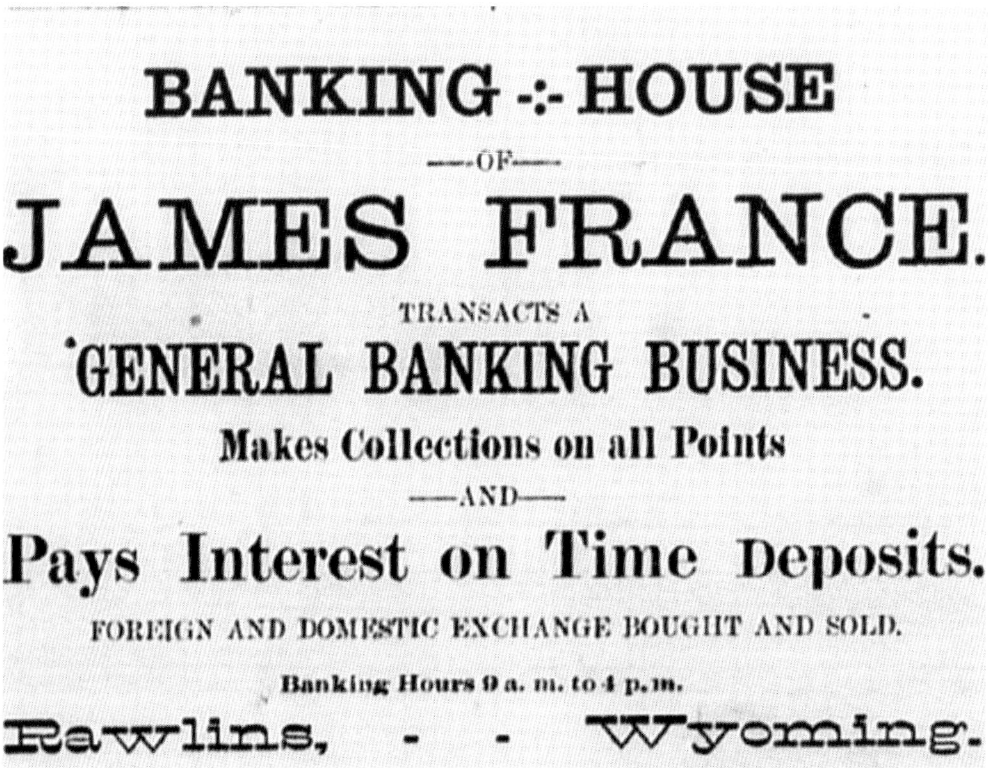

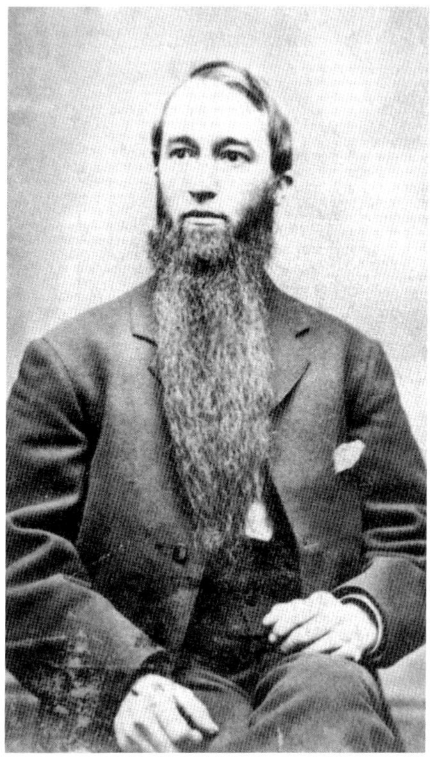

James France

James was the first France to come to Rawlins and was the first banker in town. Arriving in 1868, he operated several businesses before he opened the Banking House of James France in 1884. It is said that his success drew many people from his hometown in Pennsylvania to Rawlins—including the Rankins, who were neighbors to the Frances back home.

James served as county commissioner chair for three terms and was the second Rawlins postmaster, holding that office for 14 years. He also served in the territorial legislature. (Above, courtesy Wyoming Newspaper Project; right, courtesy Carbon County Museum.)

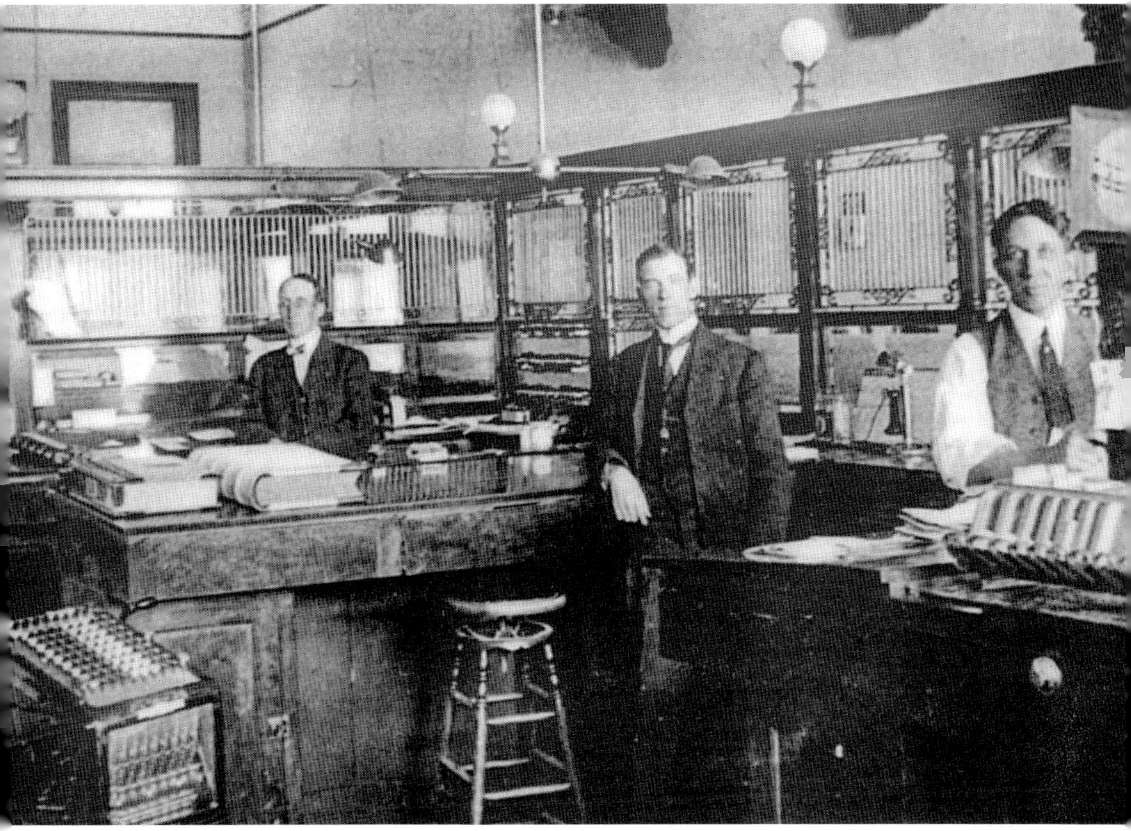

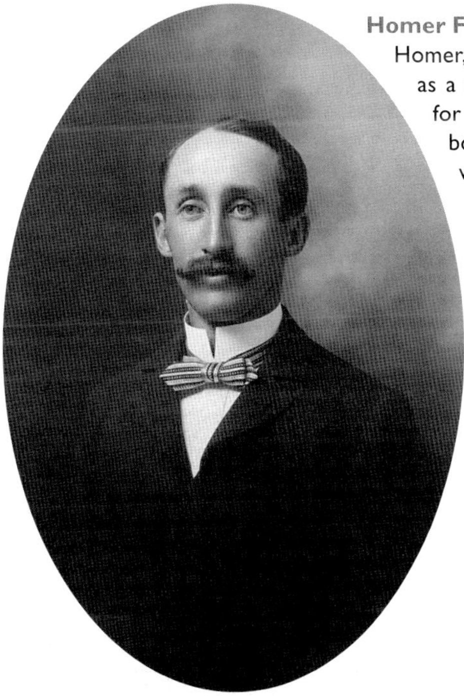

Homer France

Homer, James France's nephew, arrived in Rawlins in 1874 as a toddler to join his father, Walker, who was working for James. Homer France started his banking career as a bookkeeper and janitor for Rawlins National Bank and worked his way up to bank president in 1938. He is pictured at far left above. (Above, courtesy Rawlins National Bank; right, courtesy France family.)

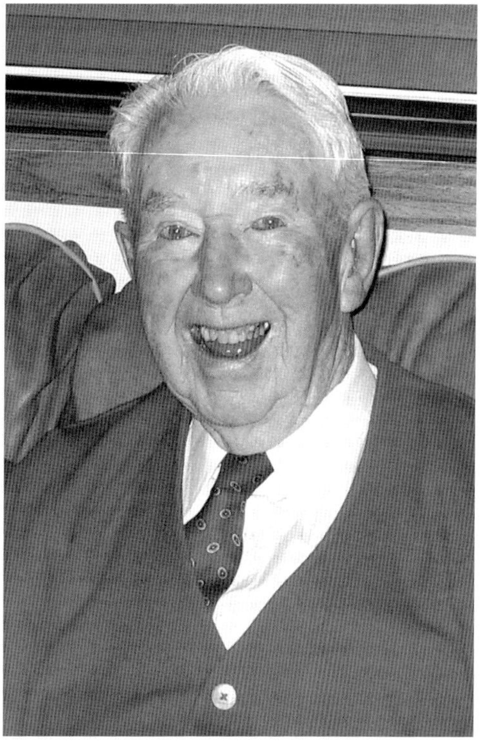

John France

Homer France's son, John, took over as Rawlins National Bank (RNB) president at age 29 and served from 1948 until his retirement in 1978. In 1984, John decided to start the Bank of Commerce because RNB was becoming more of a metropolitan-type bank. "He wanted to have a bank that had the same independent community-owned bank philosophy that he had throughout his career at Rawlins National," said his son, Sherrod. (Right, courtesy France family; below, photograph by Han Cheung.)

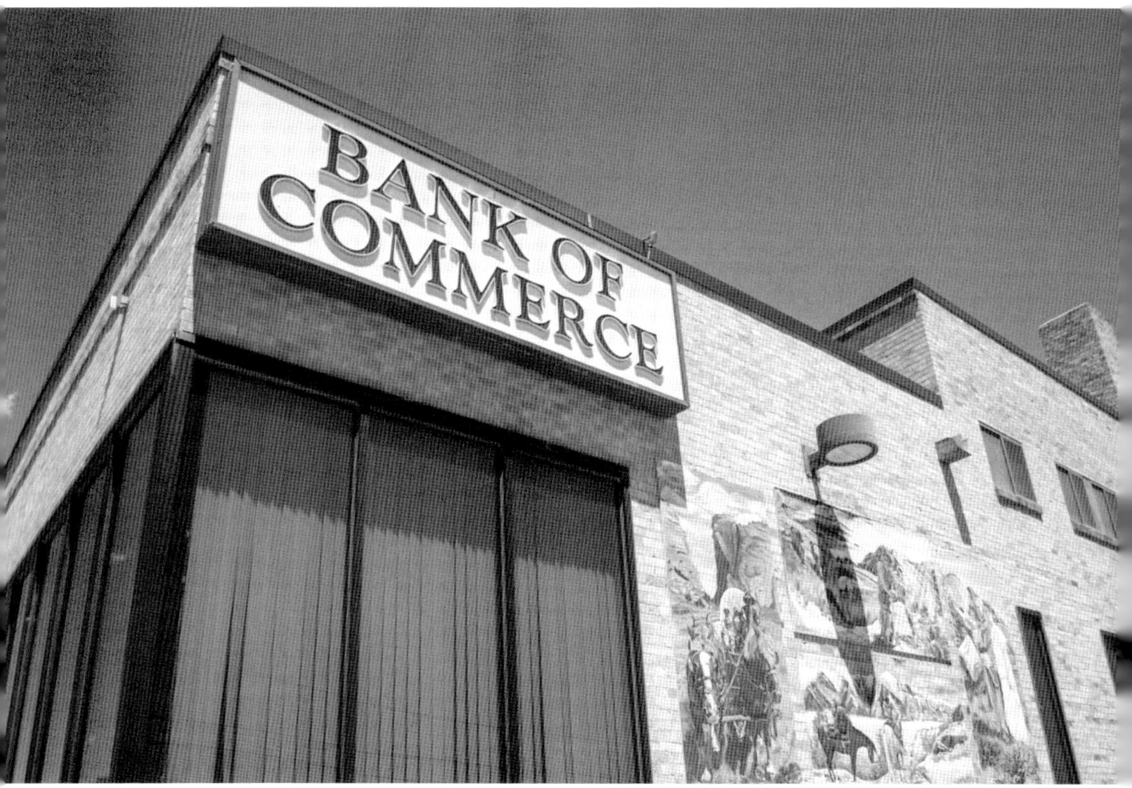

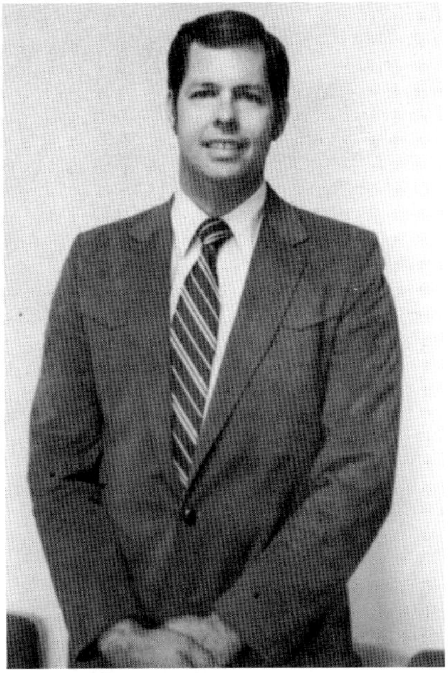

Sherrod France
John France's son, Sherrod, started his banking career at Jackson State Bank. He returned to Rawlins and became RNB president when his father retired in 1978. He left RNB in 1984 to lead the Bank of Commerce (BOC). He is retired and serves as president of the Miller Estate Company, which includes Isaac Miller's former ranch. (Courtesy *Rawlins Daily Times.*)

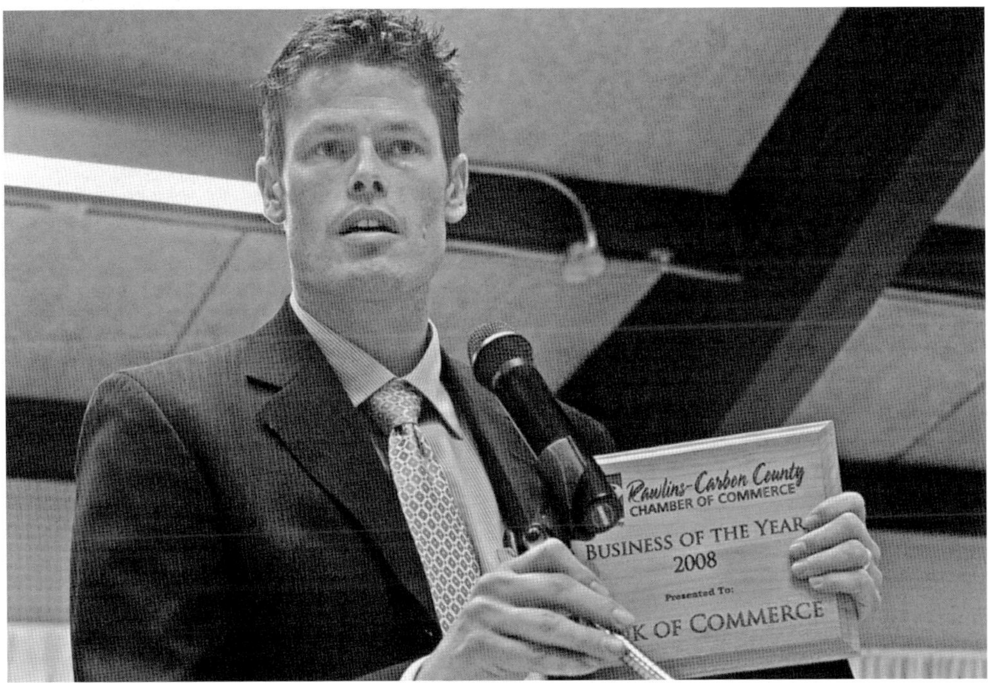

Copper France
Sherrod France's eldest son, Copper, was working as a structural engineer in Denver in 2000 when he called his father one day and said, "I'd like to come back to Rawlins and work in the bank." Copper became president when Sherrod retired. Copper stresses that BOC is locally owned by several community members. "The people of Carbon County have been loyal to us, and we are extremely grateful," he said. "It has been a very rewarding experience to come back to Rawlins and help our community grow and prosper." (Courtesy *Rawlins Daily Times.*)

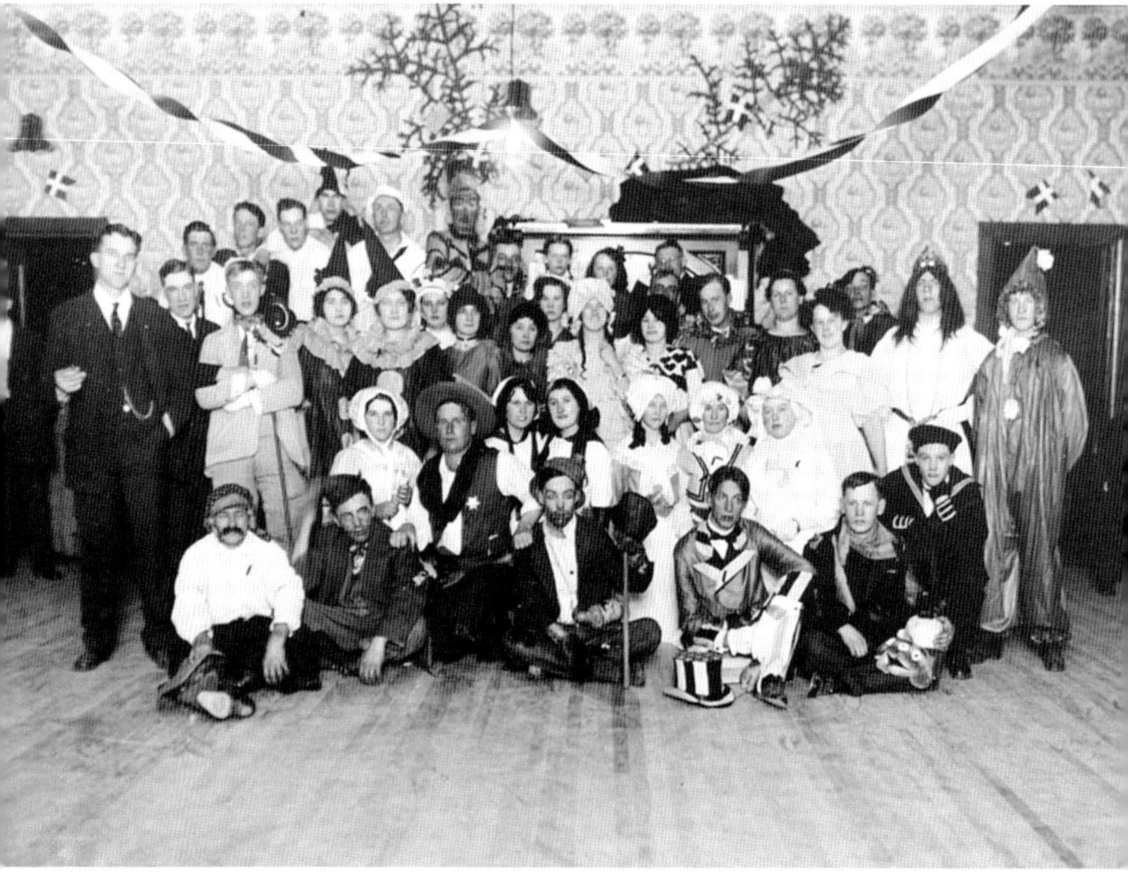

Robert O'Melia

Brothers John and Michael were the first O'Melias to come to Rawlins, arriving in 1874. Their nephew Robert followed in 1882 and found work as an engine wiper for the Union Pacific Railroad. Robert's son, Dennis, was a railroad engineer, city pumper, and night policeman.

Dennis's eldest son, Robert, followed in his father's and grandfather's footsteps as a railroad worker. In March 1918, he was one of 13 Union Pacific employees to be sent to France to fight in World War I. They dubbed themselves the "Lucky 13." Robert is pictured here fourth from left in the first row at a Halloween party. (Courtesy Carbon County Museum.)

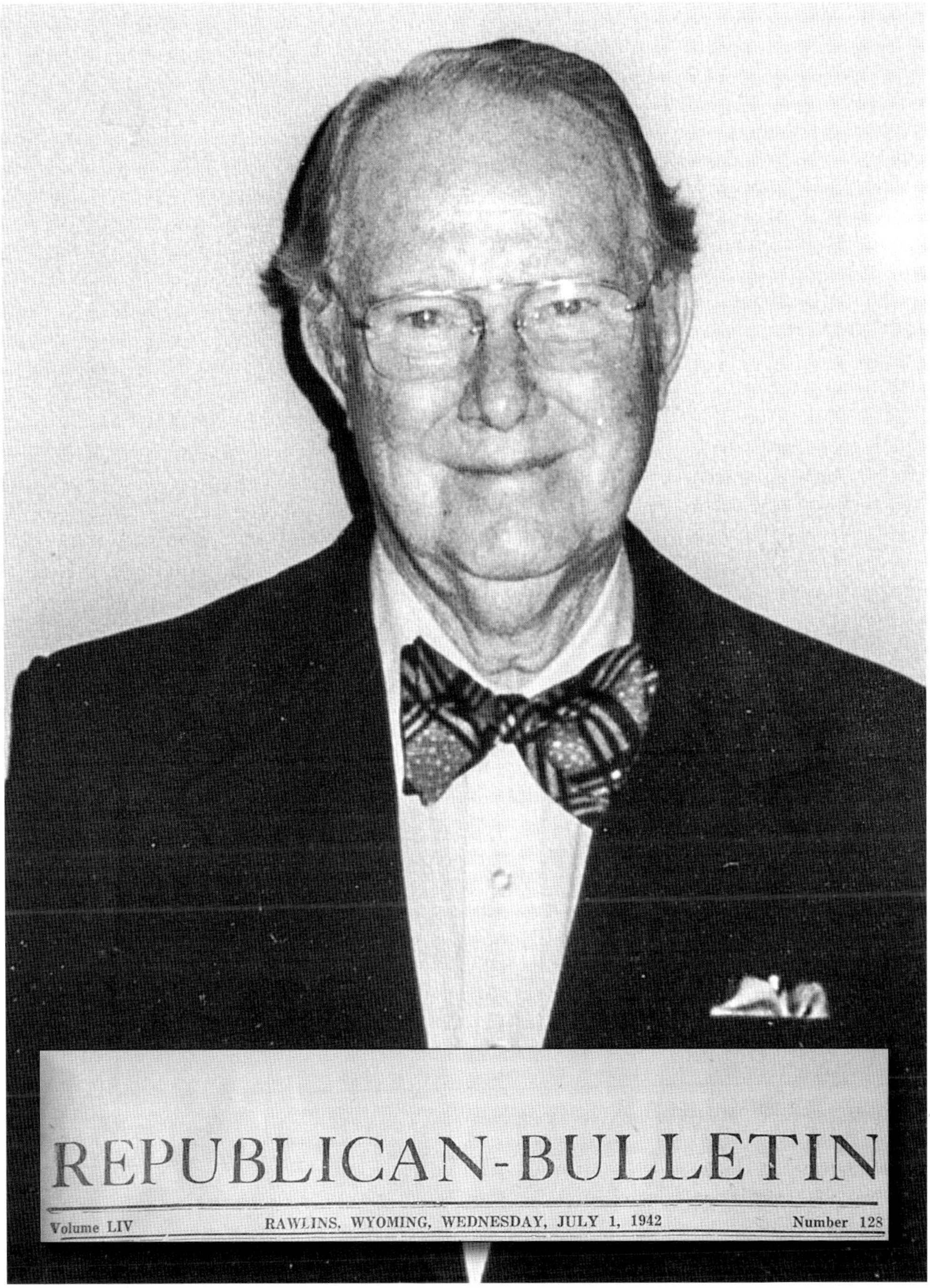

Ted O'Melia

Dennis O'Melia's youngest son, Ted, blazed his own path and became a journalist instead. In 1946, Ted returned to Rawlins from Worland, where he founded the *Northern Wyoming Daily News*. With a group of associates, Ted bought the *Rawlins Republican-Bulletin*, his hometown paper and where he started his career. (Courtesy Carbon County Museum; inset courtesy *Rawlins Daily Times*.)

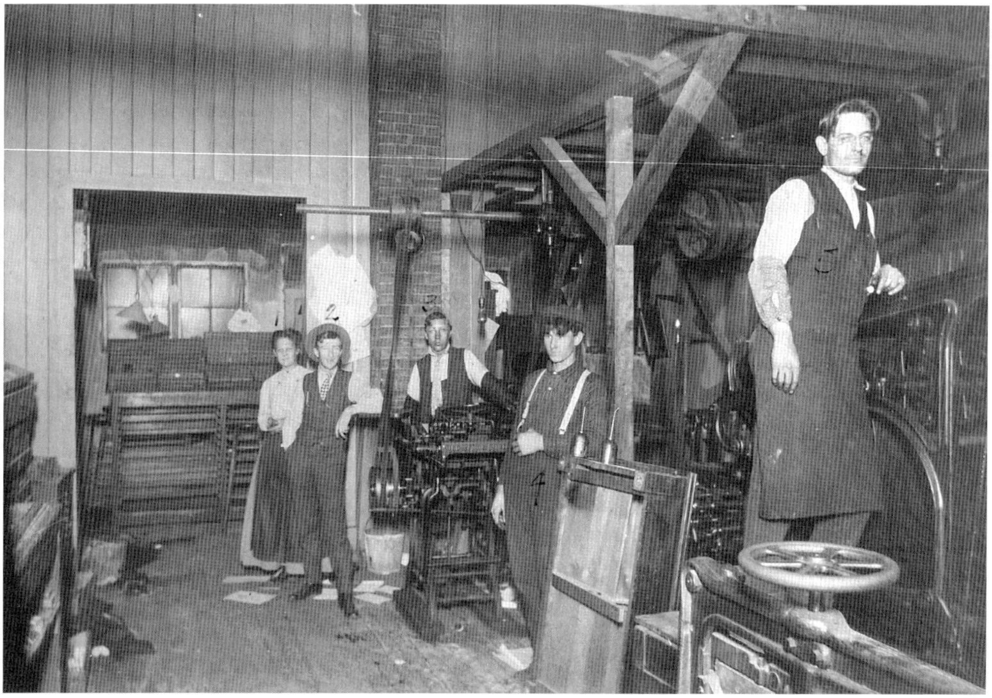

Rawlins Republican Office
The *Rawlins Republican* was founded as an eight-page weekly in 1889 by H.B. Fetz, who published and edited it until 1895. The Cheyenne newspapers described the paper as "straight republican in politics, advocating immediate statehood and the industrial development of the territory." This photograph was taken in 1906. (Courtesy Carbon County Museum.)

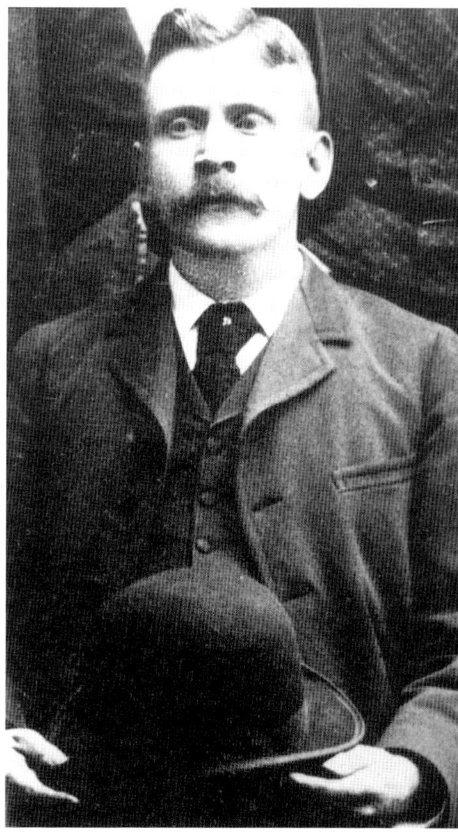

H.B. Fetz
Prior to founding the Rawlins paper, Fetz published papers in Fremont and Natrona Counties. A Laramie paper described Fetz as a young man who "takes naturally to the editorial chair," wears his hair in a pompadour, and "looks very fierce." He also took part in organizing the Wyoming Drug Co. in Rawlins. (Courtesy Carbon County Museum.)

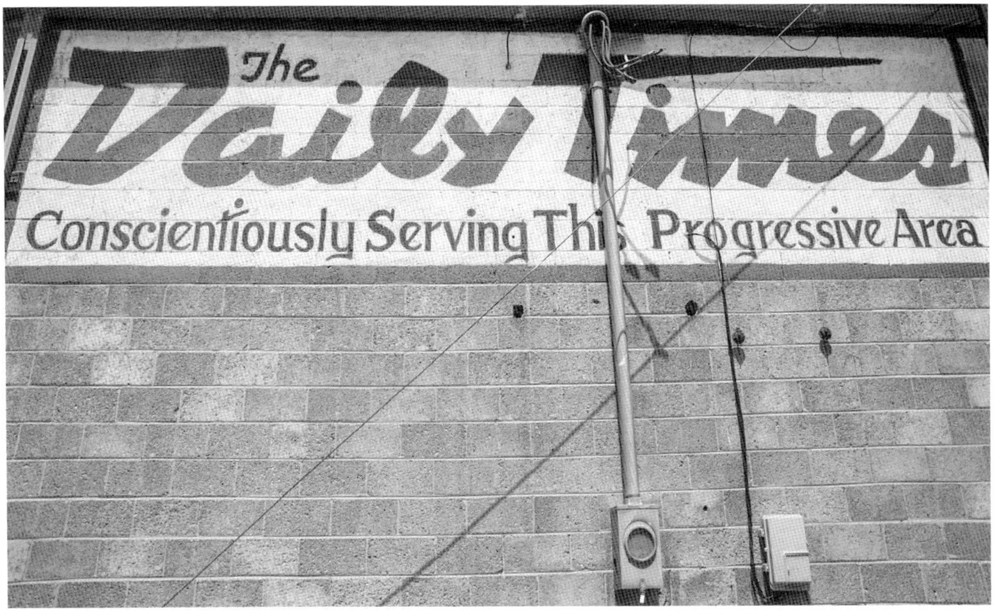

Rawlins Daily Times

Ted O'Melia explained in the first issue of the *Rawlins Daily Times* that the paper's name was changed to "reflect political independence." He was responsible for building the current *Daily Times* building in 1952. He also founded the Rawlins Broadcasting Company and radio station KRAL. Ted O'Melia died in 1997 and was posthumously inducted into the Wyoming Press Association Hall of Fame in 2005. (Above, photograph by Han Cheung; below, courtesy *Rawlins Daily Times*.)

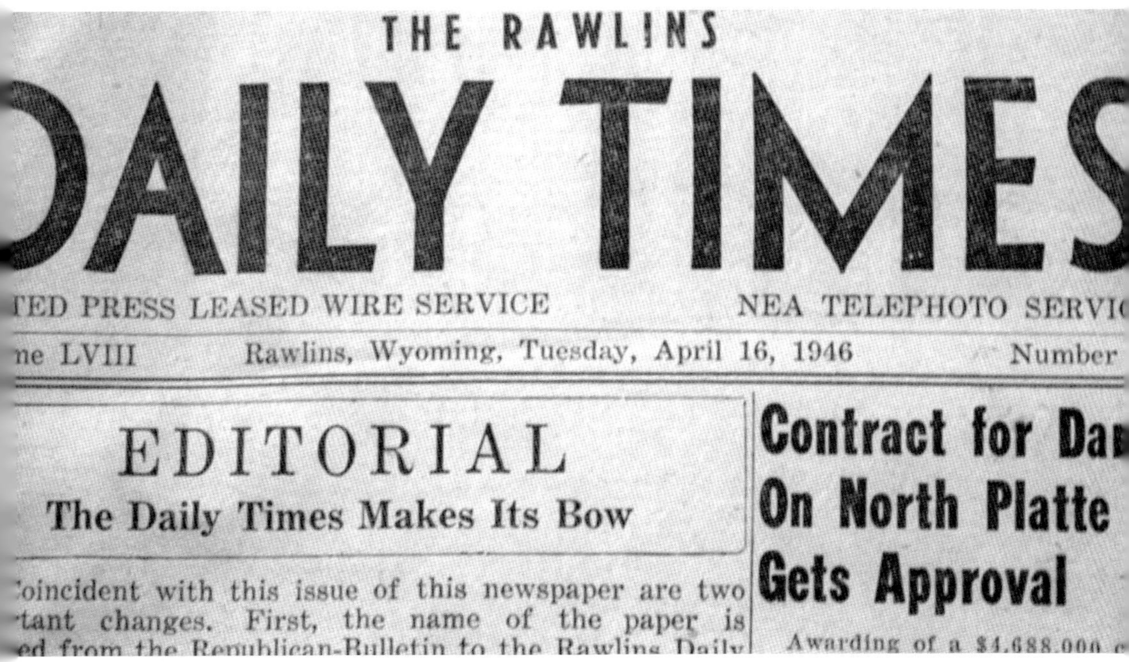

THE RAWLINS

DAILY TIMES

TED PRESS LEASED WIRE SERVICE NEA TELEPHOTO SERVI

ne LVIII Rawlins, Wyoming, Tuesday, April 16, 1946 Number

EDITORIAL

The Daily Times Makes Its Bow

oincident with this issue of this newspaper are two tant changes. First, the name of the paper is ed from the Republican-Bulletin to the Rawlins Daily

Contract for Da On North Platte Gets Approval

Awarding of a $4,688,000

Skip and Darlene O'Melia
Ted O'Melia's nephew Joseph "Skip" was the beloved principal of Mountain View and Sinclair Elementary Schools for 26 years. Affectionately known as "Mr. O.," Skip was a rare principal who would supervise the cafeteria lunch throughout his whole tenure. "That's when you get to see the kids, every one of them, every day," he would say.

Skip retired in 1999. "I've had the kids of kids I had in school here, all the way through high school," he said in his retirement article. "I figure it's time I get out of here before I have their grandkids in here."

"Mrs. O" retired in 2014 after 41 years with the school district—the last 14 as Rawlins High School activities director. She started her career in 1969 as an elementary school physical education teacher at Mountain View Elementary, where she met Skip.

"The most important thing I have told coaches, sponsors—whomever—is that these kids have four years to be at this high school. Give them the very best that you can. You can't say next year 'We will do better.' That's because some of those kids might be seniors," O'Melia told the *Rawlins Daily Times* at her retirement. (Courtesy Darlene O'Melia.)

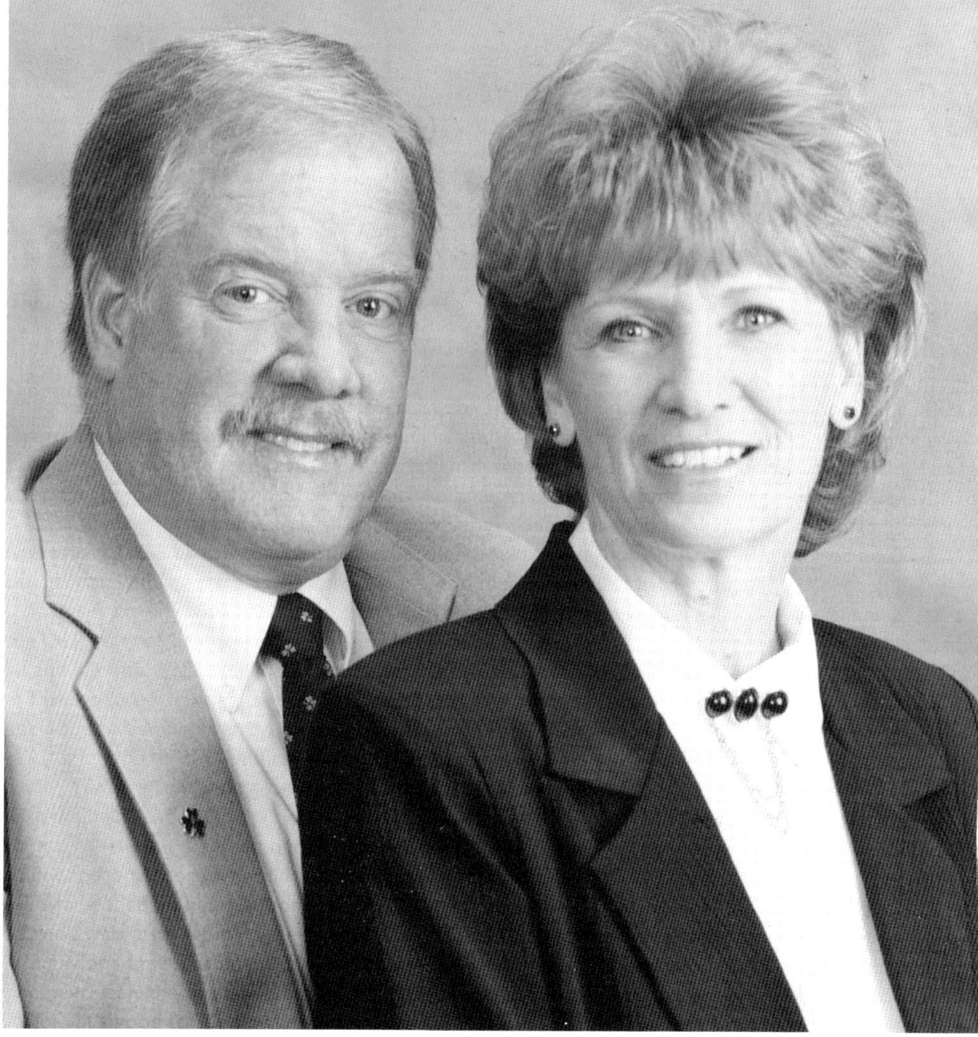

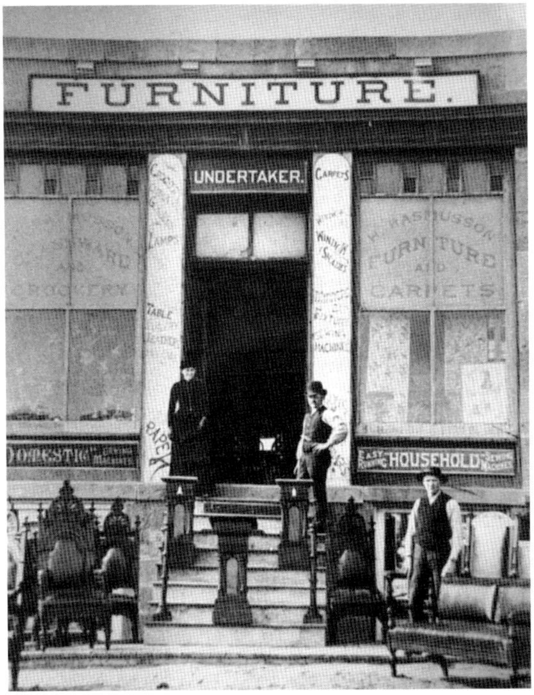

Rasmusson Furniture

Established in 1881, Rasmusson Furniture was the oldest family-owned business in town when Harold and Liz Penland bought it 90 years later. The Penlands decided to keep the store's original name, and today, the furniture store remains the oldest business in town. Pictured below are current owners Jim and Mary Penland. (Left, courtesy Rasmusson Furniture; below, photograph by Han Cheung.)

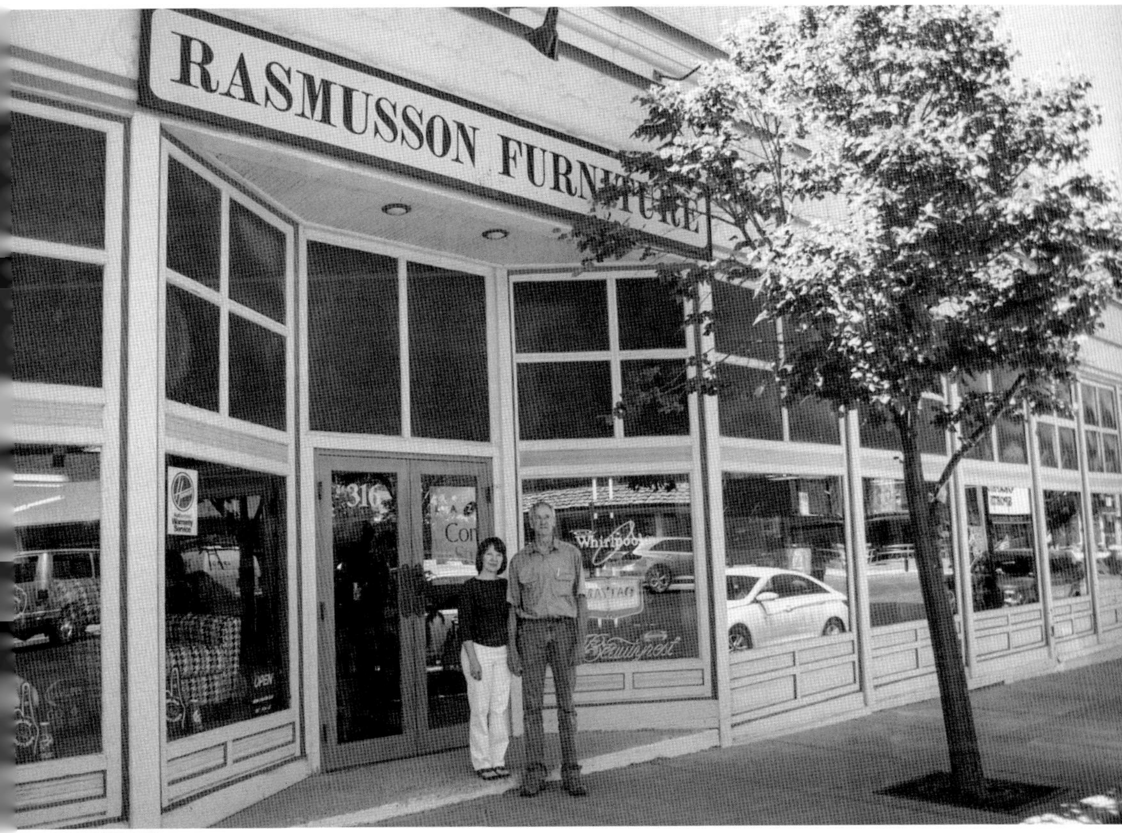

Hans Rasmusson

Hans Rasmusson came to America in 1872 and learned the cabinet-making trade in Chicago. He then headed west until he found Rawlins, which he described as "the best and most favorable place for a business."

Rasmusson opened up a furniture store and mortuary on Front Street the same year. He is said to be one of the first funeral directors and furniture dealers in the state. As business activity shifted toward Cedar Street, Hans followed suit and moved the store north in 1906.

One of the city's three Danish-born mayors, Rasmusson served from 1889 to 1892. He also served as county treasurer and city treasurer. He was instrumental in organizing the Wyoming State Board of Embalmers in 1909. (Courtesy Carbon County Museum.)

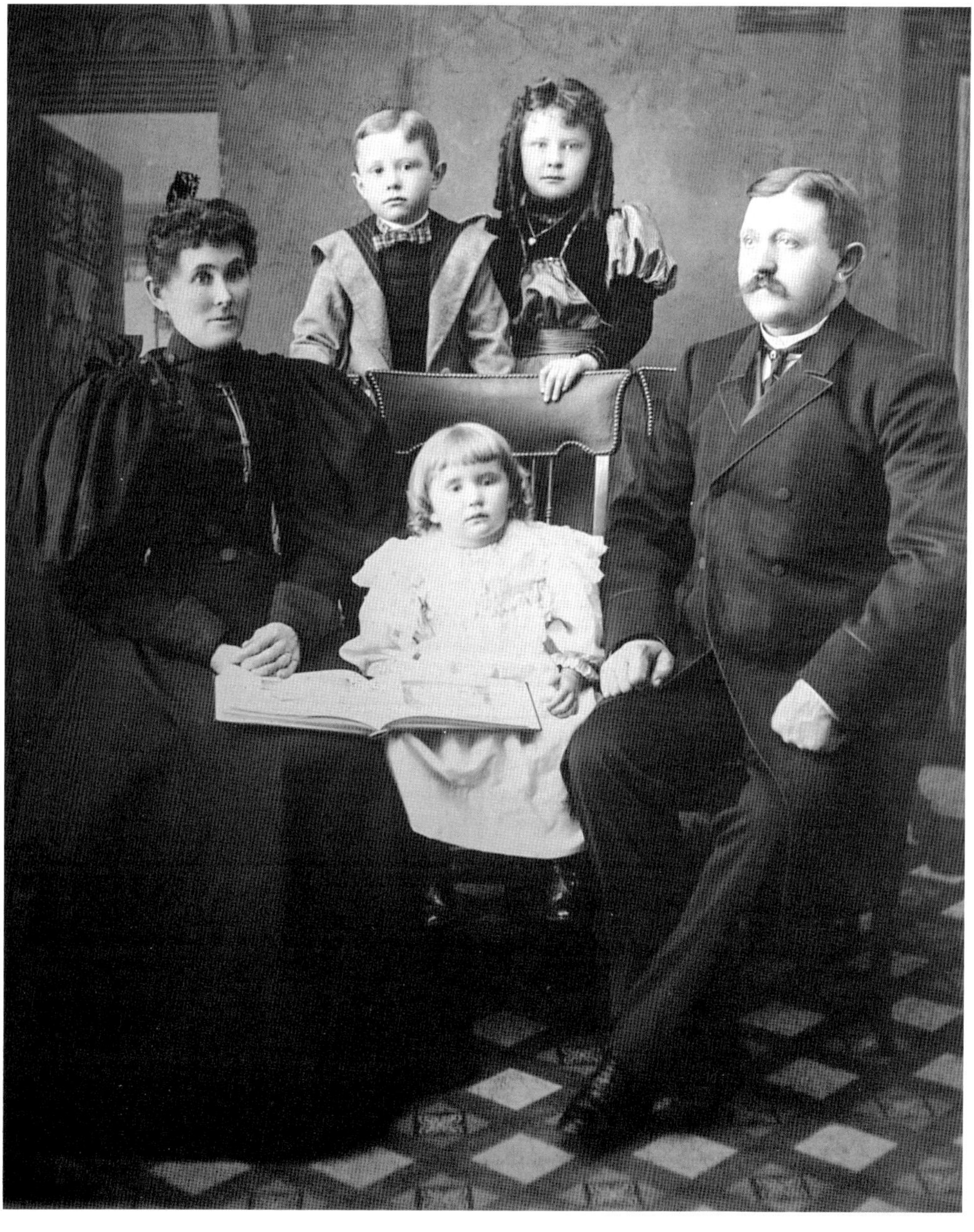

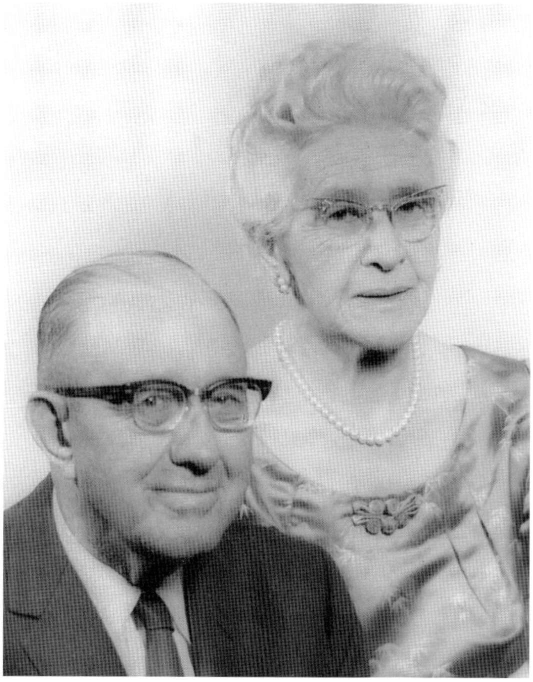

Arthur Rasmusson
Hans Rasmusson's son, Arthur, owned part of the family business, but focused his efforts on ranching. Arthur Rasmusson served as president of the Carbon County Wool Growers Association, president of the city water board, and director of the First National Bank. (Courtesy *Rawlins Daily Times*.)

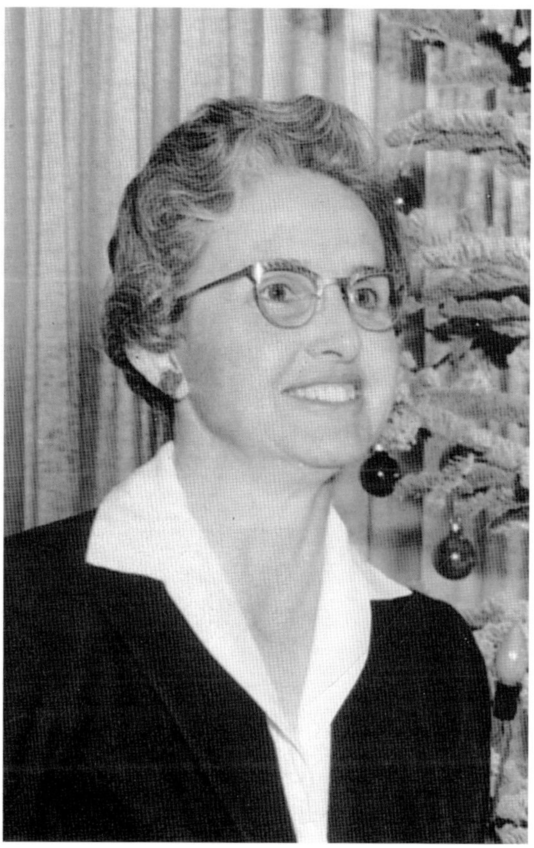

Mary Quealy (Rasmusson)
Arthur Rasmusson's daughter, Mary, was the last Rasmusson to own the store. She was a charter member of Soroptimist International of Rawlins and was known for her "loan closet" of home healthcare equipment that she lent to people free of charge—as long as they gave them back.

The Soroptimists created an annual scholarship for women in Quealy's honor after she and her husband, Stu, left Rawlins for Laramie in 2005. (Courtesy *Rawlins Daily Times*.)

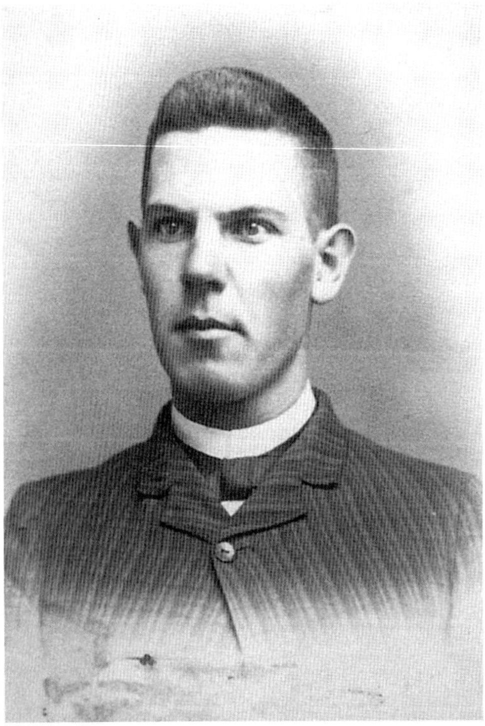

Daniel C. Kinnaman

Daniel Kinnaman was a mechanical genius, but he was perhaps known best in town for establishing D.C. Kinnaman and Son with, of course, his son Elmer. The business was a parts store, machine shop, and garage. Soon, it just focused on auto parts and became Kinnaman Supply Co. in 1957.

Kinnaman served as architect for several buildings in Saratoga and Rawlins, many of which still stand today. A lifelong Democrat, he ran in five elections and won two of them: county commissioner and school board trustee. (Courtesy Daniel L. Kinnaman.)

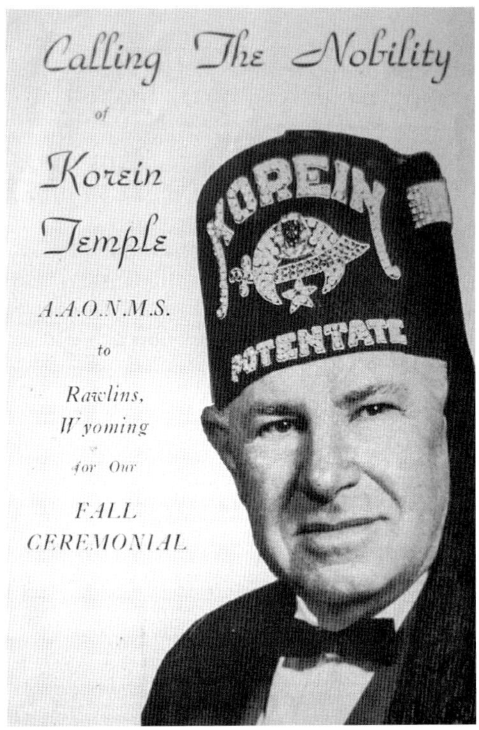

Elmer Kinnaman

Elmer Kinnaman was also a mechanic and took over the business after Daniel retired. He was more successful at politics than his father was, serving in both the Wyoming House of Representatives and Senate for a total of 34 years—a record only recently beaten.

He was named Outstanding Small Businessman of Wyoming in 1965. (Courtesy Daniel L. Kinnaman.)

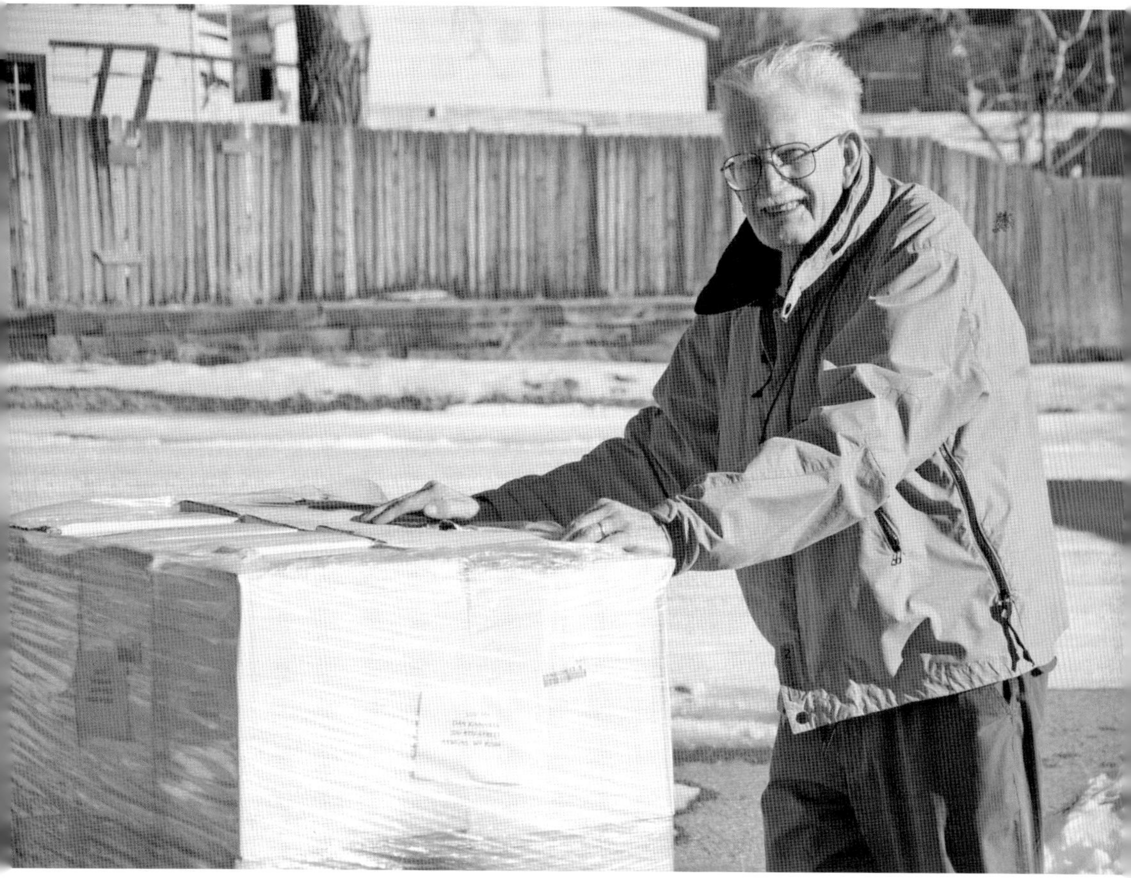

Daniel L. Kinnaman

Dan, Elmer Kinnaman's son, inherited the family business and ran it until the 1990s, when he sold it to a longtime employee.

Dan Kinnaman has dedicated most of his spare time to writing about Carbon County. He has a room full of drawers containing alphabetically organized papers detailing people who lived in and events that happened in Rawlins. "I read all the newspapers and took notes," he said. Ask him about any person or event, and he will most likely be able to find a description of him, her, or it in a short amount of time.

Dan said he started writing because his two sons, who couldn't wait to grow up and leave town, always said, "Nothing happens in Rawlins, never did, and never will." Both sons have moved to San Francisco. "This is my effort to prove them wrong," he said.

Like his father, Dan was also a Wyoming state legislator. He served on the district school board, state school board, University of Wyoming trustee board, and the state library board. (Photograph by Han Cheung.)

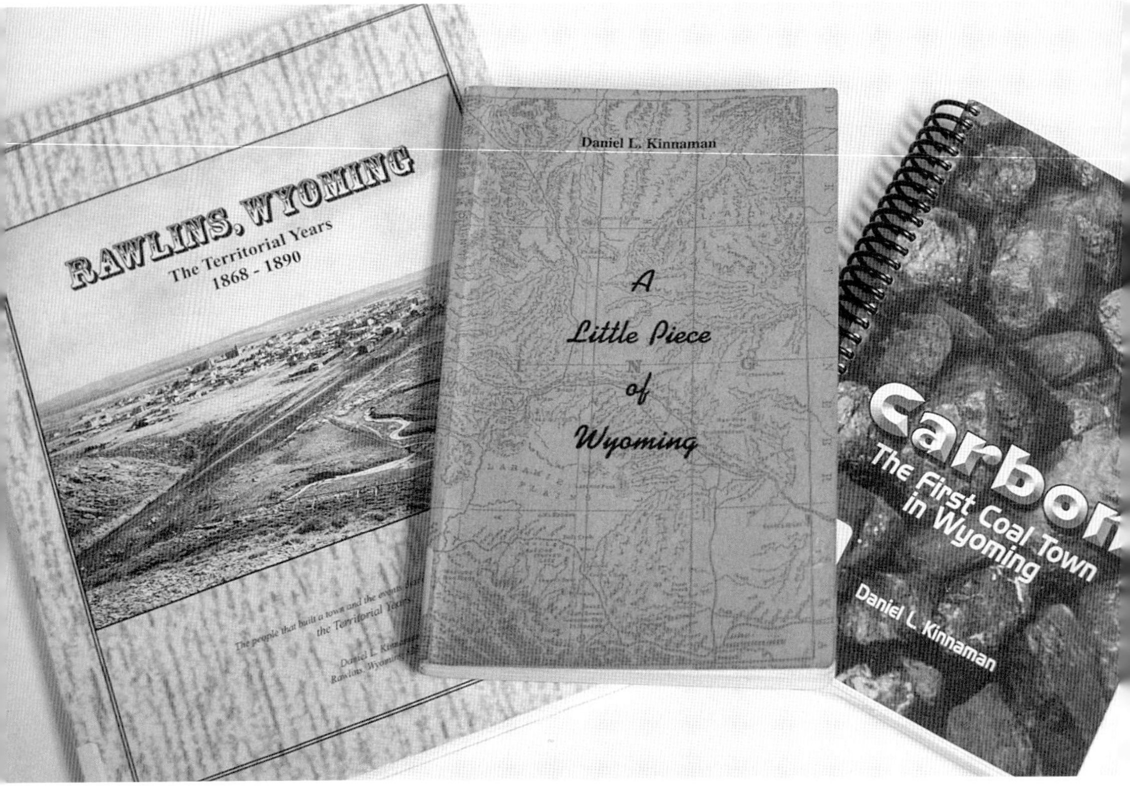

Daniel L. Kinnaman's Books

Dan Kinnaman's efforts have produced three books. His first, *A Little Piece of Wyoming*, covers Carbon County history up to 1869. The second is about Carbon, the first coal town in Wyoming. His latest, *Rawlins, Wyoming: The Territorial Years*, is a detailed description of the people who came through Carbon County from 1868 to 1890. (Photograph by Han Cheung.)

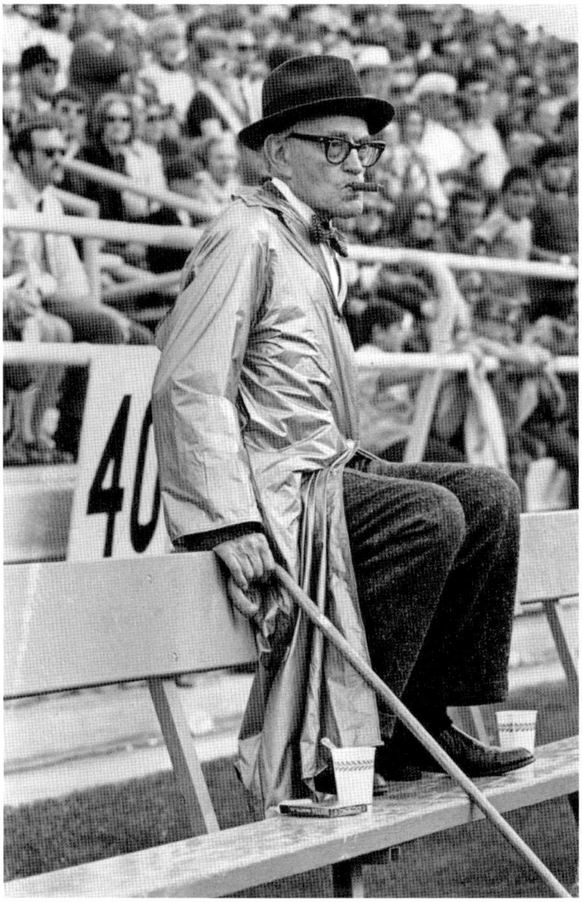

Doctor Jeffrey

It's not every day that a city dedicates an entire day to one of its residents. On July 19, 1967, Rawlins residents celebrated Dr. Jeffrey Day, which honored the iconic whiskey-drinking, foulmouthed, fun-loving local doctor and philanthropist Charles W. Jeffrey.

That night, the Jeffrey Memorial Community Center was dedicated. Dr. Jeffrey had paid the full $310,000 to have it built.

During the ceremony, resident after resident took the podium and delivered colorful anecdotes from Jeffrey's 46 years as the town doctor. One of these tales involved how Jeffrey would shove two bottles of whiskey into each cowboy boot before attending University of Wyoming football games, his favorite pastime.

A Nebraska native, Jeffrey arrived in Rawlins to take over Dr. T.J. Swisher's practice, but he didn't make his fortune by just treating patients. In 1933, A.B. Cobb asked Jeffrey to partner with him in oil prospecting in Montana. Jeffrey turned Cobb down several times before relenting, and it turned out to be the best decision of his life. A $5,000 investment had turned into a $5 million enterprise when they sold it 14 years later.

Now a rich man, Jeffrey decided to give back. His first public contribution was in 1940, when he bought a $37,500 modern fire truck for the City of Rawlins. His proudest donation is the Lincoln monument between Laramie and Cheyenne. Today, it is a popular rest stop on Interstate 80. Jeffrey City, about 60 miles from Rawlins, is also named after him.

Two years after Dr. Jeffrey Day, the doctor fell ill and moved into the local hospital, where he would spend the last five years of his life. (Courtesy *Rawlins Daily Times.*)

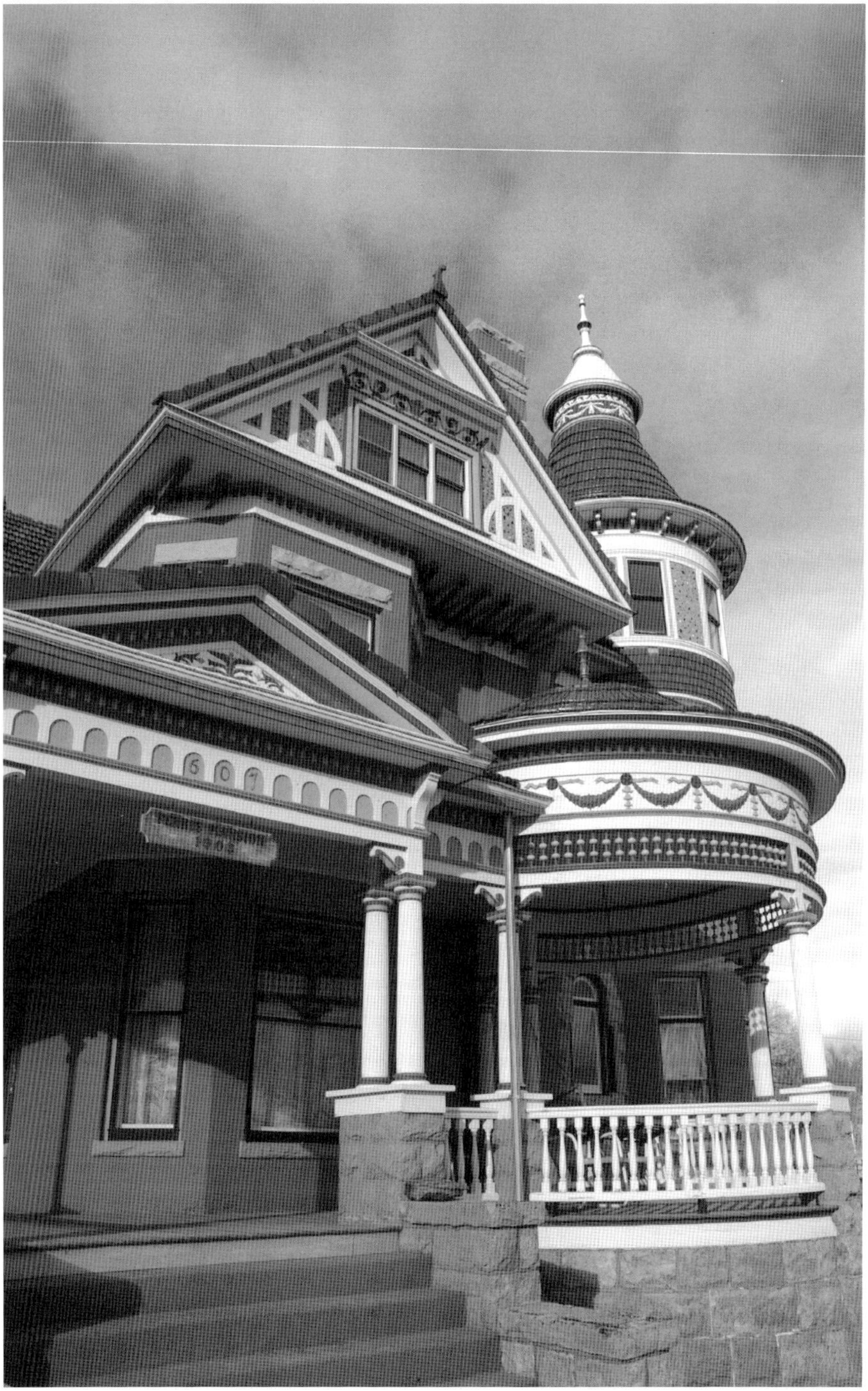

Ferris Mansion

The most beautiful building in town is arguably the Victorian-style Ferris Mansion. The home was built as a residence for the Ferris family in 1903 and later became a makeshift boardinghouse. Today, it is a popular bed-and-breakfast. (Courtesy *Rawlins Daily Times*.)

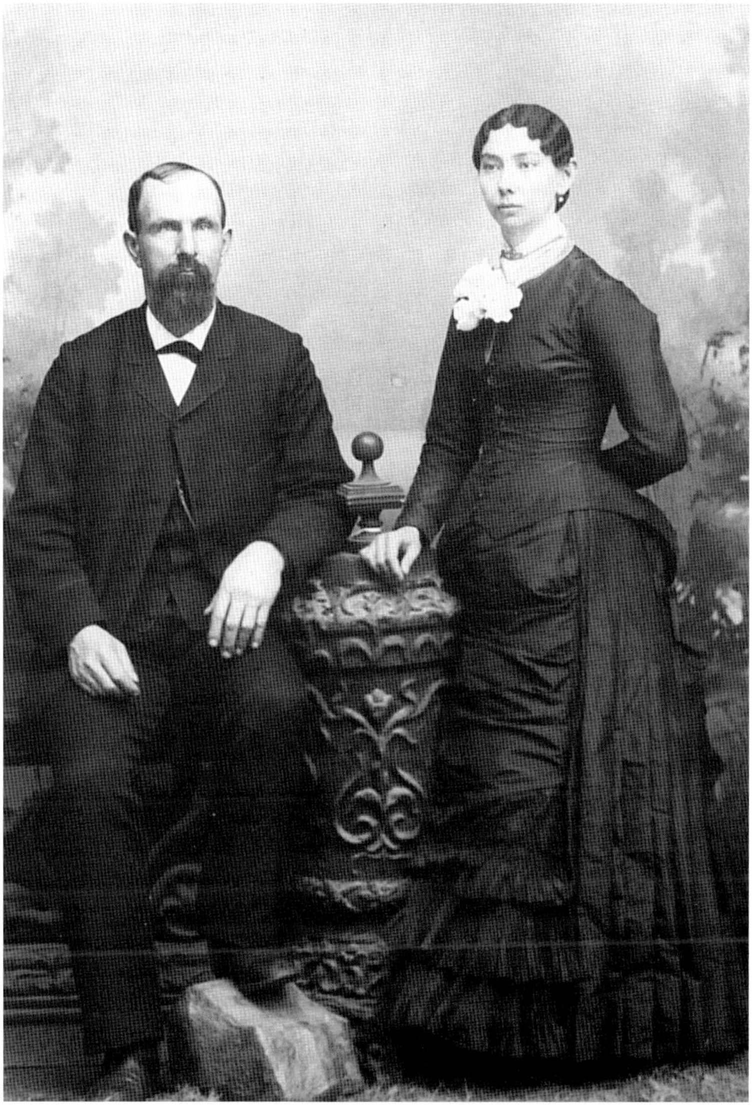

George & Julia Ferris

George Ferris, a Michigan native, first came to Rawlins in 1868 and worked as a hunter for Perry Smith. He also hauled ore from the paint mines north of town. He went back East and returned in 1875 with his wife, Julia. They lived in Rawlins for one year before moving to a ranch in the Platte Valley.

Ferris became a prominent citizen and served twice in the Wyoming legislature, and represented Carbon County at the Wyoming Constitutional Convention.

His most lucrative venture was the Haggarty-Ferris copper mines near Encampment, of which he later became the sole owner.

Flush with mining riches, the Ferris family saw an ad for George Barber's architectural firm featuring the Queen Anne–style C.R. Joy House in Keokuk, Iowa. They commissioned Barber to produce a copy in Rawlins.

George Ferris never saw the house, as he died in a buggy accident in 1900 while returning home from the mines. Julia completed the 8,000-square-foot, three-story brick mansion in 1903 and lived there until her death in 1931. (Courtesy Carbon County Museum.)

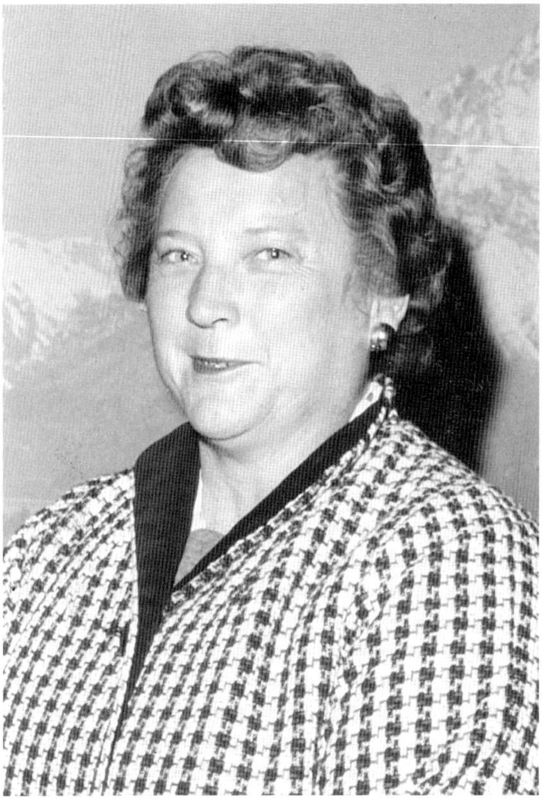

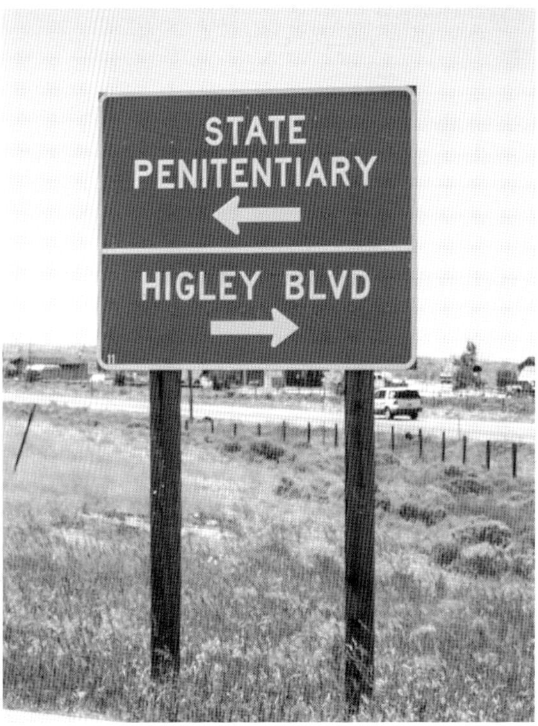

Lois Higley

Lois Higley moved to Rawlins with her husband, Bill, in 1949, and the couple ran Higley Electric until Bill's death in 1961. She was a prominent civic and youth leader, serving as president of the Rawlins Civic Association, Rawlins Community Concert Association, and the Carbon County Mental Health Board; vice-president of the Central Junior High PTA; and chairman of the Carbon County Red Cross. She was also a Cub Scout den mother, Sunday school teacher, high school substitute teacher, and city recreation coordinator, as well as the first woman to serve as city police judge. She managed the Rawlins–Carbon County Chamber of Commerce from 1969 to 1984 and served as president of the Wyoming Chamber of Commerce Executives.

Higley was included in the sixth edition of *Who's Who for American Women*. Despite her busy schedule, she always said that her children were her primary interests and was named Carbon County Homemaker of the Week in 1967.

After her retirement, she hopped in her "home on wheels" and traveled 125,000 miles, passing through each state at least once plus Canada. "She was always very honored to have Higley Boulevard named after her," stated her obituary when she died in 2007. (Top, courtesy *Rawlins Daily Times*; bottom, photograph by Han Cheung.)

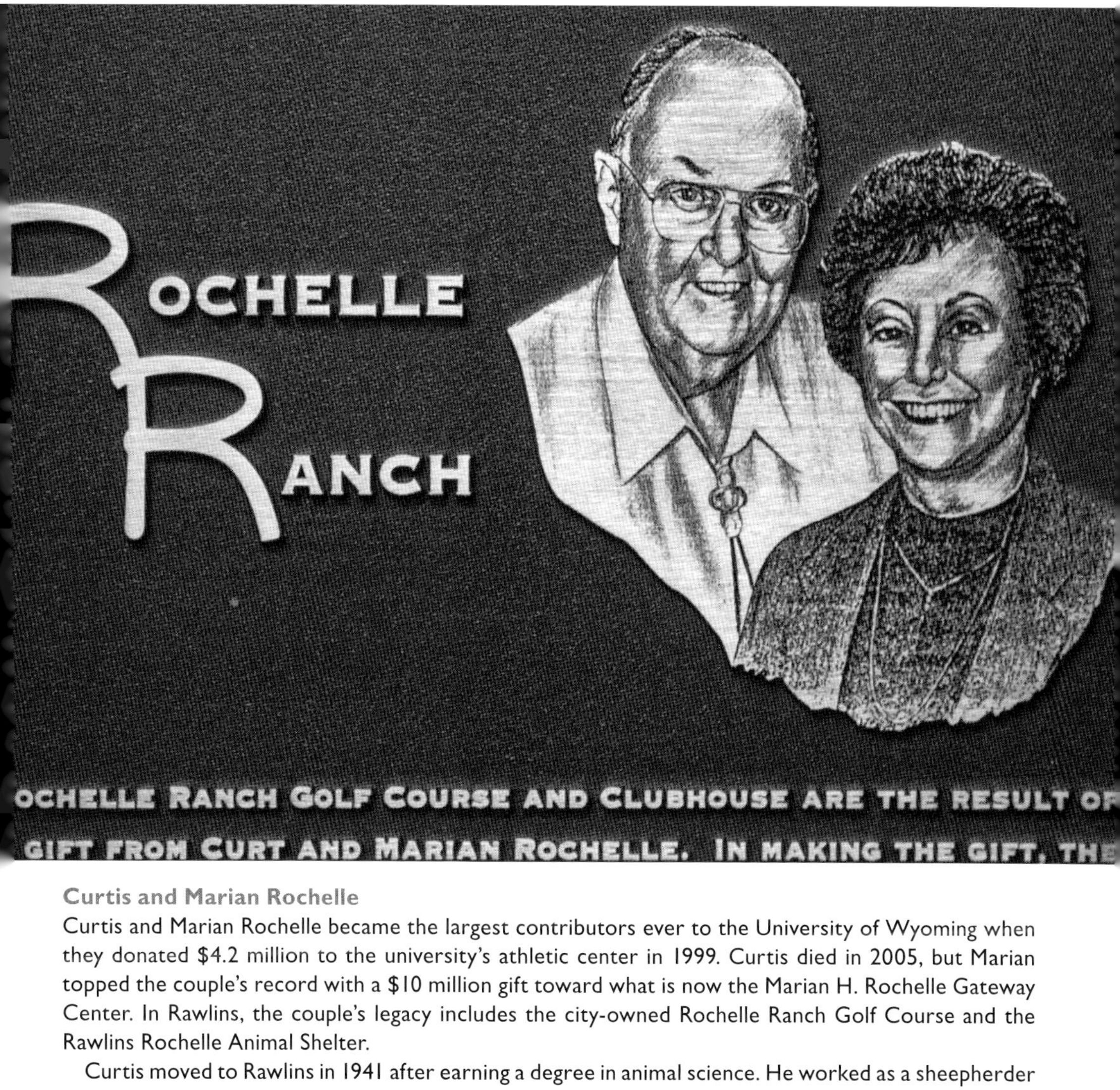

Curtis and Marian Rochelle

Curtis and Marian Rochelle became the largest contributors ever to the University of Wyoming when they donated $4.2 million to the university's athletic center in 1999. Curtis died in 2005, but Marian topped the couple's record with a $10 million gift toward what is now the Marian H. Rochelle Gateway Center. In Rawlins, the couple's legacy includes the city-owned Rochelle Ranch Golf Course and the Rawlins Rochelle Animal Shelter.

Curtis moved to Rawlins in 1941 after earning a degree in animal science. He worked as a sheepherder for the Savage Ranch. Starting out with a $1-a-day salary, he eventually bought the ranch and founded Rochelle Livestock Co. He later turned it into a cattle corporation, which is now run by his daughter and son-in-law. (Photograph by Han Cheung.)

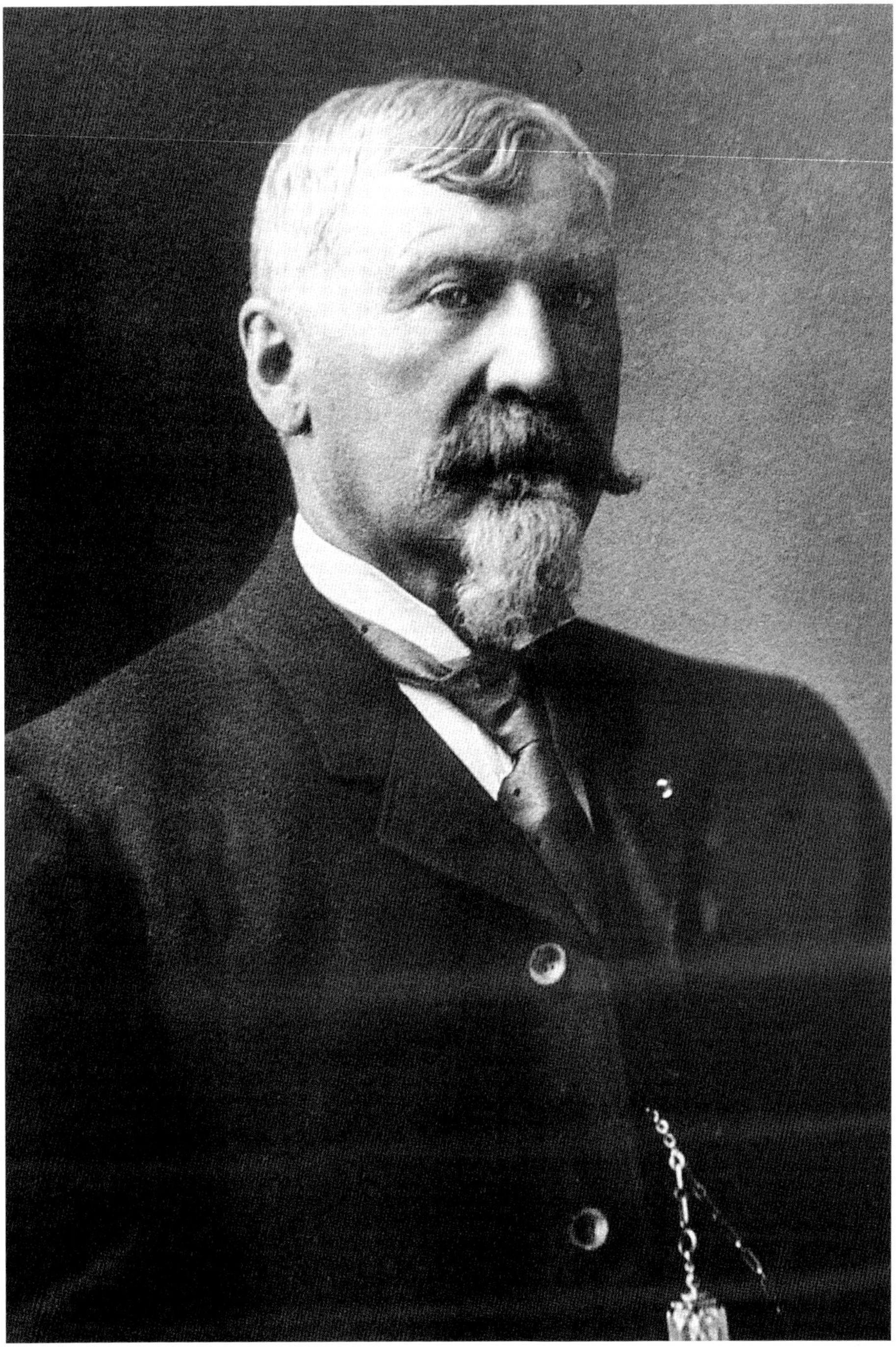

William Daley

William Daley was one of the largest livestock dealers in the area at the turn of the 20th century. He was a well-connected politician, serving as mayor in 1888. It is said that he hosted Theodore Roosevelt at his ranch during Roosevelt's bid for vice president. Daley Street is most likely named after him. (Courtesy Rawlins National Bank.)

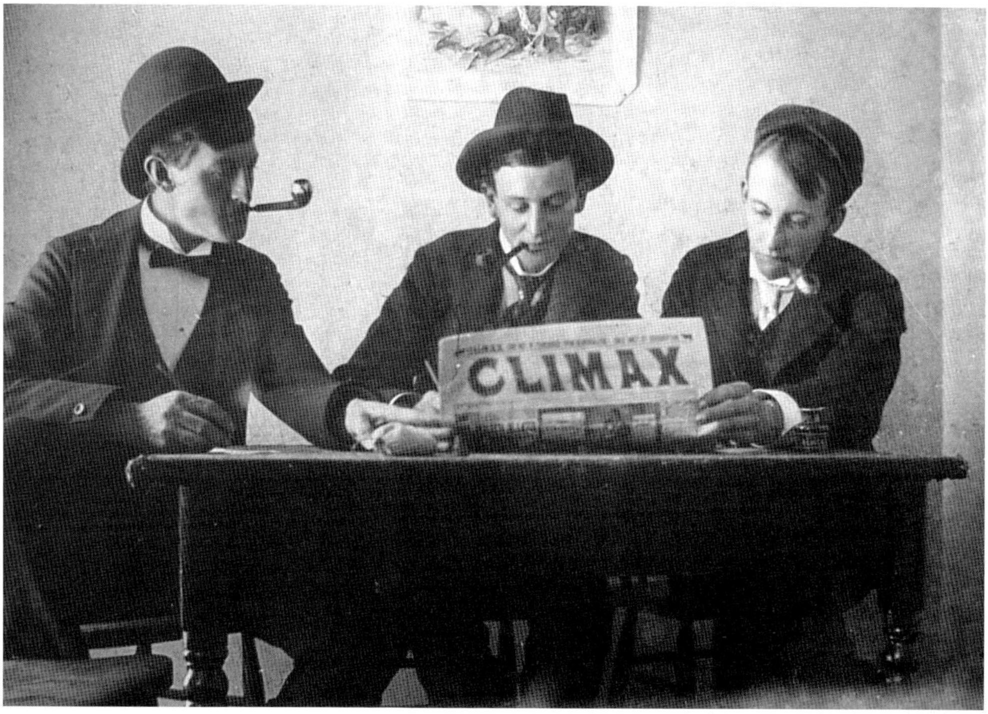

W.W. Daley

William Daley's son, W.W. (far left), was arguably more famous than his father. He served in the Wyoming Senate from 1915 to 1925 and is the one who introduced the bill creating the state flag and flower at the 14th Legislative Assembly. He owned one of the original models of the Wyoming state flag that were presented to the Senate by designer Verna Keays. The flag is now on display at the Carbon County Museum. (Above, courtesy Carbon County Museum; below, photograph by Han Cheung.)

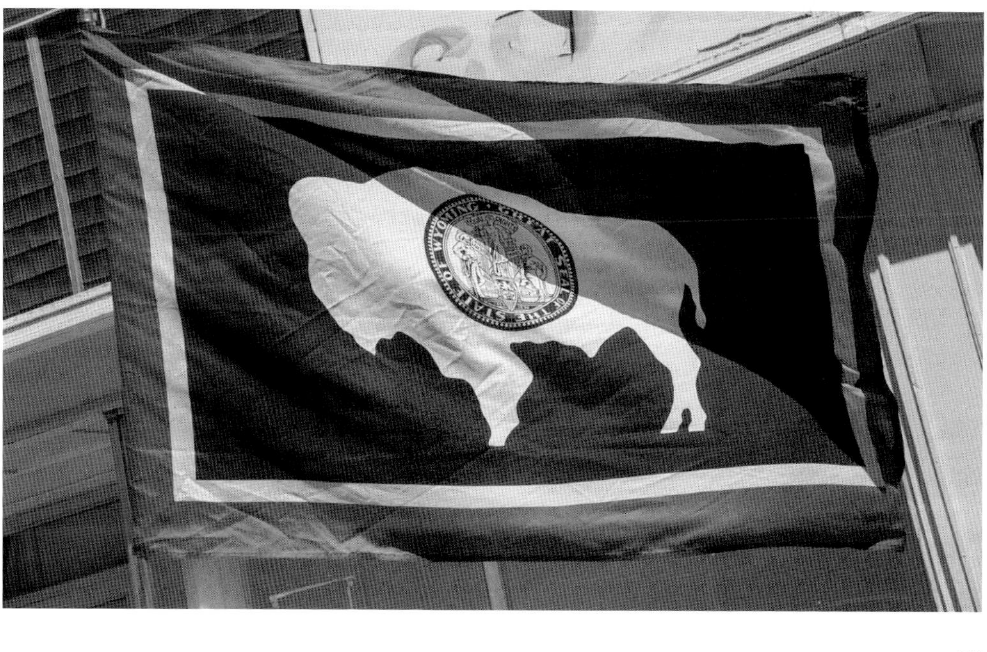

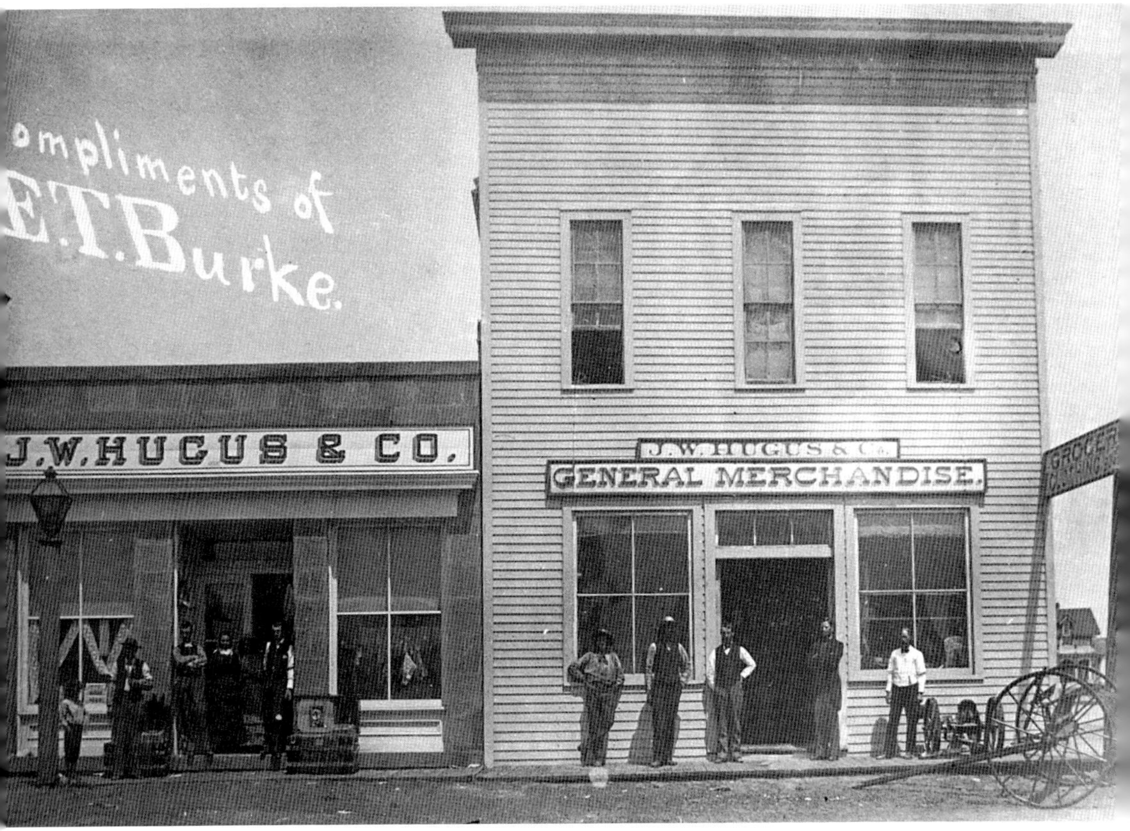
ompliments of
E.T. Burke.
J.W. HUGUS & CO.
J. W. HUGUS & Co.
GENERAL MERCHANDISE.

J.W. Hugus (OPPOSITE PAGE)
Hugus ran the J.W. Hugus mercantile at Fort Steele from 1870 to 1883. At the height of his success, there were 12 J.W. Hugus stores in Wyoming, Colorado, and Utah. Hugus moved to California in 1883, when the state was even less developed than Wyoming. He never lived in Rawlins, but Hugus Street is named after him. (Courtesy Carbon County Museum.)

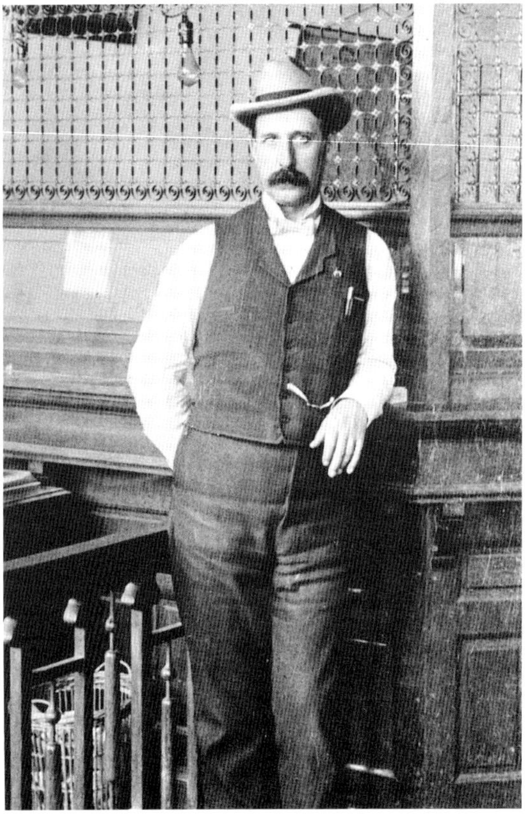

John C. Davis
The fourth mayor of Rawlins, John Davis came to town in 1881 to manage the newly opened Rawlins branch of the J.W. Hugus store. When Hugus left Wyoming, Davis took over the business and ran it from the Rawlins location. He put the first Western Union office in Rawlins and was involved in organizing the First National Bank of Rawlins. He also served as Carbon County commissioner. Davis Street is named after him. (Courtesy City of Rawlins.)

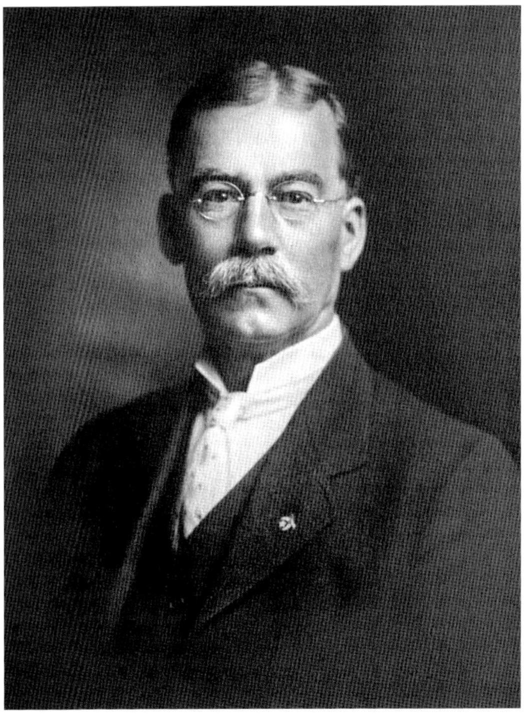

Andrew McMicken
Described by local historian Dan Kinnaman as a "rare combination of cowboy and teacher," McMicken came to Rawlins from the Snake River Valley in 1889 to work as a lawyer. He served as city attorney several times and also edited the *Carbon County Journal* from 1892 to 1895. McMicken Street is named after him. (Courtesy Carbon County Museum.)

CHAPTER SIX

War Stories

It is Memorial Day in Rawlins, and a large group of residents are assembled in the cemetery. A color guard stands proudly on top of a hill, and the many flags belonging to different organizations ripple in the wind: red for the marines; black for prisoners of war and those missing in action; blue for the American Legion; and, of course, red, white, and blue for the Star-Spangled Banner.

To the left of the hill stands a row of sharply dressed adults and children, each holding a rifle. Sheriff Jerry Colson, himself a former Marine, stands on the natural rock podium and speaks.

Rawlins residents are serious about honoring their veterans—and there are indeed many in town. Historically, Wyoming has had a high percentage of its population serve the country in combat. The first major war after Wyoming achieved statehood was the Spanish-American War in 1898. In Rawlins, 37 people signed up just a day after war was declared. "Rawlins boys are showing their valor and patriotism by signifying their desire to join the company of state militia which it is proposed to organize here to go to the front with the troops from Wyoming," the *Rawlins Republican* reported.

More than 11,000 soldiers from Wyoming fought in World War I, constituting seven percent of the state's population. Almost 30,000 fought in World War II.

The *Rawlins Republican* published letters written to long-time publisher Ross Alcorn by Rawlins trainees in various Army bases waiting to ship out to battle during World War II. For someone about to dive into the dangerous unknown, the hometown paper served as a source of comfort.

Countless more Rawlinsites served in subsequent wars—Vietnam, Korea, Iraq, Afghanistan. This chapter tells the battle stories of some of these veterans. It also mentions a few veterans' organizations in town.

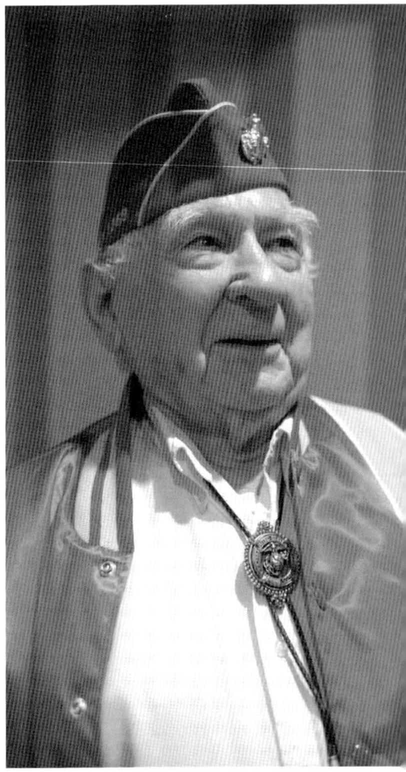

Garland "Bud" Ford

In May 2011, Ford was one of 110 World War II veterans to embark on the second-to-last Wyoming Honor Flight to visit the World War II Memorial in Washington, DC. "That was the best trip ever," he said.

As a 15-year-old in Southern California, Ford and a friend lied about their ages to get into the National Guard. Soon afterward, Pearl Harbor was attacked, and the National Guard was called into the US Army. Ford's captain, who knew he was underage, told him to go back and finish school and never mention to anyone that he had been in the National Guard. Ford obeyed the orders and went back to school. Once he turned 18, though, he enlisted in the Marines. When asked why he chose the Marines, Ford replied, "It was where all the action was."

After training, Ford was sent to the Far East theater. He would make stops throughout the South Pacific, with his primary task being loading bombs and ammunition into airplanes. While he didn't engage in close combat, his group encountered bombings, and he lost a good friend during one such incident in the Philippines.

Four months later, Ford was waiting to ship out to Japan to be, in his words, "cannon fodder." Fortunately, the war ended before they arrived. Ford then headed to China to remove the remaining Japanese from the country. (Both photographs by Han Cheung.)

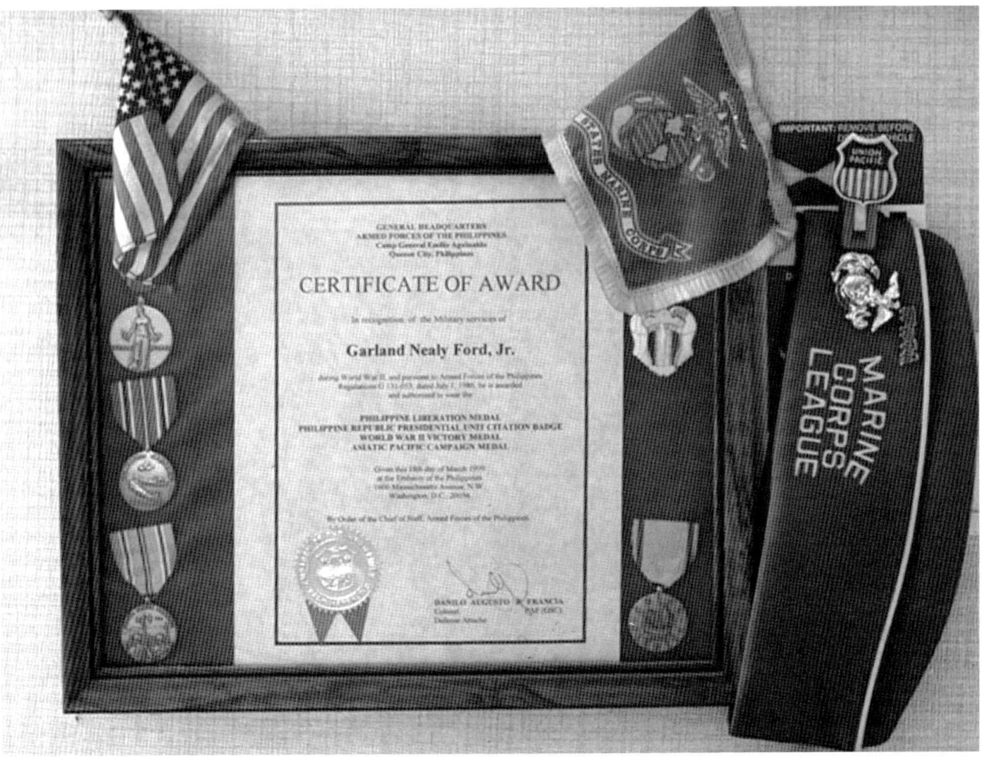

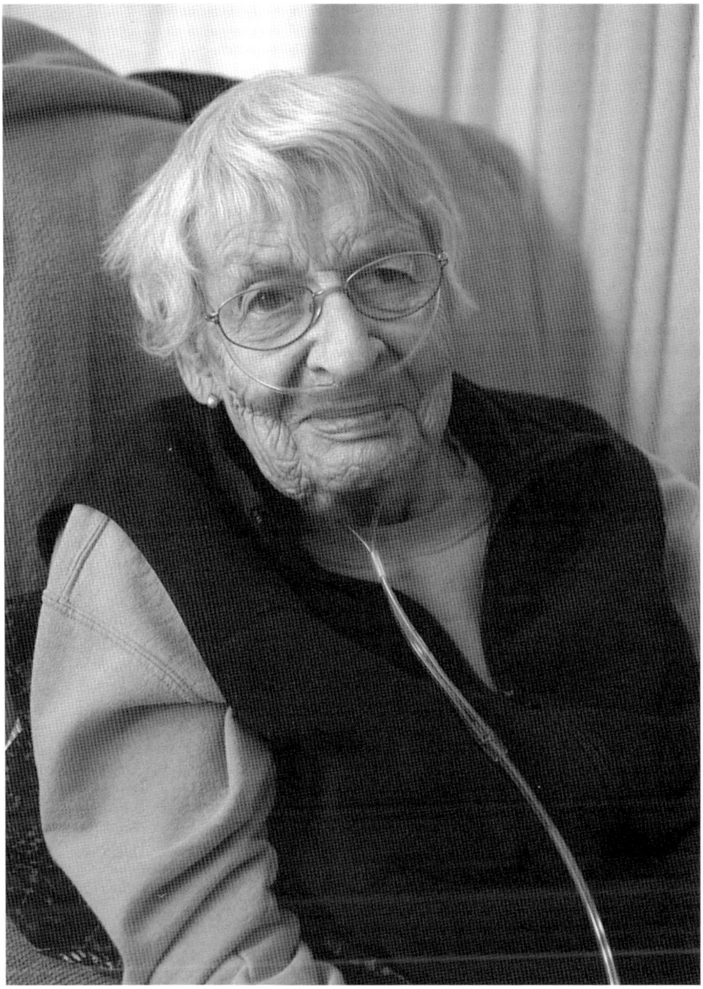

Lillian Turner
In the spring of 1945, Turner enlisted in the US Army to fight in World War II. "It was a family thing," she said. "My brother, sister, and relatives were all in the military. It seemed like the thing for me to do at that time."

Turner, a graduate of the Columbia School of Nursing, shipped out to Japan that May. En route, the war ended, and she went to the Philippines instead, where she worked at several military hospitals.

Honorably discharged in 1946, Turner focused on her nursing career, which brought her to Alaska, Seattle, American Samoa, and Aruba. In 1964, Turner decided to return to the battlefield—this time, in the Vietnam War. She completed two tours of duty and reached the rank of lieutenant commander. She spent 1969 to 1971 in the Truk Islands before heading back to Vietnam to work at military hospitals. Turner stayed there until the war ended in 1975 and earned a medal from the US Public Health Service for her efforts.

Turner traveled Asia extensively, and after all was said and done, she moved to Hanna to be closer to her family. She later became a physician's assistant and worked in clinics in both Rawlins and Hanna for many years. Turner now lives in the nursing home in Rawlins.

The 93-year-old Turner was the only female veteran on the final Wyoming Honor Flight in late 2011. Looking back at her time of service, she maintains it was just "something that was needed to be done," and she was able and willing to do the job. (Photograph by Han Cheung, courtesy *Rawlins Daily Times*.)

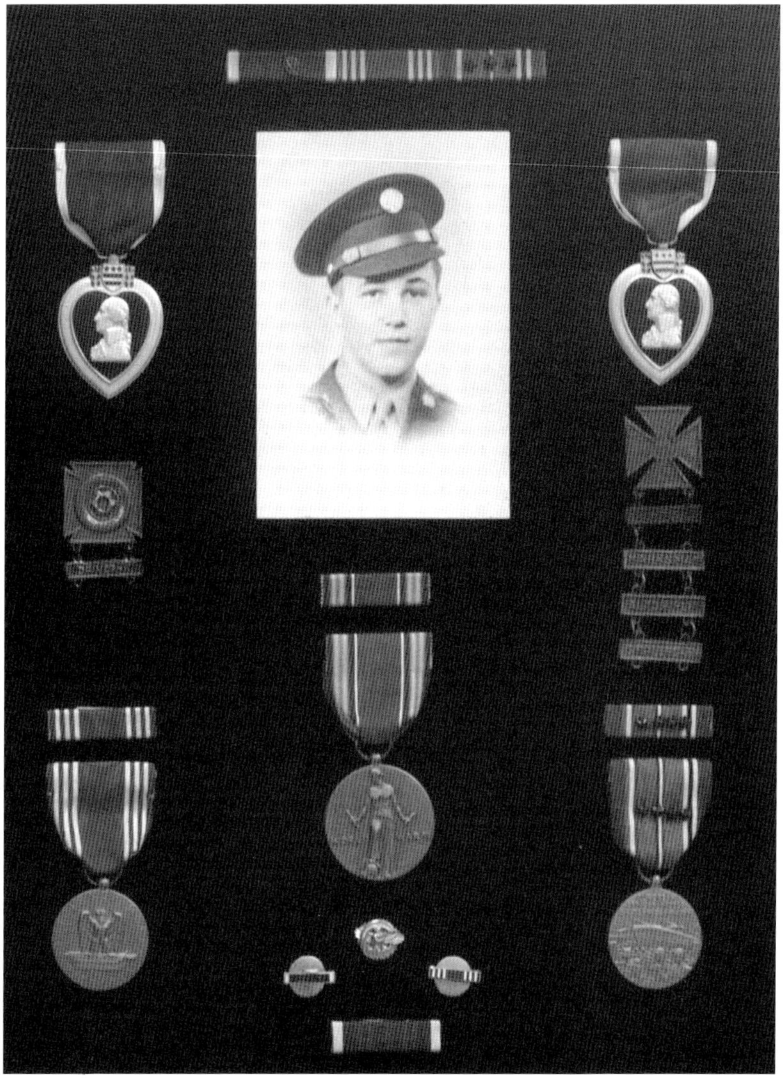

Everett Mann

Mann was a member of the first Wyoming Honor Flight in 2010. In June 1944, the 18-year-old landed in Normandy six days after D-Day. His platoon advanced through Europe in what Mann said was "combat zone all the time, except when we were looking for something to eat."

"The clothes you had on, you lived in them," Mann recalled. "If they were wet, you dried in them. I had one pair of shoes and socks on for a month before I took [them] off." This led to severe frostbite, and the second time it happened, he was sent to a hospital in England and later sent home. "I was discharged on V-E Day," he said.

One of Mann's more memorable stories happened on his way home. He and a friend from Sinclair entered the service together and didn't see each other again until the war was over. "On my way to England, I was in the USS *George Washington*," he recalled. "I was lying in the bunk looking at names all over the wall. Here it was, Doug Mitchell, Sinclair, Wyoming." It turns out Mitchell was transported to the war zone on that same ship, which later became a hospital ship and transported Mann away from the action. And it just happened that the two men were assigned to the same bunk. (Photograph by Han Cheung.)

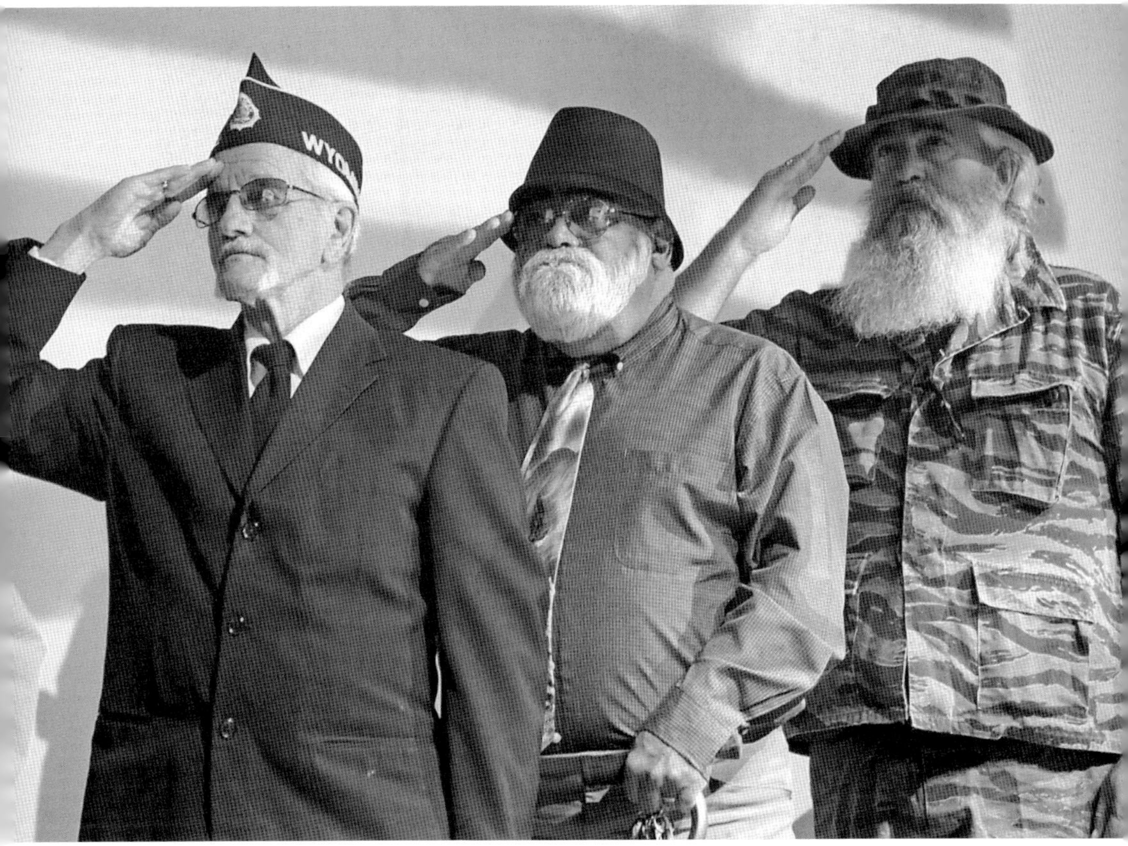

Frank Lucero

Frank Lucero (center) was hit by shrapnel in 12 places in Vietnam and returned home alive. He developed diabetes from exposure to Agent Orange during the war, and 31 years later, can still walk and lead an active life.

The most significant thing Lucero took back from the war was a strengthened faith in God. "I learned to appreciate God's protection," he said. "I survived by God's grace. Because of my experience, I have a deeper love for my lord and savior Jesus Christ."

On February 18, 1971, he deployed to Vietnam with the 101st Airborne Division, also known as the "Screaming Eagles."

"When I got there, I thought I had died and gone to hell," Lucero recalled. He was wounded during action twice, on March 22 and 23, in a close-combat battle in Khe Sanh. After recovering from his injuries in a hospital in Quang Tri, he returned to the troops and managed to complete his 10-month tour.

"I appreciated the fact that I came back," he said. "We had guys coming back with no legs."

Lucero now serves as chaplain for the America Legion Post 122 in Rawlins and starts and ends each meeting with prayer.

In his spare time, Lucero enjoys taking long walks. "When I'm walking, I'm always praying," he said. "One thing that I learned in life is God never forgets." (Photograph by Han Cheung, courtesy *Rawlins Daily Times*.)

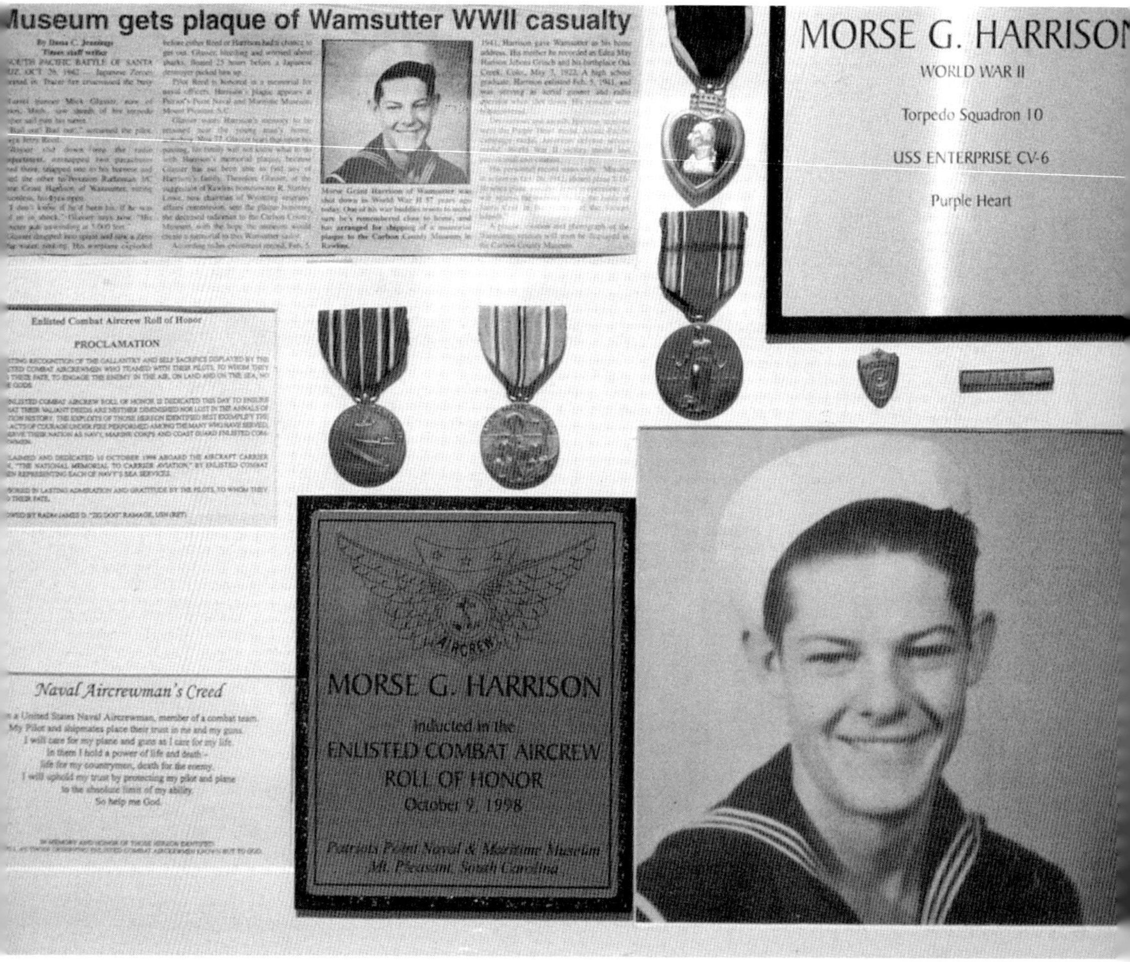

Morse Grant Harrison

Harrison enlisted in the US Army shortly after graduating from Rawlins High School in 1940 and was deployed to World War II's South Pacific Theater as a radio operator on a torpedo bomber.

On October 26, 1942, his plane was shot down during the battle of Santa Cruz. Both Harrison and the pilot lost their lives. Harrison's remains were never found, and he was mostly forgotten until 1998, when Michael Glasser started sending letters searching for Harrison's relatives.

It turns out, Glasser was the tail gunner and only surviving soldier from Harrison's fallen plane. He had been inducted in 1997 to the Enlisted Combat Aircrew Roll of Honor at the Patriots Point Naval and Maritime Museum in South Carolina, and believed that his fallen comrade deserved the honor as well.

"I feel deeply about having this recognition for Harrison, especially since I survived and he did not," Glasser wrote in a letter to the *Rawlins Daily Times*.

Glasser never found any of Harrison's relatives and accepted the plaque in his place. In 1999, he donated it to the Carbon County Museum, where it is still on display in the military room. (Courtesy Carbon County Museum.)

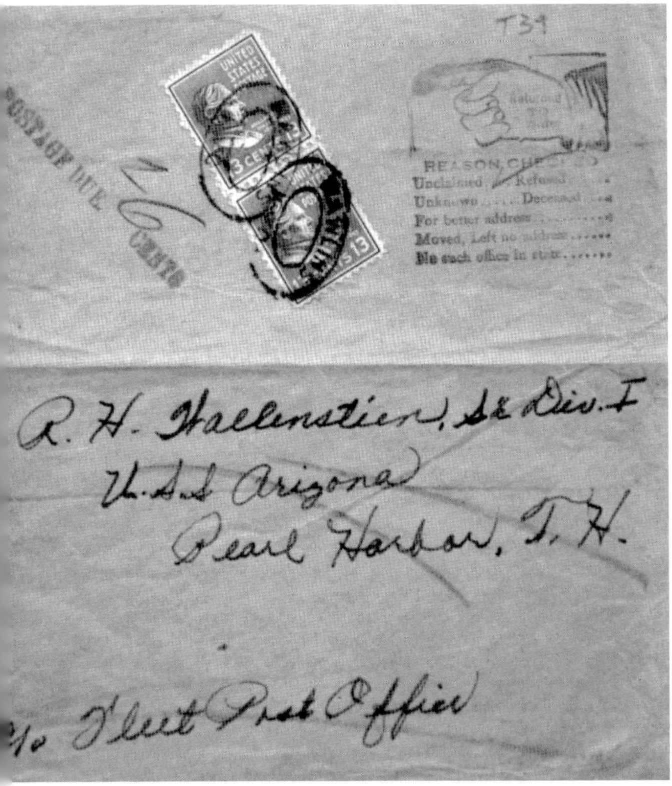

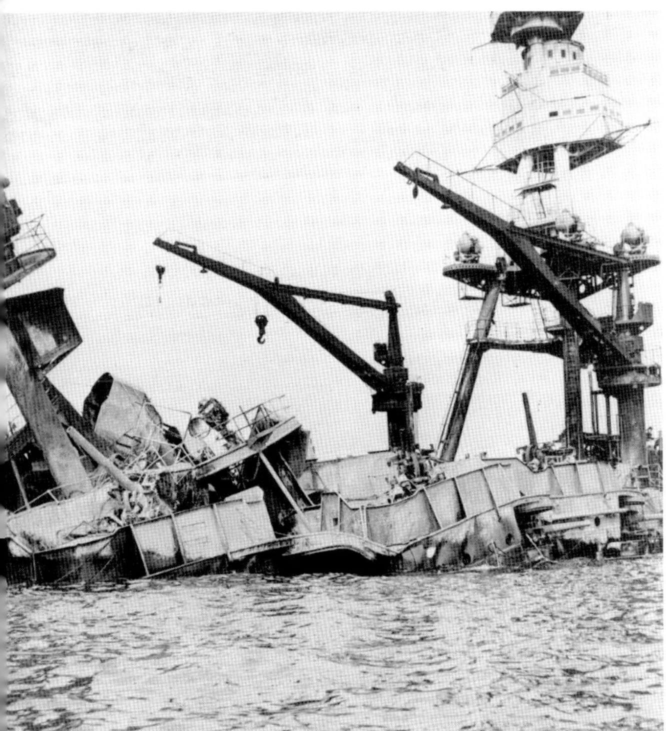

Richard Wallenstein

The USS *Arizona* was one of the battleships destroyed during the Japanese attack on Pearl Harbor. Out of 1,512 sailors and marines onboard, 1,177 perished.

In the summer of 2013, Carbon County Museum employees came across a piece of the front of an envelope while reorganizing the military room. It was addressed to Pearl Harbor and was sent back to Rawlins after nobody claimed the letter.

The addressee was R.H. Wallenstein, USS *Arizona*.

Dick Wallenstein's obituary was featured on the front page of the *Rawlins Republican-Bulletin* on December 23, 1941. He joined the Army upon graduating high school, and was 18 years old when he died.

Wallenstein's name is engraved in a memorial built across the *Arizona*'s remains, which is now a national shrine. The museum is still trying to find out who sent the letter and who donated it. (Top, courtesy Carbon County Museum; bottom, courtesy Library of Congress.)

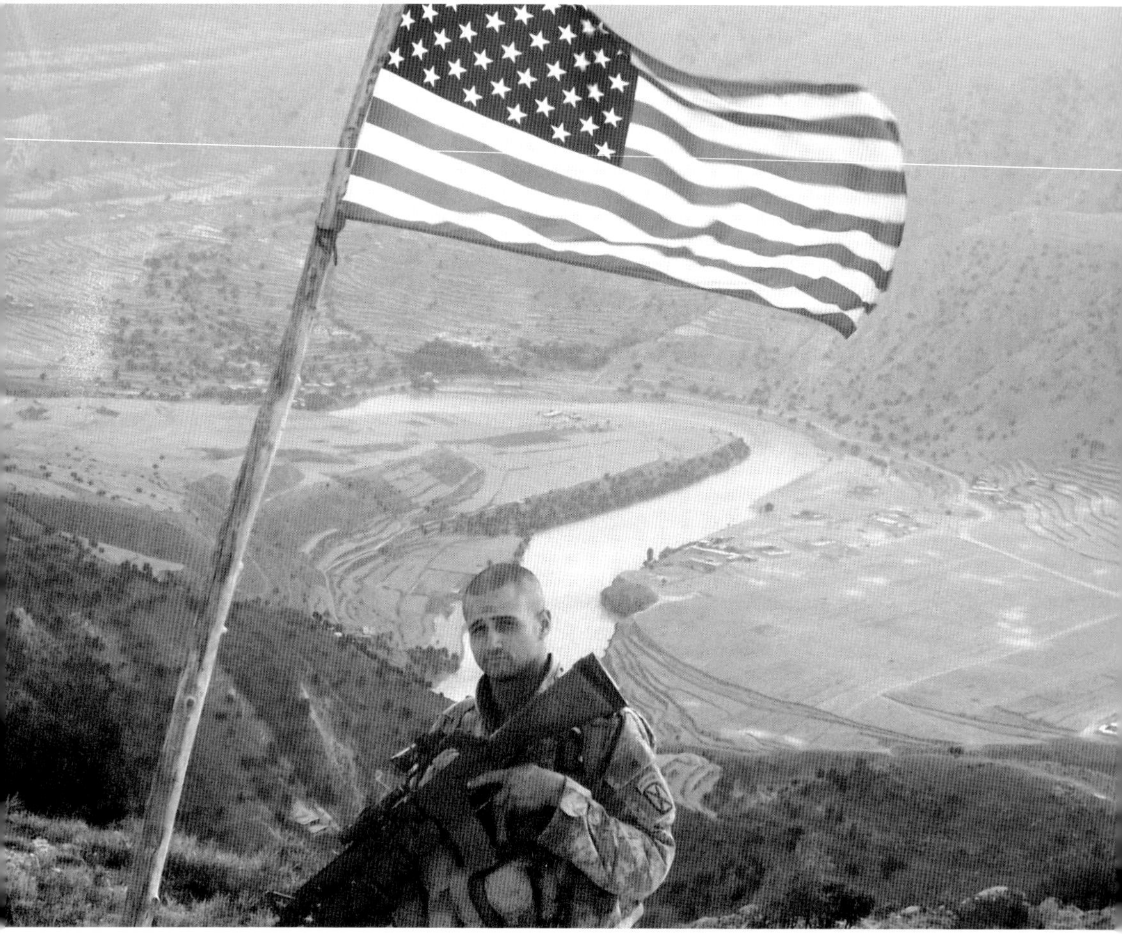

Joshua Weickum
Weickum described himself as the "epitome of a spoiled American kid" before he joined the US Army in 2004 at age 19.

"I grew up and became a man in a five-month period," he said. "I got cultured and saw the other side of the planet. You have a pretty narrow view of the world until you've been abroad. It gave me a taste of real life."

After five uneventful months in Afghanistan, Weickum's platoon was sent to the Pakistan border, where "things got real." He remembers the confusion the first time they were shot at, as only two people in his platoon had actual combat experience.

After eight months, Weickum took two weeks off to watch his wife in Rawlins give birth. He was ready to go back, but the Army told him to stay home.

"I was so close to ending my tour, and it was too much money to send me back," Weickum said. He believes this is the reason he is still alive.

After he left, a man one foot taller than Weickum took over his position on the gun hatch and took a bullet through his neck. "It didn't kill him," Weickum said. "It missed the arteries and spine."

The next soldier who took over was one foot shorter than Weickum. This man was shot at in an ambush and the bullet went through his Kevlar.

"If it were me, it would have been a kill shot," Weickum said. "They were lucky to be the height they were, or they definitely would have been dead. I believe my son is my savior, being born then." (Courtesy Joshua Weickum.)

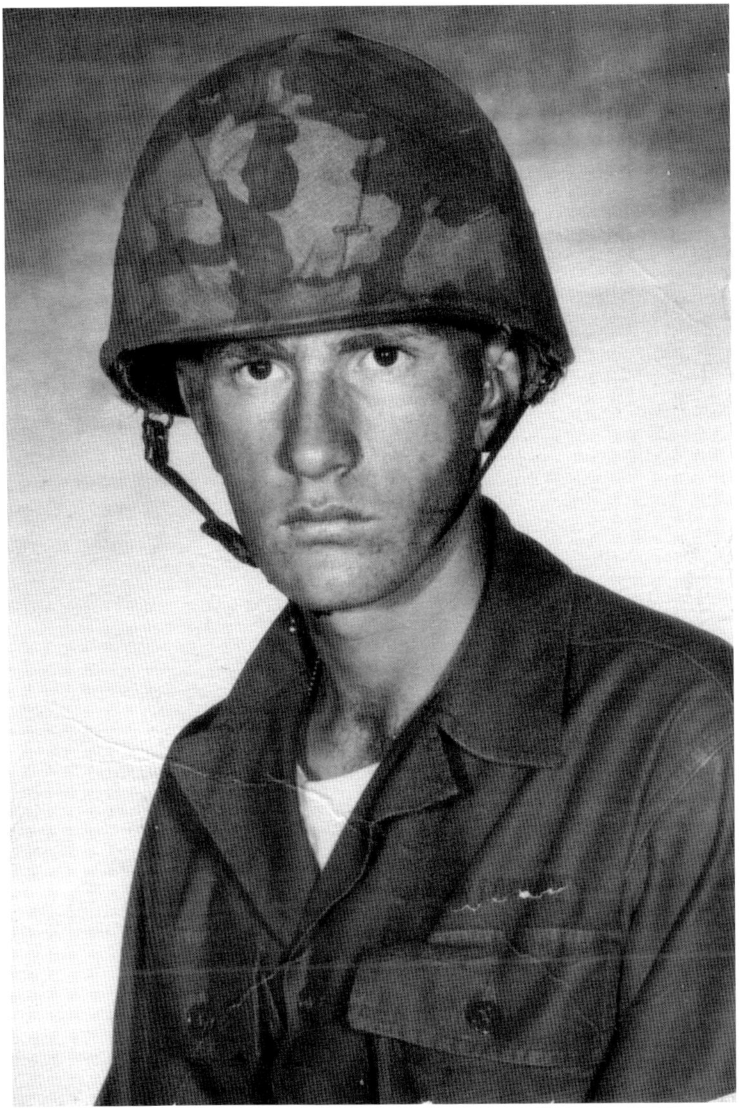

Jack Lowrance
Lowrance was named after a Marine—his uncle Jack Jernigan—and it wasn't surprising when he decided to enlist in the corps himself as soon as he was old enough.

During the Vietnam War, Lowrance was one of 5,000 Marines who took park in Operation Double Eagle I in January 1966—the largest amphibious operation since the Korean War.

Luckily, the landing was uncontested; otherwise, Lowrance believes it would have been a disaster. Lowrance was a member of the mortar platoon, which meant in addition to his 70-pound rucksack, he had to carry a part of the 81-millimeter mortar, which weighed between 23 and 40 pounds.

Lowrance spent six months in Vietnam and saw frequent combat. "You are never really ready for it, and of course, you adjust real fast," he said. He recalls being without food for days and fellow soldiers wearing the same clothes and boots for so long that the materials rotted onto their bodies. He said many soldiers had to be shipped out of the war zone because they weren't able to obtain new supplies.

After the war, Lowrance worked in the uranium mines in the Shirley Basin for many years. He also served for 15 years as Carbon County deputy sheriff. (Courtesy Jack Lowrance.)

Mike Sherr

Sherr joined the buddy program right out of high school and served in the National Guard after completing his basic training. At age 19, he enlisted in active duty and volunteered to go to Thailand for seven months to train border police to patrol drug traffickers.

"It was right after the Vietnam War, and there were still booby traps in, and we engaged in firefights with insurgents," he recalled. They were isolated in the jungle, and Sherr clearly remembers the last cold Pepsi he had before he returned to the States.

Sherr was able to see the world through the military, making stops in Grenada, Panama, Honduras, El Salvador, Nicaragua, and Okinawa. He also toured Europe, and his favorite place was Germany because that was where his grandparents were from. (Photograph by Han Cheung, courtesy *Rawlins Daily Times*.)

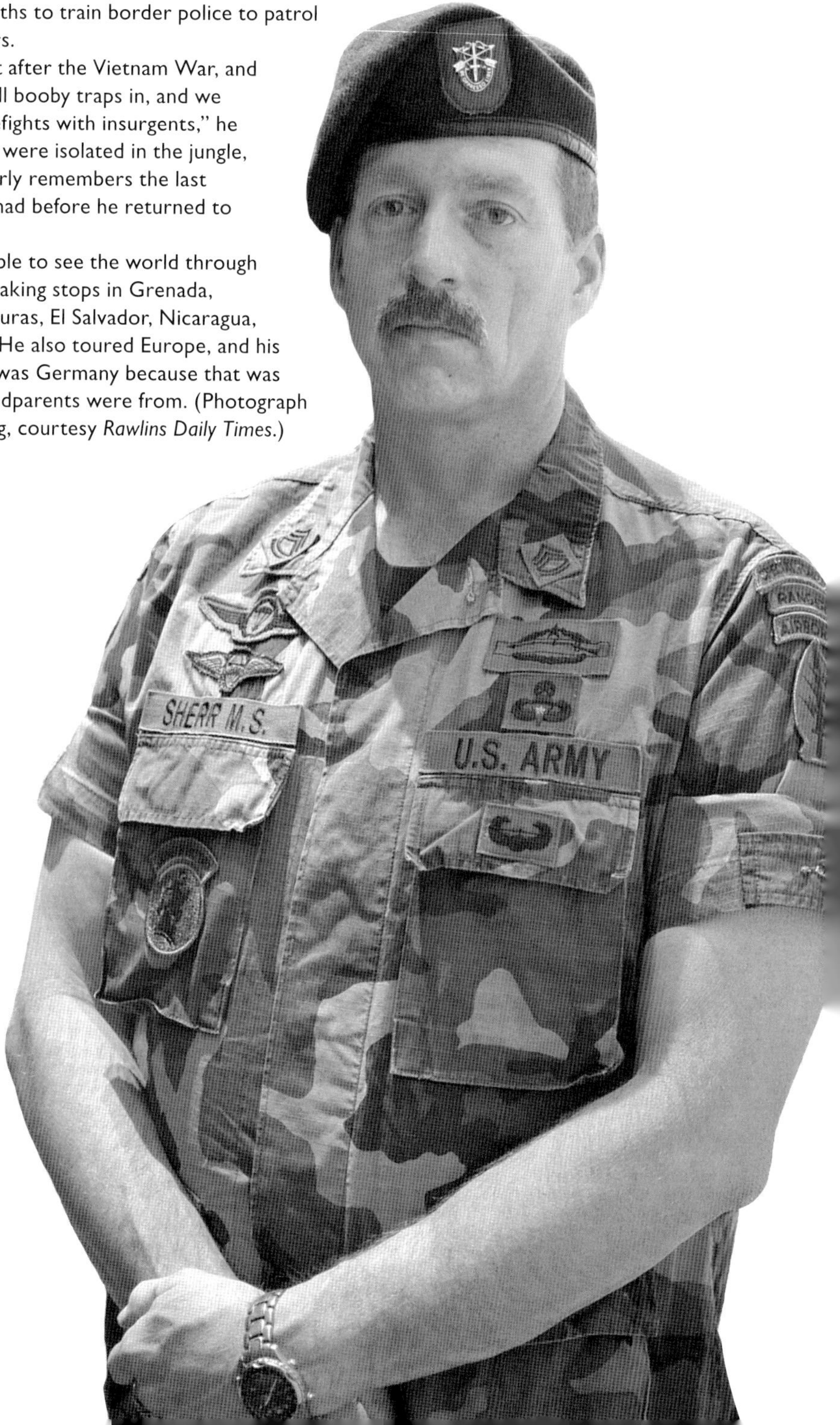

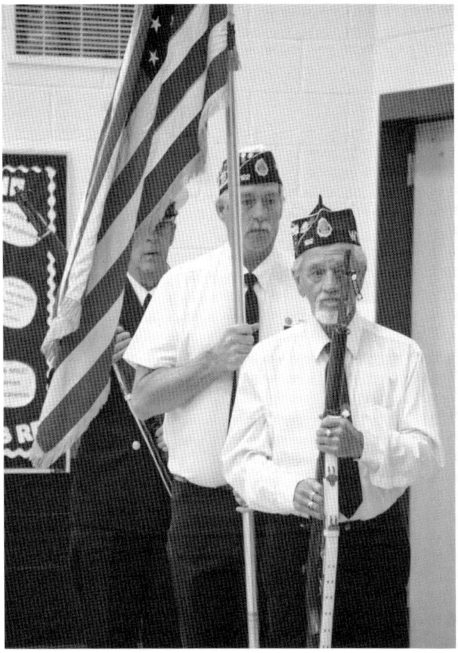

American Legion

Mike Sherr revived an inactive American Legion and serves as both post commander and district commander. The American Legion organizes color guards, helps other veterans, does community service, and also has a little-league baseball team. "I decided that I wasn't done with the service," Sherr said. "I still wanted to serve, and the legion is a good way to do it." (Both photographs by Han Cheung, courtesy *Rawlins Daily Times*.)

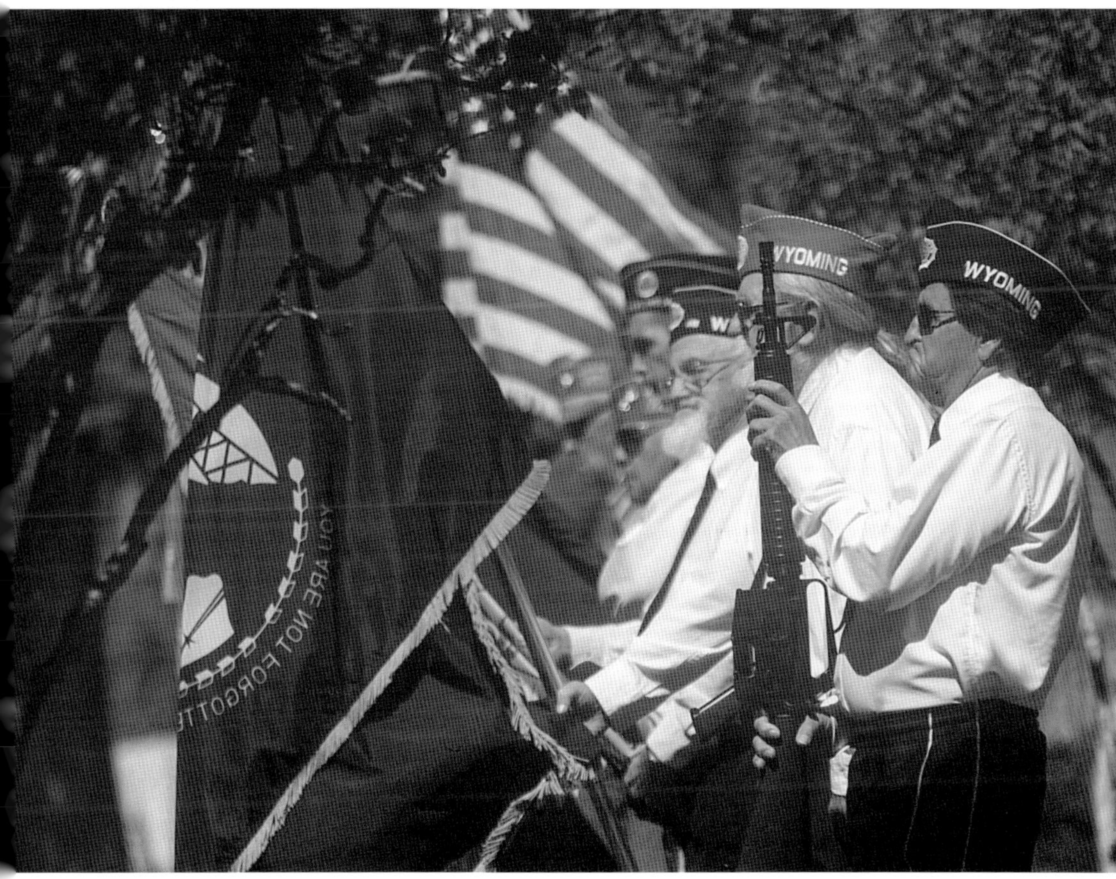

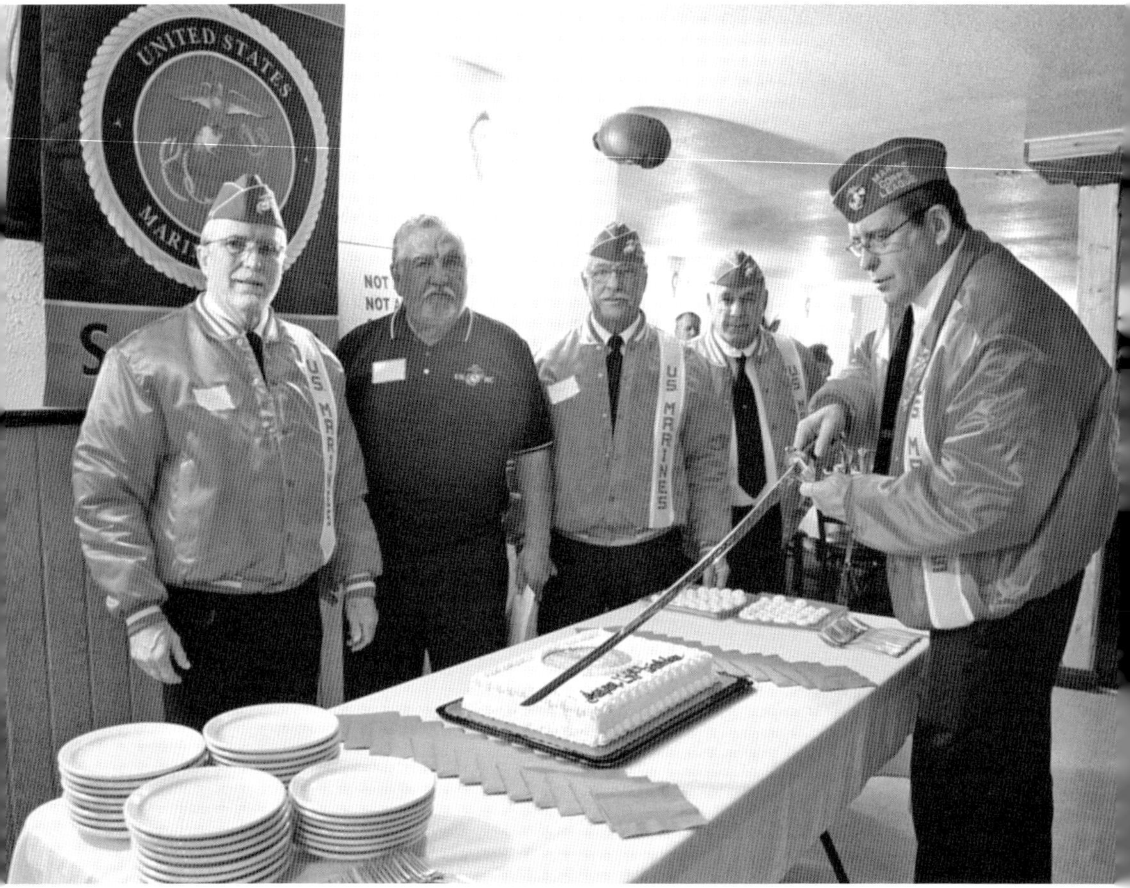

Marine Corps League

The Marine Corps League, Pronghorn Detachment 1359, was formed in Rawlins in 2009. The group is open to Marines and Navy fleet marine force corpsmen.

"It's a way to keep all former marines and navy corpsmen connected," commander Jerry Colson (far right) said. In addition, the group focuses on community service and performing military honor duties. "We're building on trying to make a difference in the community," Colson said.

Colson, who is also Carbon County sheriff, served in the Marines from 1975 to 1979 and spent 16 months in the Philippines and Panama. "I'm proud to serve my country," he said. "Once a Marine, always a Marine." (Photograph by Han Cheung, courtesy *Rawlins Daily Times*.)

CHAPTER SEVEN

Mentor and Student

In small towns, there are always those teachers who have taught virtually everybody, as well as everybody's kids and grandkids. Whether you are 25 or 45, if you grew up in Rawlins, you probably had Bill Williams as your art teacher. Talk to anyone involved in the performing arts, and he or she will almost always mention Larry Moore.

Sure, academics are important, but extracurricular activities like sports and the arts are the venues in which all students can shine. Several residents expressed that Rawlins was a good place to grow up because they were able to participate in pretty much whatever extracurricular activity they wanted to without the competition that big cities might have.

When there were games or performances, it seems like almost half the town would show up wearing red, black, and white in support of their beloved Outlaws and Lady Outlaws.

One story tells of how a girl was banned from choir practice because of a suspension. She ended up leaving the school because choir practice was the only thing that kept her attending.

This is the kind of effect that a teacher strives to have on a student. Teachers experience no greater joy than when their students follow in their career footsteps. The only better scenario is when the student comes back to town and takes over the teacher's role years later.

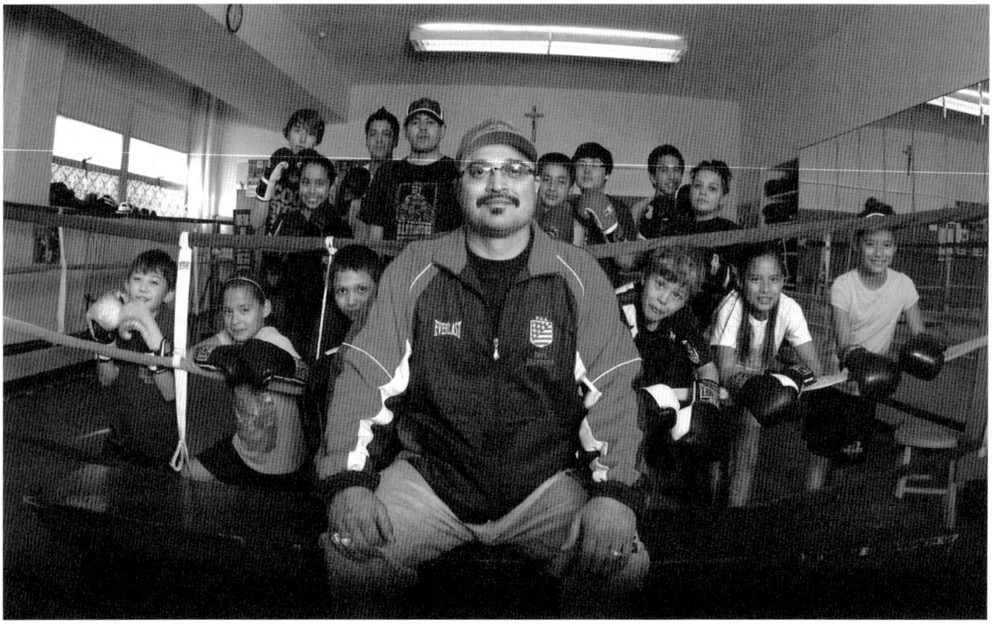

Bert Hererra

Hererra, an ex-boxer and wrestler, founded the Gladiators Boxing Club in 2000 to give his relatives a chance to box and get local youth off the streets. "I knew that boxing was one of the main things that kept me out of trouble," he said. That first year, the club won six state championships and a 14-year-old Sammy Martinez went all the way to the national finals.

Hererra believes more than 200 young pugilists have come through his doors, and Martinez is now helping him train the newcomers. "What little kids see from Sammy is that they can go somewhere," said Hererra shortly after Martinez's return. (Photograph by Gavin Elliott, courtesy *Rawlins Daily Times*.)

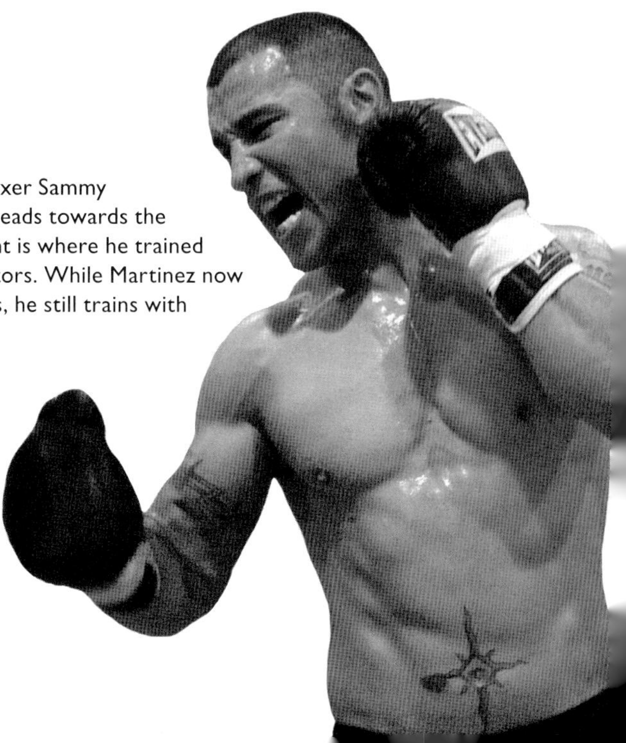

Sammy Martinez

After a 12-hour workday, professional boxer Sammy Martinez takes a brief rest at home and heads towards the St. Joseph School. The building's basement is where he trained as a teenager with Bert Hererra's Gladiators. While Martinez now has a 7-0 pro record with four knockouts, he still trains with Herrera in the same basement.

Martinez's tale is the stuff of boxing movies: troubled Rawlins kid joins his cousin's boxing club, exorcises his demons, straightens up, and joins the Marines. He makes the All–Marine Corps boxing team, fights all over the world, comes home, and turns pro. (Photograph by Han Cheung, courtesy *Rawlins Daily Times*.)

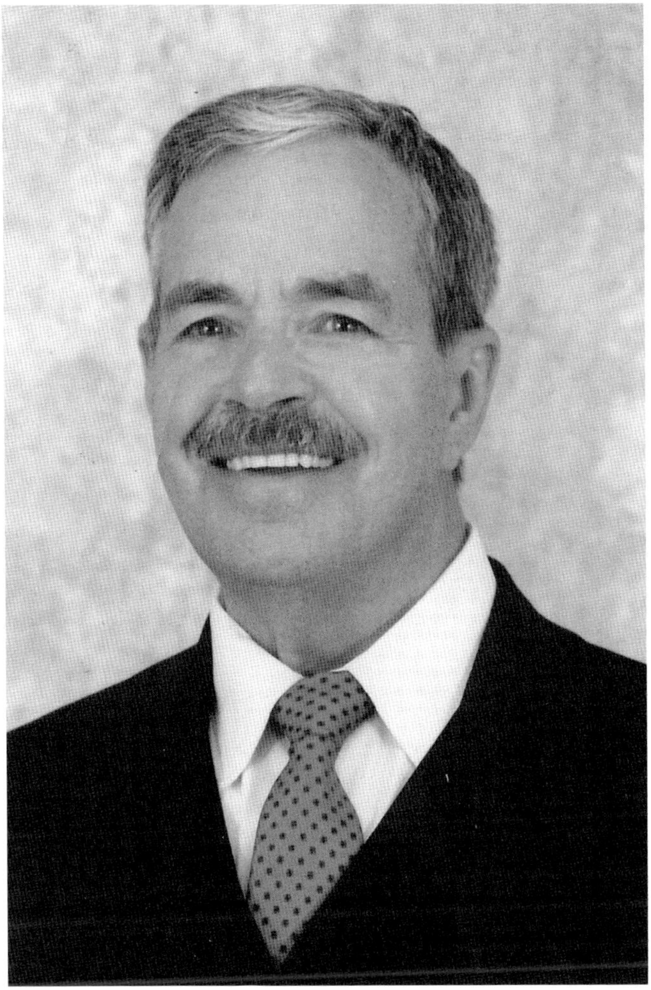

Larry Moore

If there is any theater-related activity in town, chances are that Larry Moore is involved in one way or another. After all, Moore coached Rawlins High School drama for 38 years and is the one responsible for the team's glorious run at the state level.

Moore acted through high school and college and was hired as an English teacher at Rawlins High School in 1967. He took charge of the drama club in his second year.

There was no state drama tournament back then, so Moore decided to start one the next year. "Over 10 years, Rawlins had more first places than any other school, including 4A schools," said Moore.

Under Moore's tutelage, the RHS drama club was selected in 1993 and 1999 as one of 10 drama clubs in the country to perform on the main stage at the International Thespian Conference at Ball State University.

Moore was named the first ever Wyoming High School Theatre Director of the Year in 1996.

He cared about his students' experiences a lot and would take them to New York to watch shows. One night, after watching four productions and attending an MTV show, they walked past a film crew in Times Square on their way back home. "For the next two hours, we were running back and forth across Times Square as extras," he said. "It's moments like this that made their experience more memorable."

The drama program didn't do so well after Moore retired, but in 2012, former student Brandon Taylor moved back to Rawlins from New York City to take the reins. (Courtesy Larry Moore.)

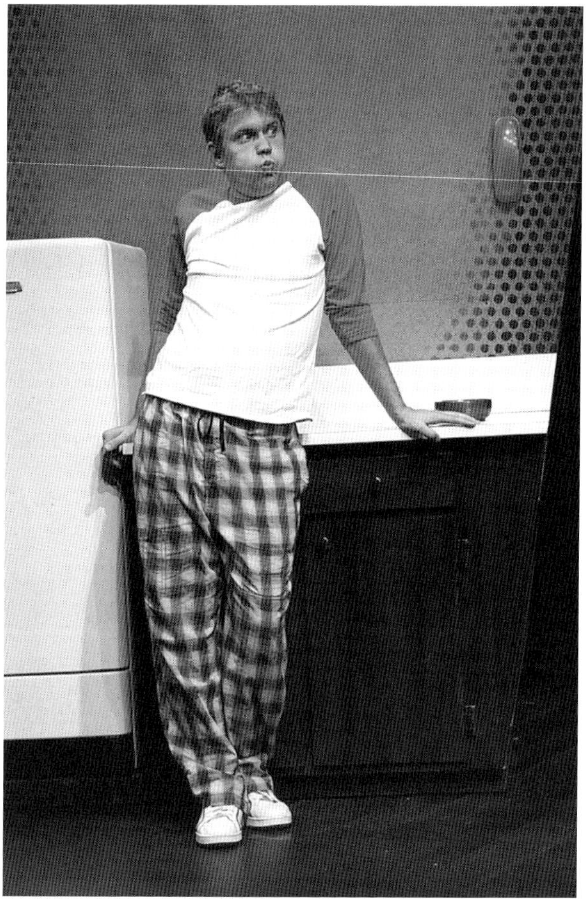

Brandon Taylor
Larry Moore's son, Travis, directed Taylor's first high school play in 1996. "I remember Larry saying, 'You've got to keep going,' " Taylor said. "He was the ultimate recruiter. After that it was nothing but plays."

"Larry was very strict," Taylor recalled. "Someone missed an entrance, and we did it 50 times for two hours. Larry didn't know the theory, but he knew what he was looking for. What I learned from him was the passion you have to give to a character—and that's incredibly hard to teach."

Taylor went on to major in theater at the University of Wyoming and earned a master's degree from the University of California–San Diego. He was active in the Los Angeles acting scene for a while before he and his wife, Callie, decided to pack up and try their hand in New York.

Taylor's career highlights included being listed in the original cast of the play *Election Day*, which was published by Samuel French, and being a costar on the TV show *Criminal Minds*.

After the birth of their first child, the Taylors decided to move back to Wyoming to be closer to family. Taylor was planning on taking a break from theater, but Moore convinced him to get involved with the high school.

"It wasn't what I remembered," he recalled. "When I left, it was in good shape." Few students auditioned, and those who did frequently missed practice.

Taylor ended up helping more and more until he became the director of the 2013 spring play. "I just couldn't walk away from it," he said. And slowly, he's turned the drama program around.

In Taylor's first year at the 2013 State Drama Tournament, Rawlins won only an honorable mention. The next year, the drama club finished third overall in the 3A division, prompting a rival coach to tell Taylor, "It's good to see Rawlins as a strong competitor again." (Courtesy Brandon Taylor.)

Bill Williams

When Williams was a freshman in high school, his principal decided to buy some oil paints so the "bad kids" had something to do during study hall. Williams thought it looked like fun. "I asked Mr. Hopkins if I could check the oils out during breaks," he recalled. "He said, 'But you're not a troublemaker.' I replied, 'I could be.' "

There was nothing to paint on, so Williams went to the lumberyard and found some wood scraps—thus began the career of the legendary Rawlins artist and art teacher.

About five years later, Williams was failing out of college. When he told his father he wanted to change his major from business administration to art, his father pointed at some buckets of paint and told him to paint the house.

The art department was full, and Williams graduated as an education major with an art minor. "When I got into art, I could compete," he said. "It was night and day."

In 1960, Williams landed a job as a junior high and high school art teacher in Rawlins—a job he would keep for the next 36 years.

Williams's teaching philosophy was an equilateral "golden triangle" of the student, parent, and educator. "Put these things together, and you'll really get things done," he said.

He also made sure he was boss. "I had few rules, but they weren't negotiable," he said. "I would tell them, 'Look, you and I can be friends, but not buddies. My name is Mr. Williams.' Some called me Mr. Will—and I let that stand."

Williams's art, which is mostly of nature subjects, has been a mainstay in the community through the various art galleries that have come and go. One of his more recent projects is the "Walk in the Forest" series, for which he paints a forest scene on a piece of wood cut from a stump in the same forest. His favorite piece, however, is his photograph of Aspen Alley.

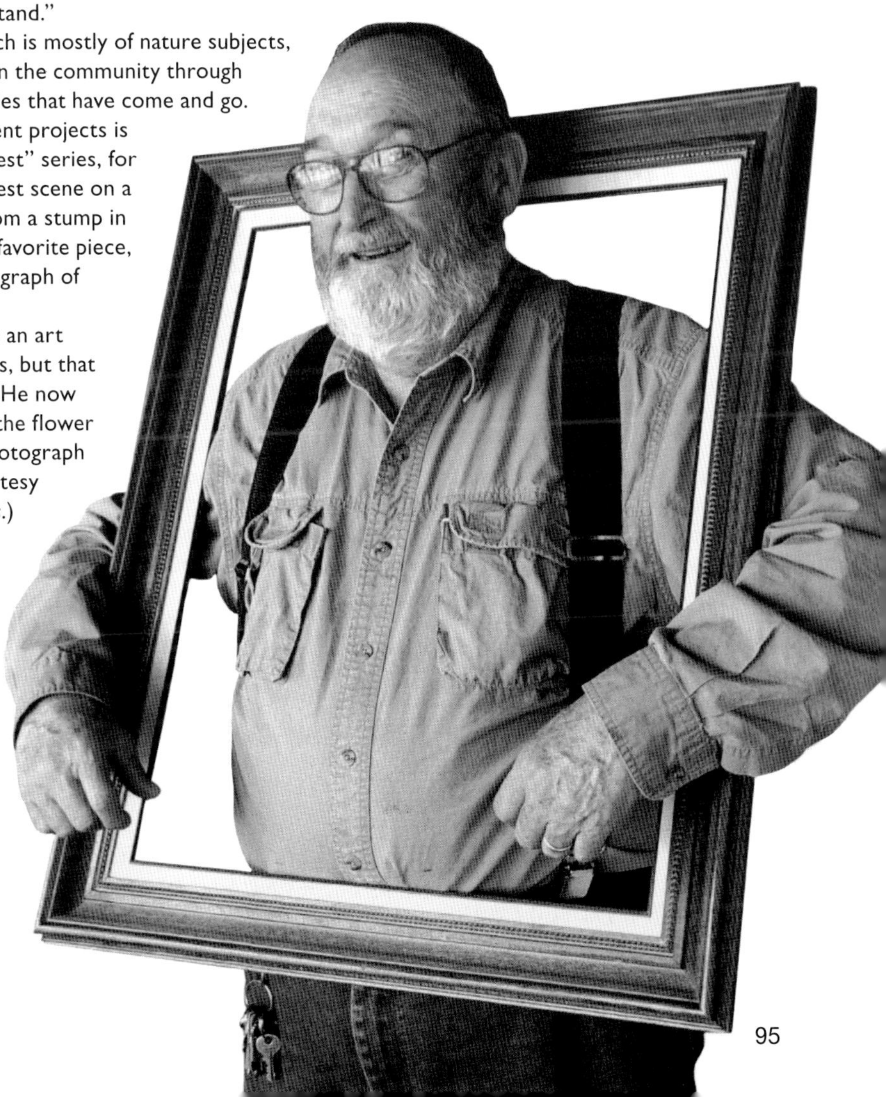

Rawlins didn't have an art gallery for many years, but that didn't stop Williams. He now showcases his art in the flower shop downtown. (Photograph by Jerry Raehal, courtesy of *Rawlins Daily Times*.)

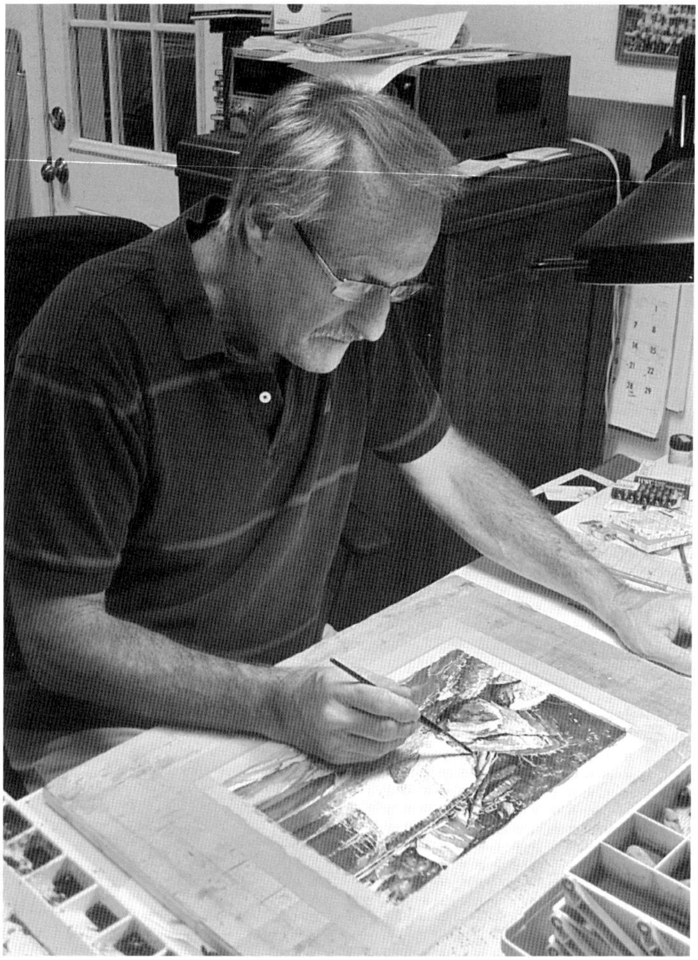

Joel Johnson

Bill Williams is proud of how many former students went on to be art teachers. He said that at one point, there were 27 working in art education. Joel Johnson is one of them.

Johnson, a Florida-based watercolor painter, also started his career as a high school art teacher. Today, he is a full-time artist but still teaches classes regularly at the Vera Beach Museum of Art and conducts workshops around the globe.

Johnson met Williams in his seventh-grade art class. "I copied a drawing of Ben Hur from the film," he recalled. "That kind of started my association with him."

"He was great at analyzing your work critically. That was his great gift—he could verbally let you know what you needed to do to strengthen the work. Not a lot of artists can do that." Johnson said that aspect of Williams has influenced him a lot as an educator.

Johnson was primarily an oil painter until he was working on his master's of fine art exhibit in 1987. "I was doing both oil and watercolor, and the committee told me I couldn't do an exhibition in multiple mediums. I don't know even to this day why I chose watercolor."

It was probably the right decision. Johnson is now a signature member of two of the "big three" watercolor societies in the country, the National Watercolor Society and Transparent Watercolor Society.

Johnson said becoming a full-time artist was a "very difficult decision to make." "You have to motivate yourself constantly to create, yet if you're teaching on a full-time level, then you never really know what it is you can do," he said. (Courtesy Joel Johnson.)

Roy and Becky Dahlinger

For many years, Becky Dahlinger would direct the middle school choir, and when her students got to the high school level, they were coached by her husband, Roy.

The Dahlingers retired in 2012 and moved to California. Their daughter, Rachel, is now carrying on the family torch as a music education major. Their son, Blake, is pursuing a musical career in a rock band.

"We encouraged them, but we didn't force them," said Roy. "They naturally took to it, which is great."

Roy has had a storied 36-year career at Rawlins High School and is responsible for starting many of the programs in place now, including the Jazzco choir. "At one point, I had six choirs going," he said. Roy also brought a community choir back to Rawlins, one that is still active today.

Roy said it was great having his wife direct the middle school choir. "There couldn't have been a better pairing," he said. "Becky was incredible at what she did and getting kids involved. I always knew I had a strong group of kids coming up because of what she was doing at the middle school. That made the program as strong as it was."

Roy moved to Rawlins first in 1976, and Becky followed a year later after they got married.

"She gives me great feedback, and I do the same thing," he said. "It wasn't all professional talk, but we passed ideas off each other. We were both involved in community theater. It was fantastic."

Roy was the 2012 Wyoming Music Educator of the Year. (Courtesy *Rawlins Daily Times*.)

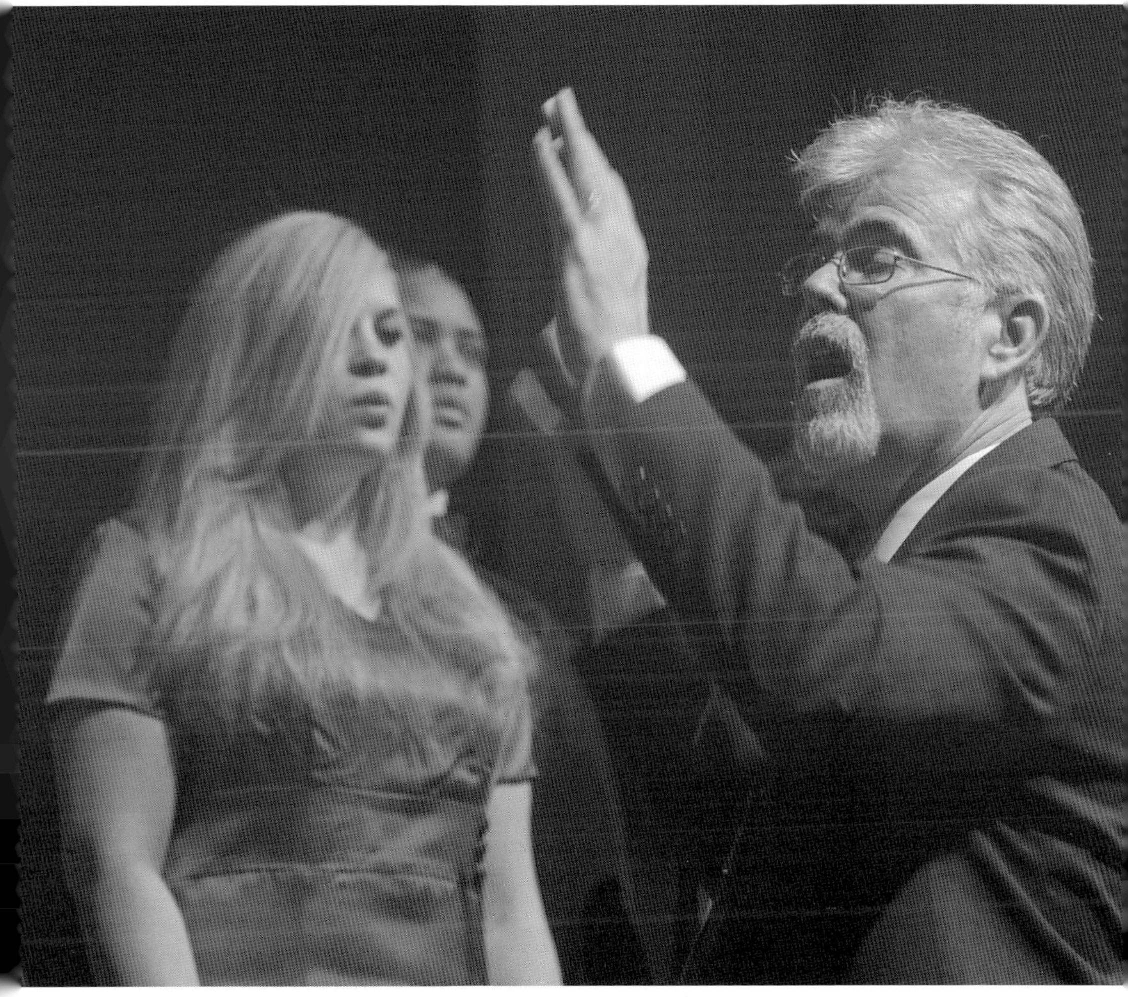

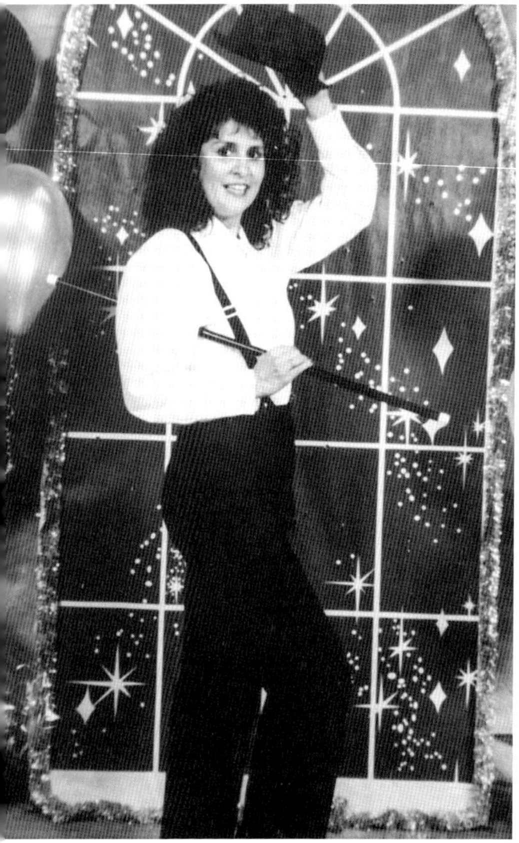

Babbette Mathill

After 40 years of teaching and a lifetime of dancing, the owner of Babbette's School of Dance, Baton, and Tumbling shows no signs of slowing down.

Just last year, Babbette Mathill opened a new studio in Riverton and now splits her time between the two towns. "Most people my age are thinking of retiring," she said. "I'm going full steam ahead."

Mathill is now seeing the third generations of the same families come through her doors. She is also proud of the former students who have followed her path: 12 dance teachers, 14 with degrees in dance, and 6 gymnastic teachers. "Watching students fall in love with their discipline and achieve challenging steps are some of my most exciting rewards of teaching," she said.

While Mathill has led her students to 12 national championships in tumbling and trampoline and 62 baton state championships, she said her studio is a place "where every child is a champion."

Mathill has taken her students to several cultural exchanges overseas, including a 28-day homestay in Japan during which they performed at the world fair, and two weeks in Australia.

Mathill recently achieved one of her most important goals: she has taught all eight of her grandchildren: Meadow, Remington, Kalli, Kody, Josie, Timbree, Kimber, and Aspen. (Both courtesy Babbette Mathill.)

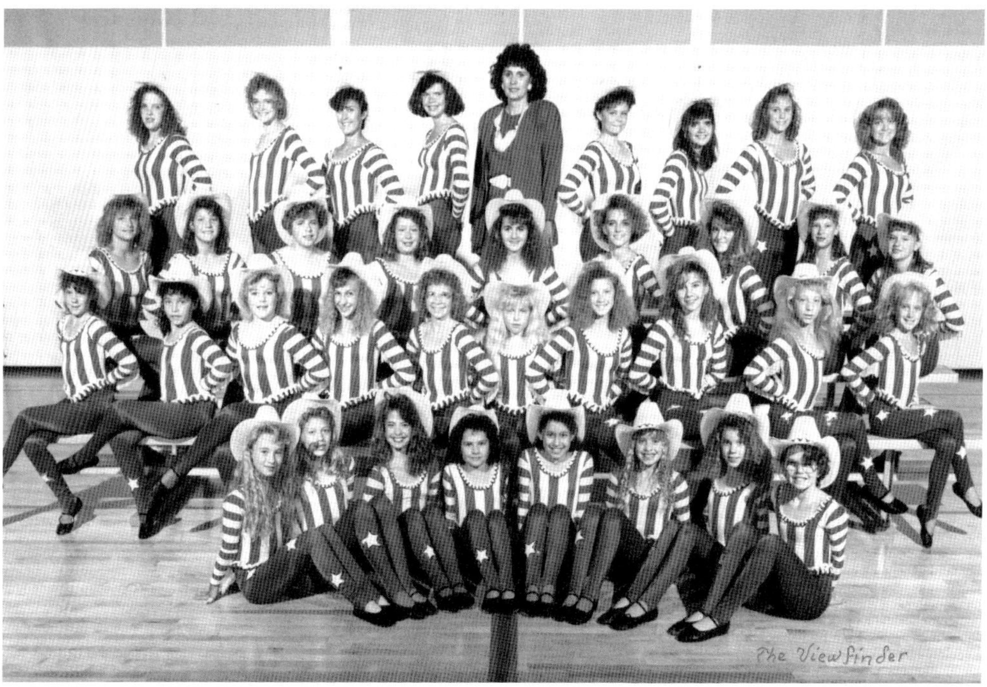

CHAPTER EIGHT

To the Big Stage

Many Rawlinsites live here because they enjoy the open spaces and easy access to outdoor activities. Some just don't like big cities, and others stay here to be close to family.

But small towns are not for everybody. Kids with big dreams can't wait to grow up and leave for a bigger city where there are more opportunities.

Most young people first leave town to either go to college or join the military. From there, they forge their own path.

After they make it on the big stage, the hometown newspaper tracks them down and calls them up. "I never thought a small-town kid from Rawlins, Wyoming, would make it this far," they usually say. But when the reporter probes further, they also say that they believed in themselves from the beginning.

The reporter then asks if they have any words for the youth of Rawlins. The responses are often similar.

"Dream big," said Hollywood actor Jesse Garcia. "Dream as big as you can."

This chapter covers people from Rawlins who found success on the big stage in a variety of fields. It includes a US senator and his wife, who became one of the first female politicians in the state capitol; a Hollywood actor; a father and son who both became federal judges; a record-breaking track star; and several successful musicians and artists.

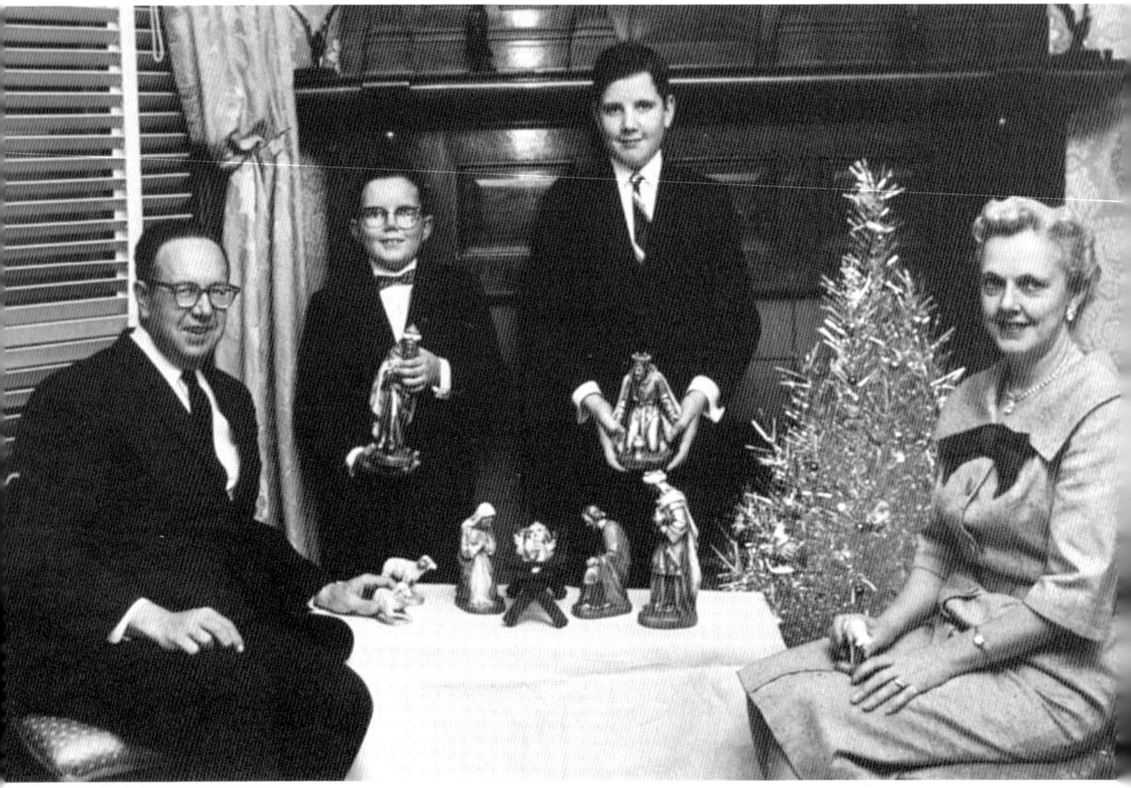

John "Joe" Hickey & Wynne Hickey

When John Osborne assumed office as Pres. Woodrow Wilson's assistant secretary of state in 1913, the next Rawlins native to make it big in the national political scene was two years old.

John "Joe" Hickey returned to Rawlins after receiving his law degree and established a private law practice. He started his political career as county treasurer and later became county attorney. In 1949, he was appointed US district attorney for Wyoming.

In 1958, Hickey was elected the 24th Wyoming state governor. He resigned his post in 1961 when he was appointed to the US Senate to fill the deceased senator-elect Keith Thomson's vacant seat. This made him the first Carbon County native ever to serve in the US Senate. He lost the bid to keep his Senate seat in 1962.

Commonly known as "Wynne," Winifred Hickey was the niece of Clare Espy (the early Rawlins cowboy). After her husband's death, she remained in Cheyenne and delved into politics herself.

She was the first woman to serve as a Laramie County commissioner and served in the Wyoming Senate until her retirement in 1990.

Her many accolades include an honorary doctor of laws degree from the University of Wyoming, Cheyenne Chamber of Commerce Person of the Year, and the Papal Medal for extraordinary service to the Catholic Church. (Courtesy Carbon County Museum.)

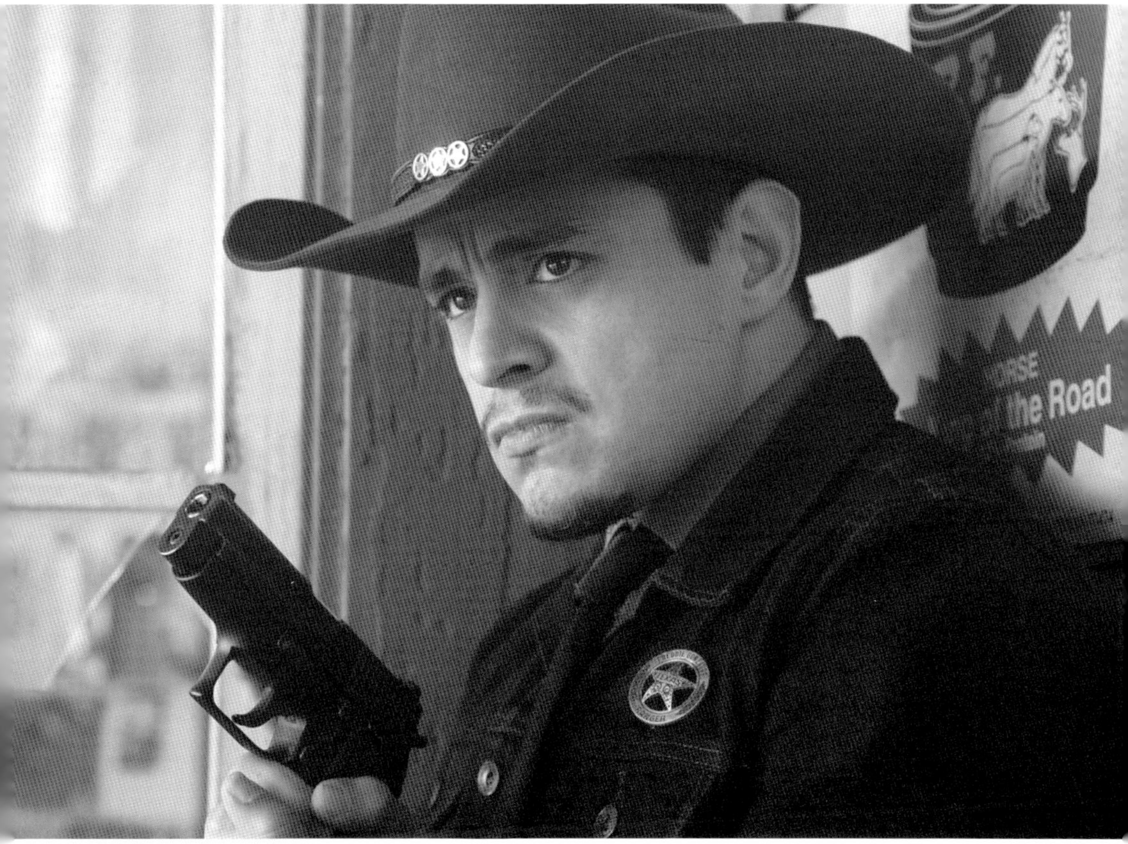

Jesse Garcia
Jesse Garcia had his big Hollywood break in 2005 as one of the two protagonists in *Quinceañera*. That film won both the Grand Jury Prize and Audience Award at the 2006 Sundance Film Festival in the Dramatic Independent Feature competition. Garcia's performance earned him Best Actor at the 2007 American Latino Media Awards.

Garcia moved to Rawlins from Hanna during middle school. During his time here, it never crossed his mind that he would become an actor. After graduating from Rawlins High School, he pursued an exercise science career.

His life changed when, on a whim, he decided to go with one of his friends to Atlanta to study acting. "Otherwise, I'd probably be a massage therapist or holistic medical practitioner," he said. Three years later, Garcia moved to Los Angeles to try to make it as an actor—and he did, in just over a year.

Garcia most recently appeared as one of the main characters on Robert Rodriguez's cult classic turned television series *From Dusk till Dawn*. You may not have noticed him, but he had a brief cameo in 2012's *The Avengers* as one of the pilots of the S.H.I.E.L.D. helicarrier. (Courtesy El Rey Network.)

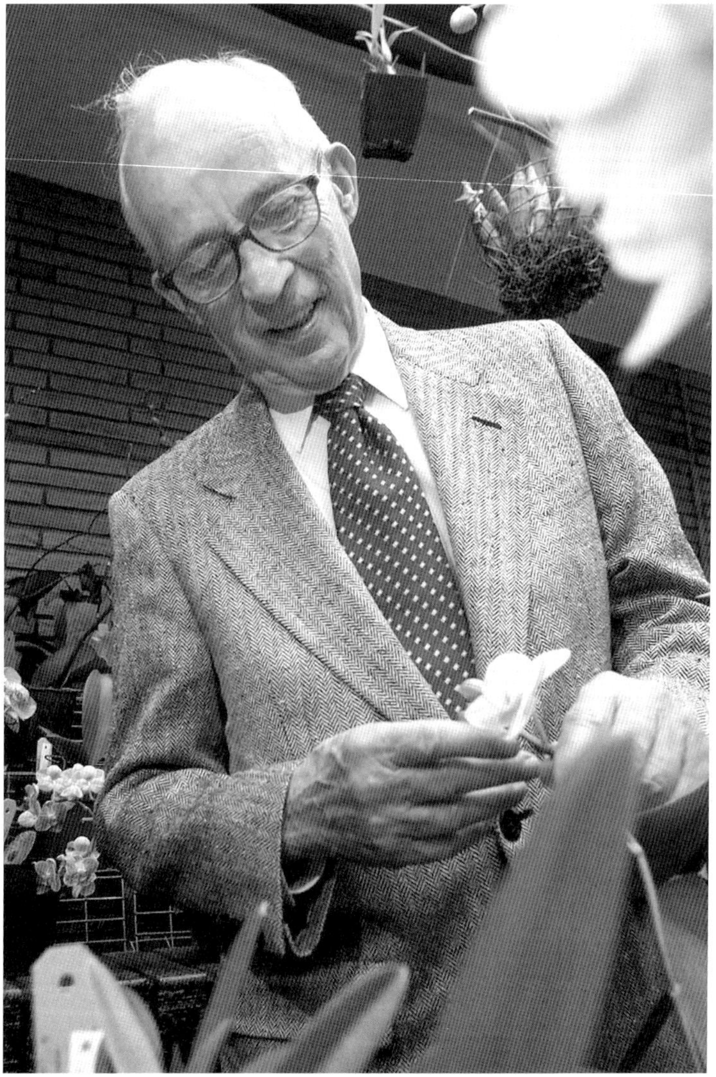

Clarence "Bud" Brimmer

Known as the "Grand Old Man of Wyoming Law," Brimmer retired in 2013 after 38 years as US federal judge for the District of Wyoming. He had a private law practice in Rawlins for 24 years before becoming Wyoming state attorney in 1971.

Brimmer made headlines in 2003 for issuing a nationwide injunction prohibiting the US Forest Service from implementing the roadless rule, which would ban construction and logging in 58.5 million acres of federal land, mostly in the West.

Brimmer continuously ruled against the roadless rule for the next several years. It wasn't until the Supreme Court rejected Wyoming's bid to allow the court's full panel to review the rule in 2012 that Brimmer lifted his injunction.

The case was an example of Brimmer's self-described "pro-Western" stance. "I know that in my career, I have decided cases for the West," Brimmer told the Associated Press after his retirement. "And that's because I've always felt that this area needed help in representation, that just two senators and a congressman only, couldn't do it all. And so I've pitched in too." (Photograph by Dan Cepeda, courtesy *Casper Star Tribune*.)

Phil Brimmer

The first time anyone called him Judge Brimmer, Phil Brimmer thought, "That's my dad's name." When the assistant US attorney was named US federal judge for the District of Colorado in 2008, the elder Brimmer was still serving in the same position for Wyoming.

This marked only the 11th time in history that the child of a sitting federal judge had also been appointed to the bench.

Brimmer lived in Rawlins for the first 12 years of his life. "I have great memories of Rawlins," he said. "The outline of the hill behind our house is etched in my mind."

According to Brimmer, you don't plan on becoming a federal judge. "You're setting yourself up for disappointment if you do," he said. "It just happened to work out."

As a federal judge, Brimmer enjoys the variety of cases he gets to preside over. "Federal judges always have mixed dockets, and that's what makes the job interesting. There are new challenges all the time."

In particular, he has enjoyed working on intellectual property cases. "I've had some interesting patent and trademark cases, and that's been a fun area to gain some knowledge in," he said. (Courtesy Phil Brimmer.)

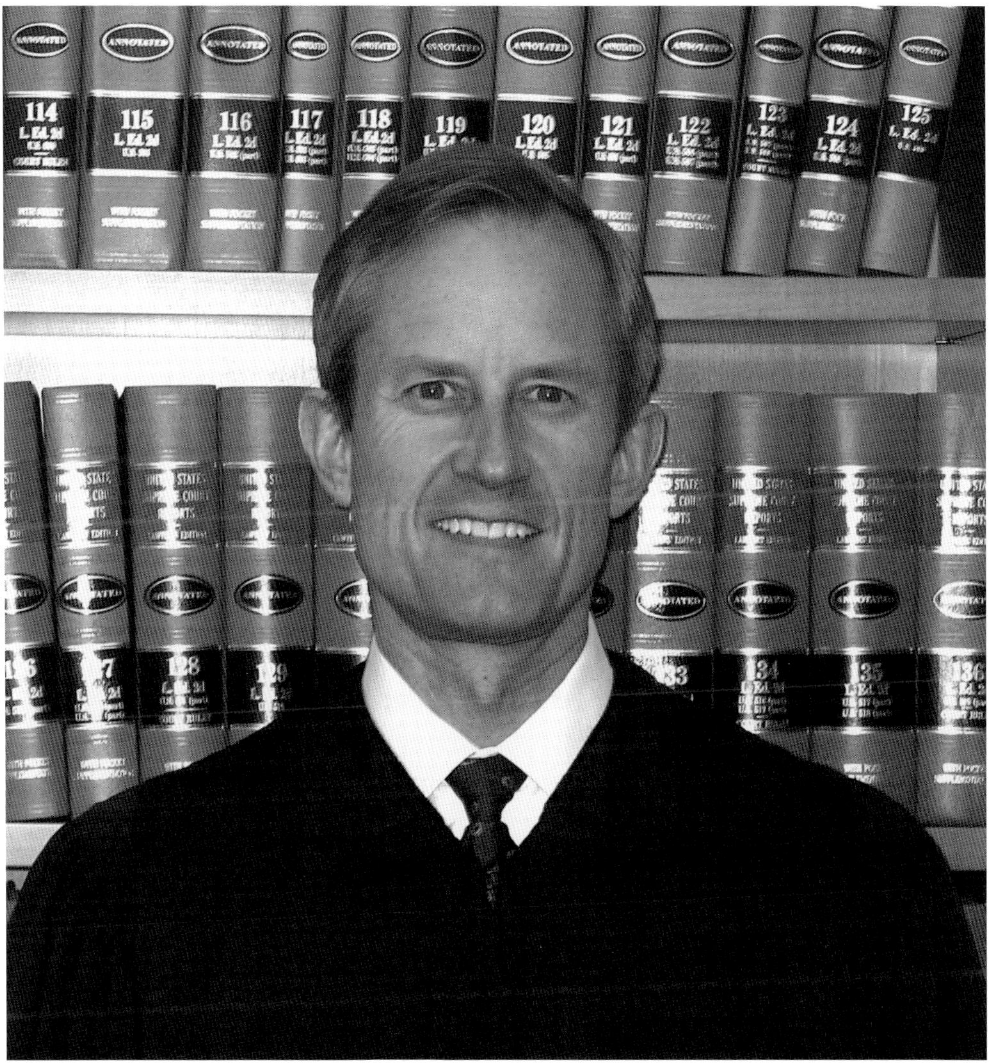

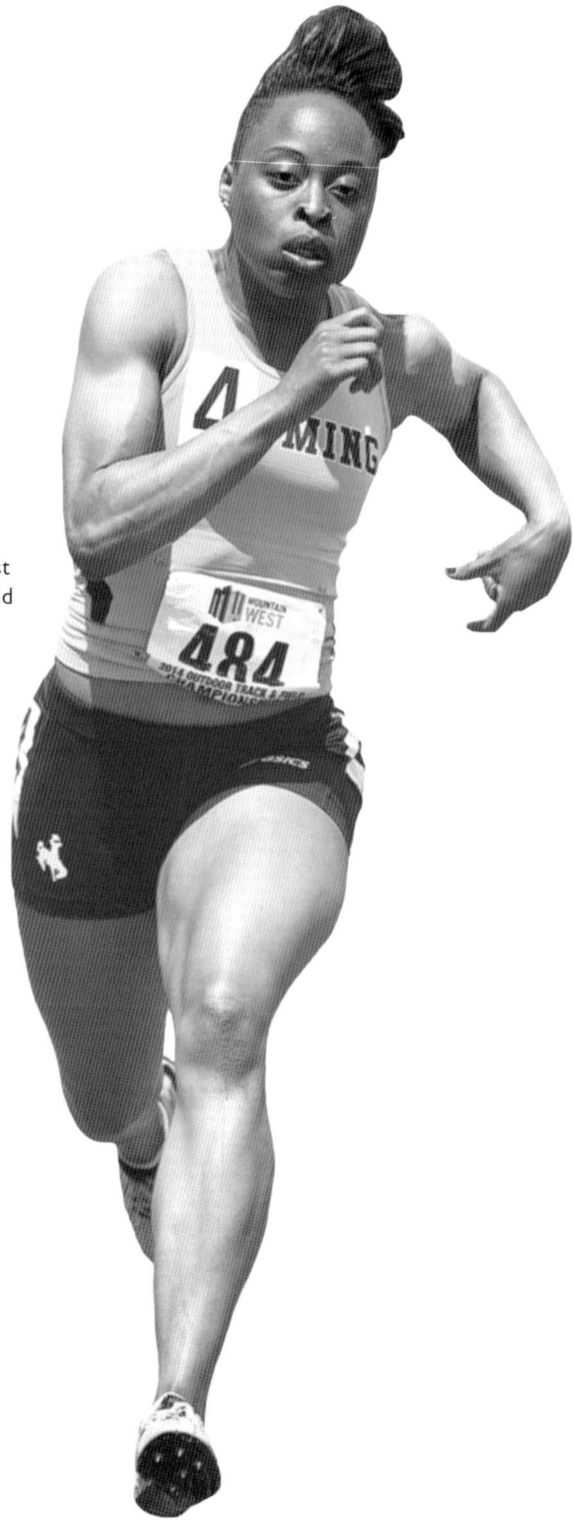

Kereston Thomas
A former Rawlins High School track star, Kereston Thomas has continued her success at the college level as arguably the fastest female runner at the University of Wyoming. In May 2014, the sophomore broke her own university all-time record in the outdoor 100 meters, clocking in at 11.57 seconds. She holds the second-fastest times for the indoor 60 and 200 meters and the fourth-fastest time in the outdoor 200 meters.

Thomas finished her Rawlins years with a perfect high school track record at the state level, winning titles in all 13 state events that she participated in over four years. She also broke the 3A division records in the 100 and 200 meters.

On top of her athletic success, Thomas is majoring in cultural anthropology and plans on going to law school. (Photograph by Jeremy Martin, courtesy WyoSports.)

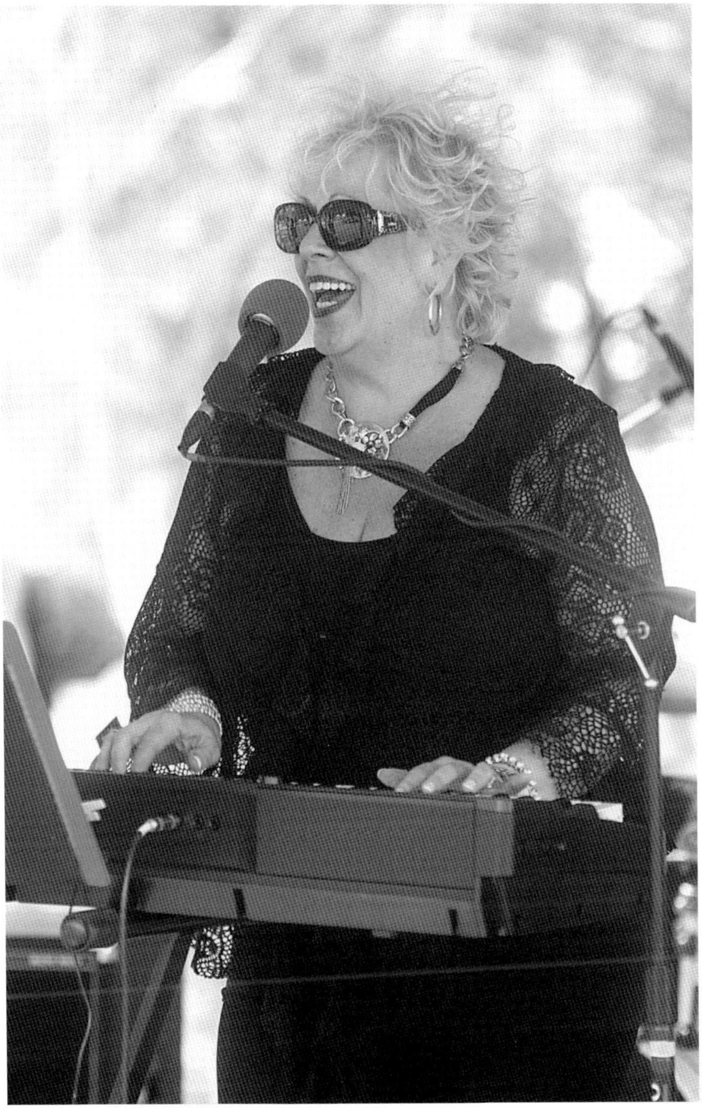

Shannon Gunderson
After watching a Peter, Paul, and Mary concert in Colorado as a sixth grader in 1964, Shannon Gunderson knew she wanted to become a musician.

"A light went on in my head—'Oh, yes, that is what I will do for the rest of my life,' " she recalled. And she did just that.

If there was anything music related in Rawlins, Gunderson was part of it. She even had her own local television show called *The World of Music with Shannon Whitehead.*

Gunderson left Rawlins for college in Nebraska in 1973. She was active in the music and theater scene, but ultimately decided to drop out and hit the road with the band Bijou Revue.

For the next eight years, Gunderson toured the country with the band and even went on a USO tour in the Mediterranean.

After that ended, Gunderson got married and moved to Virginia, Minnesota, where she continued her career as a performing artist and music teacher. "How ironic it was not to finish college and become a teacher," she laughed. (Photograph by Han Cheung.)

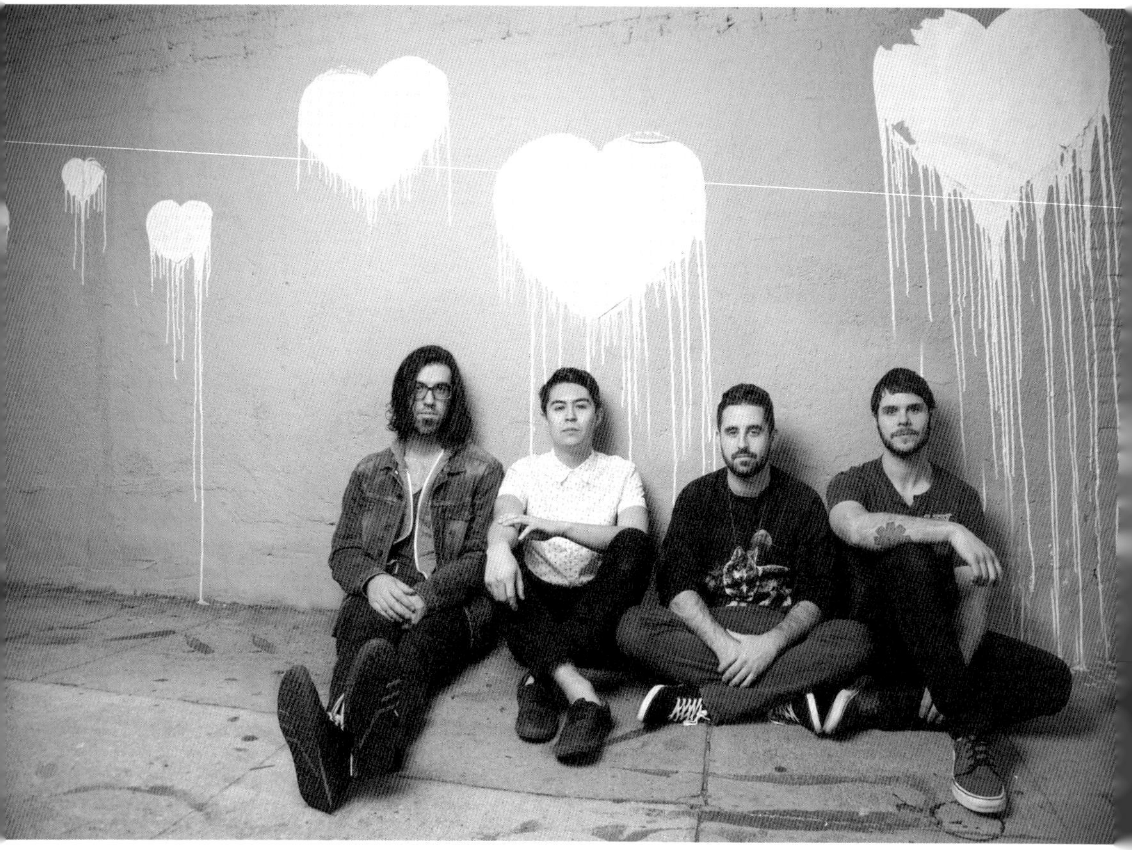

Blake Dahlinger

Growing up in Rawlins, I the Mighty drummer Blake Dahlinger (far left) always wanted to become a musician and tour with a rock band.

With the band signed to his favorite record label and being selected to play alongside some of his favorite bands in the 2014 Vans Warped Tour, it's been dream come true after dream come true for Dahlinger.

"I've just been extremely fortunate," said Dahlinger. "It's hard to find people who want to write the same music you want to—let alone find people you get along with."

Dahlinger moved to San Francisco after graduating from the University of Wyoming to pursue a musical career. "New York was just really far away and unfamiliar, L.A. is where everyone goes," he said.

Dahlinger met his future band mates at a concert in a dive bar. The musicians eventually got together for a jam session. "We instantly hit it off," he recalled. The band has been together for six years.

As the band works on its latest album, Dahlinger has his sights set on yet another dream: "We're not at the point yet where this is all we do," he said. "We still have day jobs when we're not on tour. We're working toward the point where we have I the Mighty be the way we make our career." (Photograph by Megan Thompson, courtesy Equal Vision Records.)

Molina Speaks

Adrian Hulberto Molina, aka Molina Speaks, is a writer, poet, hip-hop artist, community educator, and university professor. Molina wrote his first rap song at the age of 16 in loving memory of his cousin and best friend, fellow Rawlins native Randy Esquibel. He recorded his first track in the home of D-Mind of Rawlins rap group Loco Mente. Molina credits another Rawlins native, Dominic Martinez, for helping him get to college, teaching him about the Chicano movement, and encouraging his education and activism.

Molina is the performance director and a lead instructor at Youth On Record, a nonprofit in Denver that empowers at-risk teens through for-credit high school music production, poetry, and audio engineering classes. Molina is a featured artist on Arts Education projects funded by the National Endowment for the Arts and has enjoyed several artist residencies. He also teaches Chicano studies, hip-hop studies, and media justice courses through the University of Wyoming.

Molina calls himself an "artist of the people." "I speak to the people and the love of the people, the struggles and triumphs of the people," he explained. "I do not limit myself as an artist. My music comes from the heart. It is never for fortune or fame. It's about life, every angle of life." Molina served as music supervisor for *Papers the Movie*, a documentary about undocumented youth. (Photograph by Ric Urrutia.)

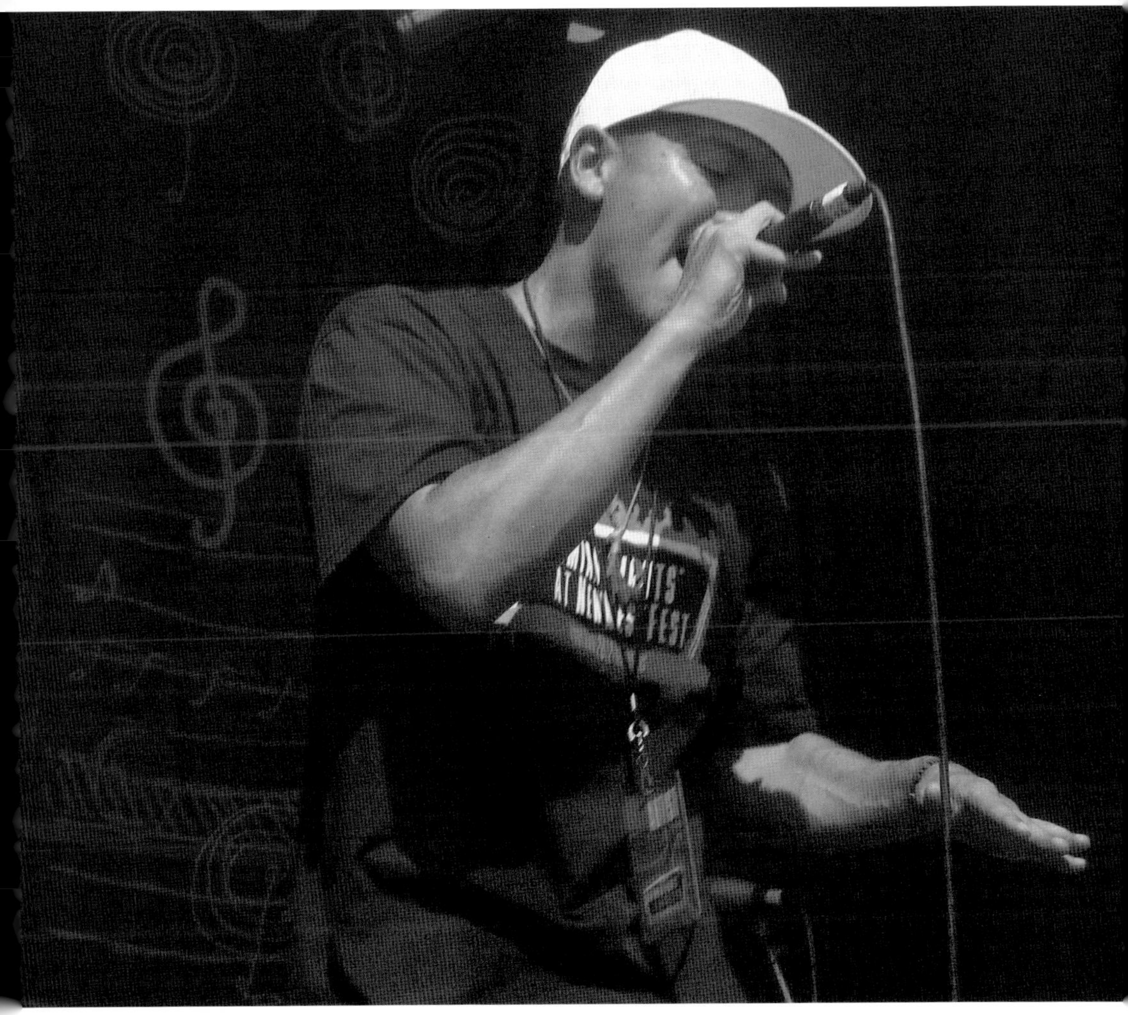

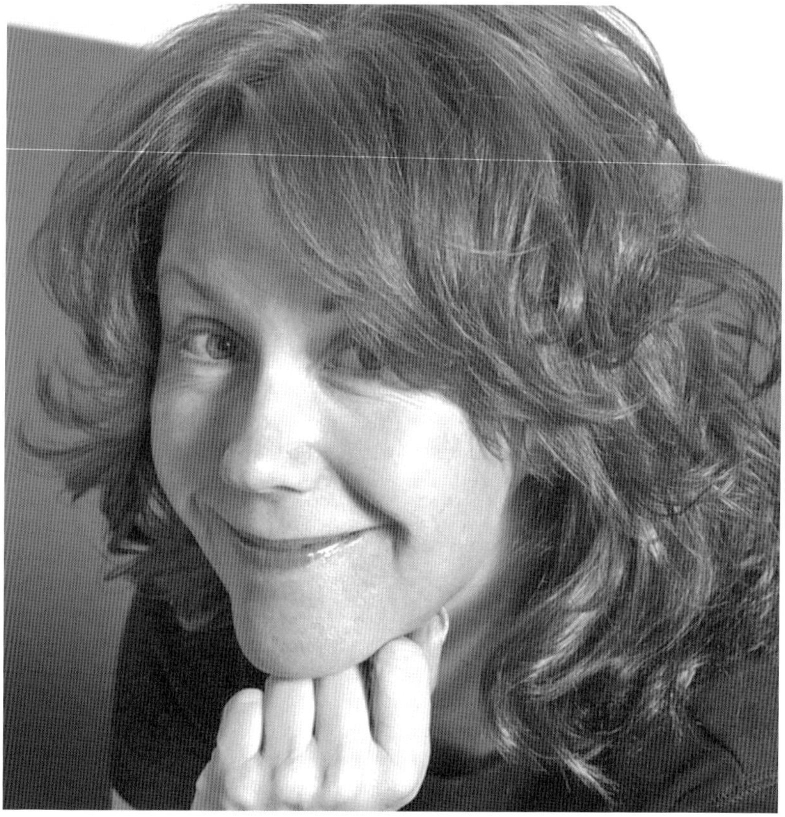

Lori Pate

After more than a decade in New York City enjoying a successful broadcast design and consulting career, Lori Pate recently moved back to the West. "I've been doing what I'm doing long enough that I can live pretty much wherever I want," she said. "Colorado is a little isolated from NYC, but when I'm looking out over the golf course at the big blue sky, I really have very little stress—and that's a big change from living in the city."

Today, Pate functions as a connector between media companies and creative talent, and she's worked with "pretty much every network" in the United States. "Because I know all the clients and networks and that sort of stuff, I can put teams together to work on projects," she said. "We've worked in Australia, a lot in Canada and Mexico, we launched news networks in India in both Hindi and English . . . we get to work around the world."

Most people probably have unknowingly seen Pate's projects somewhere on television. She points out one production that might stand out in people's minds: the graphics for The Who's 2010 Super Bowl halftime performance.

After stints in Denver as art director at the NBC and CBS affiliates, Pate moved to Houston with her husband and became a consultant at CBS, which had hired hurricane expert Neil Frank as weatherman. They asked her to make the graphics, and she taught herself in an era when designers had to basically write their own code. "It was challenging, but true to my Wyoming teachings, if you tell someone you can do it, you gotta figure out how to do it," she said. "Once it got all done, people started calling the station. They were giving my name out, so I would go all over the U.S. working with weathermen to improve their weathercasts.

"From there, I realized I could do consulting in television on my own and have control of my schedule. It has worked beautifully with balancing family life with my professional career and has led to lots of amazing adventures along the way." (Courtesy Lori Pate.)

CHAPTER NINE

Community Warriors

Rawlins has come a long way in the past few decades.

Residents recall there being junkyards at the entrances to the city. The downtown was suffering, with many empty buildings and blighted properties. The city's 100-year-old historic depot was abandoned and falling apart. What is important is that people cared. They rallied and fixed things. They planted trees. The city government launched projects to clean up derelict structures and crush abandoned cars. The historic downtown is fresh off a makeover, and a façade easement project for historic structures is on the horizon.

In a community where everyone knows everyone, people often rally for those in need or those who are fighting for a cause. Benefits, raffles, and fundraisers for community members are common.

Again, due to the boom-and-bust nature of the town, many community organizations disappear when people leave town. Ask people what happened to the county's Special Olympics team, and nobody remembers.

But there are always new arrivals who notice something missing in town and decide to revive the organization of their interest. When Roy Dahlinger was asked about starting the current community choir, he said, "No, I restarted it."

And that may just be the nature of the town. A Special Olympics team is being organized and may be competing soon. The community theater group is back after many years. A community orchestra is going strong. An art gallery and bookstore recently made their return.

This chapter includes people who just love the town and won't hesitate to show some Rawlins pride, even when visiting a foreign country.

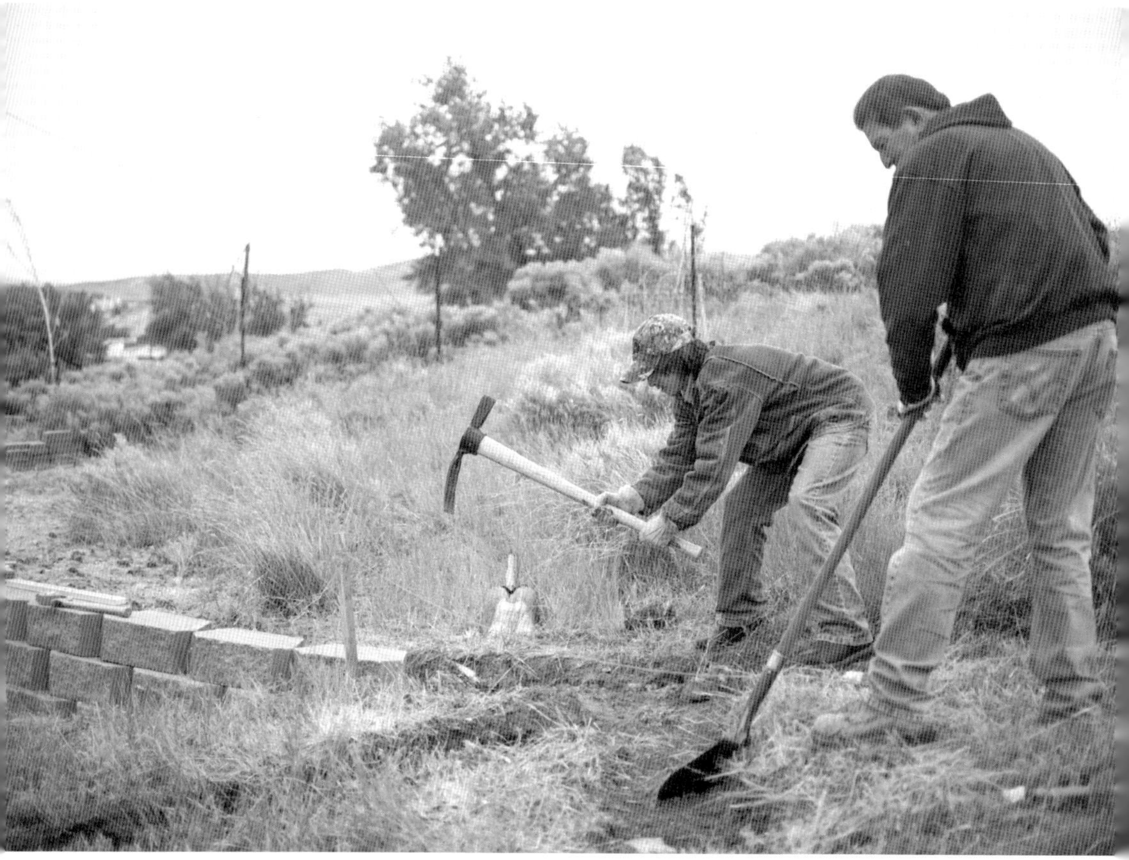

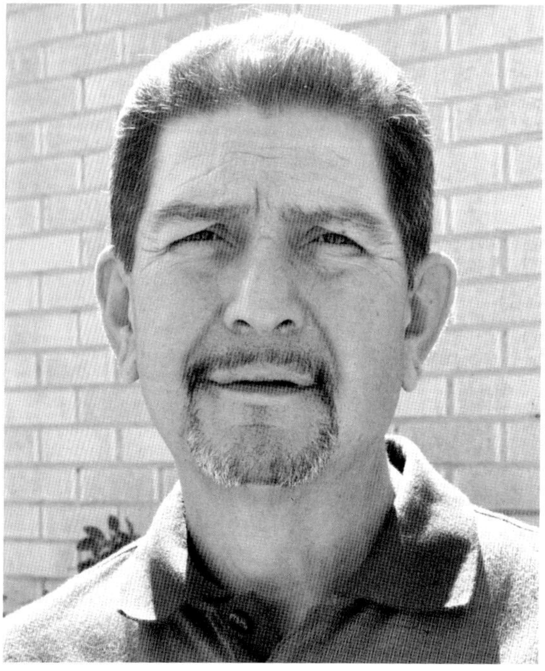

Louis Espinoza's Phoenix Project
Before Councilman Louis Espinoza started his "Phoenix Project," the hills along the railroad north and south of the Washington Street tunnel were covered with anthills and coal cinders from the railroad's steam engine days.

Starting around 2005, Espinoza was often seen on the hill, shoveling away by himself using his own money and resources. Slowly, people started to pitch in, donating topsoil, bricks, and labor. Eventually the city and Union Pacific got on board as well. The project is still in progress—59-year-old Espinoza said it will probably be complete when he is 70—but there are now decorative blocks, planters, and benches, and most importantly, there is vegetation everywhere. This is why the project name is so fitting: Espinoza literally built a garden out of ashes. (Above, photograph by Han Cheung; left, courtesy *Rawlins Daily Times*.)

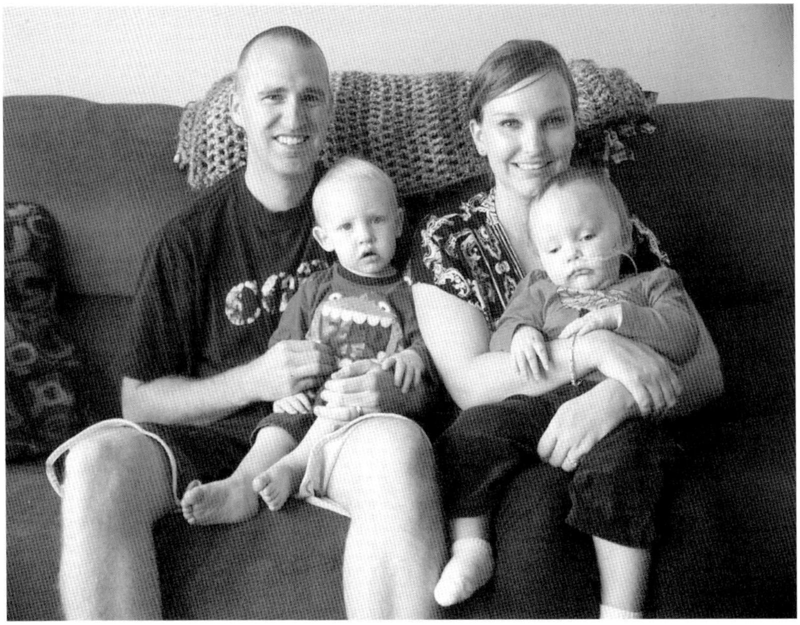

Olivia Caldwell Foundation
In October 2013, twenty-month-old Olivia Caldwell passed away after battling brain cancer for almost her entire life. During her treatment, her parents Katie and Brett noticed now little funding and awareness there was for pediatric cancer. A month after Olivia's passing, they started the Olivia Caldwell Foundation.

"We just wanted to remember Olivia," said Katie. "We want to have something that's still all about her. She was never really healthy—even in remission—and always had developmental delays. Our life used to be packed with appointments and everything was about her."

The foundation has had a wildly successful first year. Three days after the first anniversary of Olivia's passing, the Caldwells handed a $40,000 check to the Children's Hospital Colorado's pediatric neuro-oncology research lab.

"People see the need," said Katie. "It's the research that will actually save lives. We want to do something that can help other kids like her so other families don't have to bury their kids." (Both photographs by Han Cheung, courtesy *Rawlins Daily Times*.)

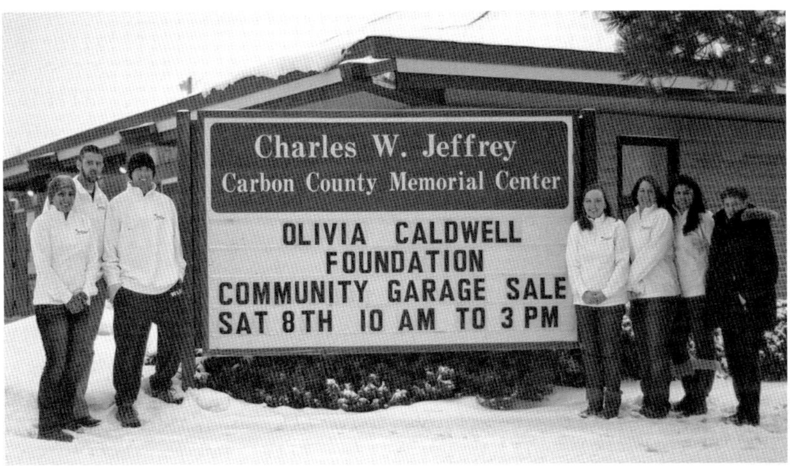

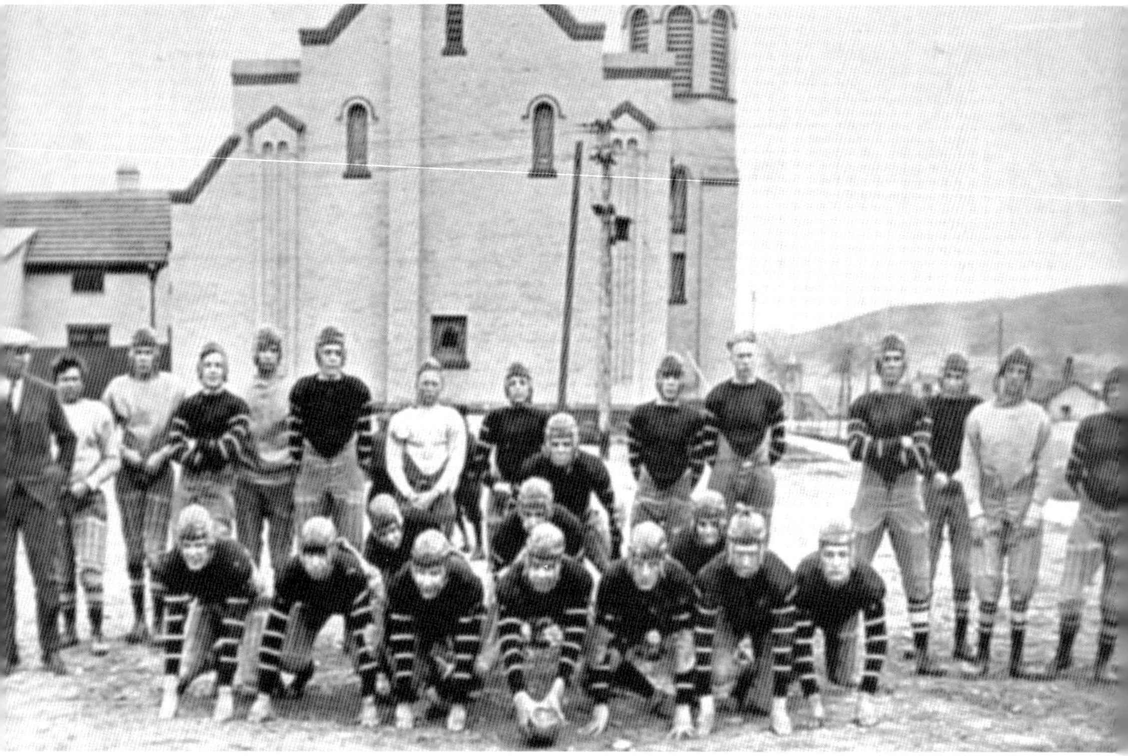

Outlaw Spirit

In a town without a university, Rawlins High School sports and other activities have always been a source of pride for residents. There were no organized high school sports until 1910, when a boys' basketball team was formed. A girls' team followed shortly after. In February 1911, the boys' team notched its first win by beating a University of Wyoming team.

The name for the school's teams, the Outlaws, first appeared in the Rawlins High School annals in 1921. This photograph shows the Outlaws football team in its second season in 1925. RHS principal H.H. Moyer came up with an "Outlaw Day" in 1931 that has since expanded to "Outlaw Week." (Courtesy Carbon County Museum.)

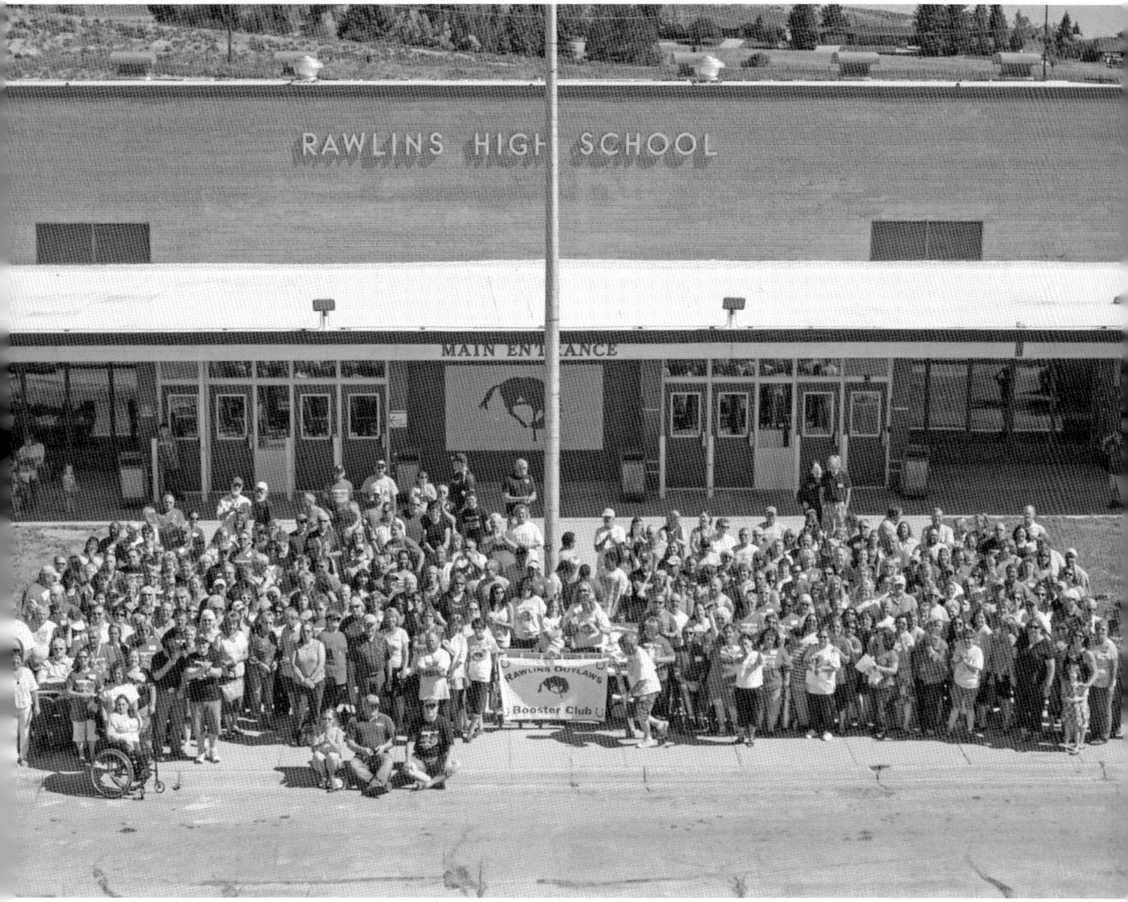

Round Up the Outlaws
The current Rawlins High School building was dedicated in 1959. With the upcoming construction of a new building, a group of RHS alumni led by Vice-Mayor Patty Schuler decided to organize an all-school reunion in the summer of 2014. This photograph was taken during the reunion. (Photograph by Han Cheung, courtesy *Rawlins Daily Times*.)

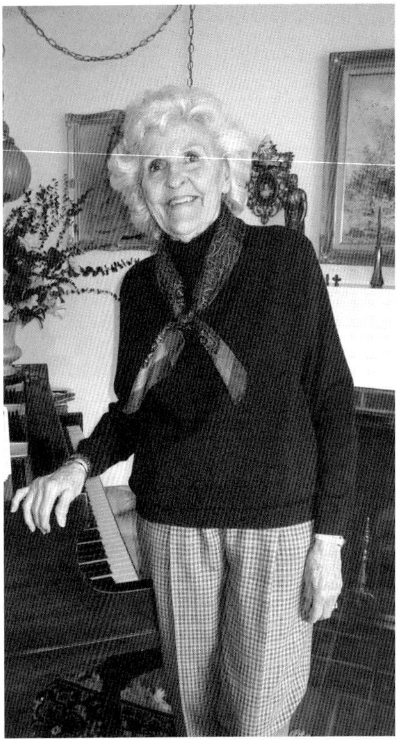

Della Vivion

Rawlins has had its share of female firsts in the state, but the town didn't see a female mayor until January 7, 1987, when Della Vivion was elected by her fellow city council members.

A Sheridan native, Vivion moved to Rawlins with her husband, Vern, to work on the family ranch. The Vivion family was well known in town, and Vern served three terms in the state legislature and was past president of the Wyoming Wool Growers Association.

Vivion started the Cedar Chest, a jewelry, gift, and accessory shop and art gallery, in 1976. While the store is gone, the sign still remains on a downtown building.

Vivion was the first president of the first Downtown Development Authority board in 1991. The organization's first tasks were to renovate blighted properties and fill vacant downtown storefronts, but Vivion's favorite project was the restoration of the Rawlins Historic Depot, originally built at the turn of the 20th century. Depot Park was later built across the street on abandoned lots.

"Depot Square was my vision," Vivion told the *Rawlins Daily Times*. "Being part of saving the Depot was my greatest achievement." (Left, courtesy *Rawlins Daily Times*; below, photograph by Han Cheung.)

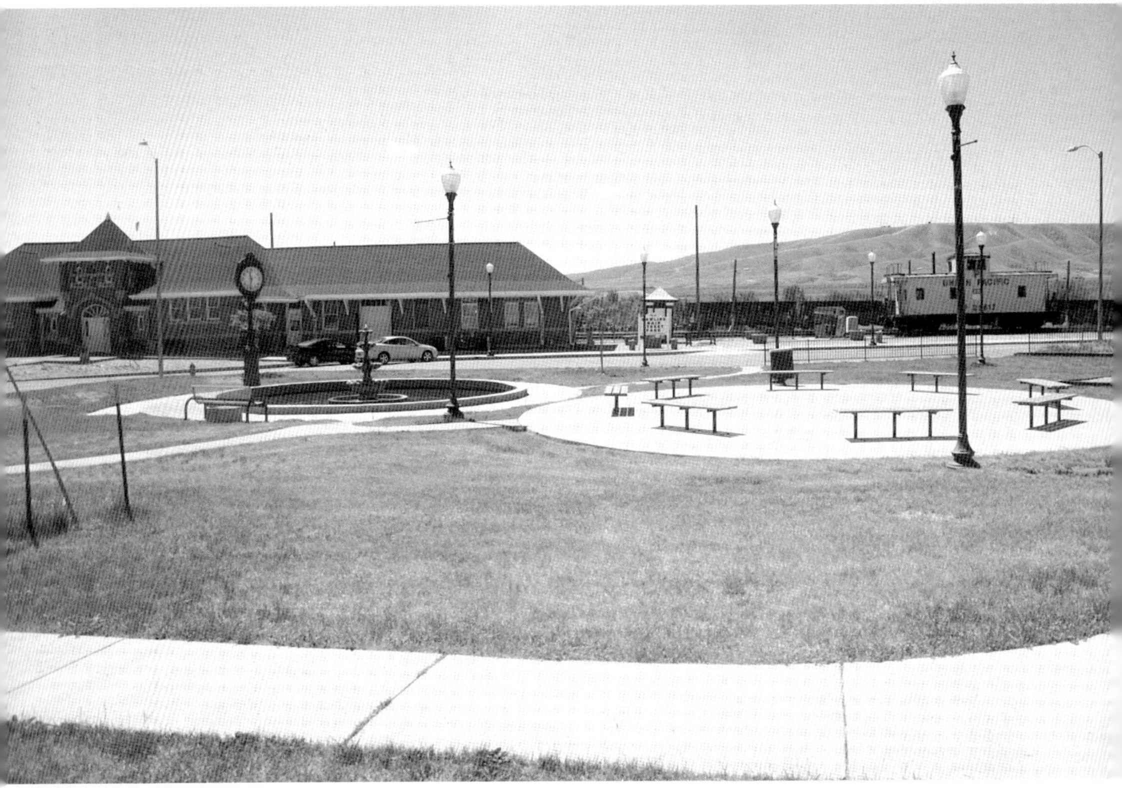

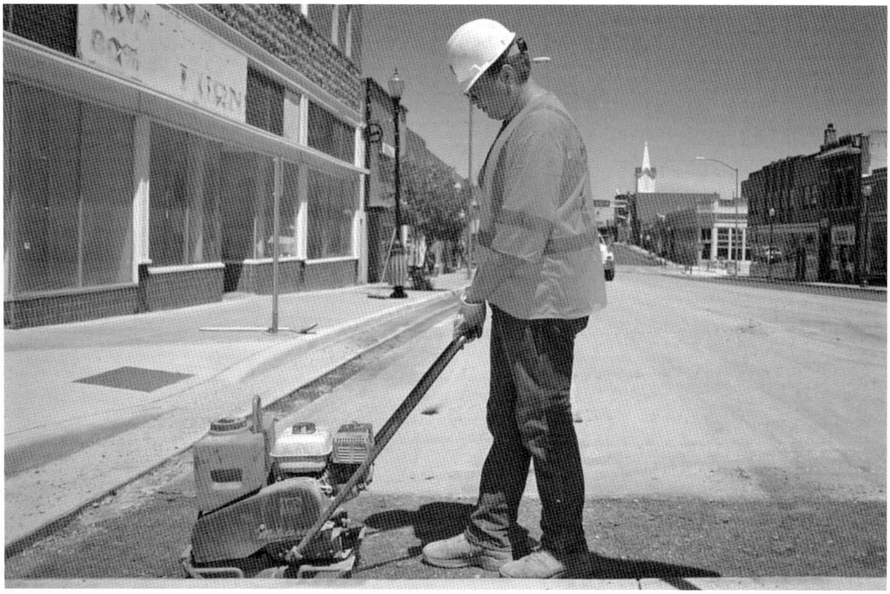

Revitalizing Downtown
The Downtown Development Authority (DDA) is going strong. In 2006, Rawlins became a certified Main Street community, and DDA adopted the Main Street approach. Now led by Executive Director Pam Thayer, the organization wrapped up a street makeover project in the summer of 2014 and unveiled the first public sculpture on a downtown street in July.

Over the past several years, DDA/Main Street has overseen a drop in the downtown's building vacancy rate from 45 to 10 percent and completed 55 private and public rehabilitation projects.

In early 2014, DDA was chosen as one of 10 semifinalists for the Great American Main Street Award, a first for any Wyoming Main Street community.

The organization also puts on several annual events, including SummerFest, Rawlins's largest downtown street festival. (Both photographs by Han Cheung, courtesy *Rawlins Daily Times*.)

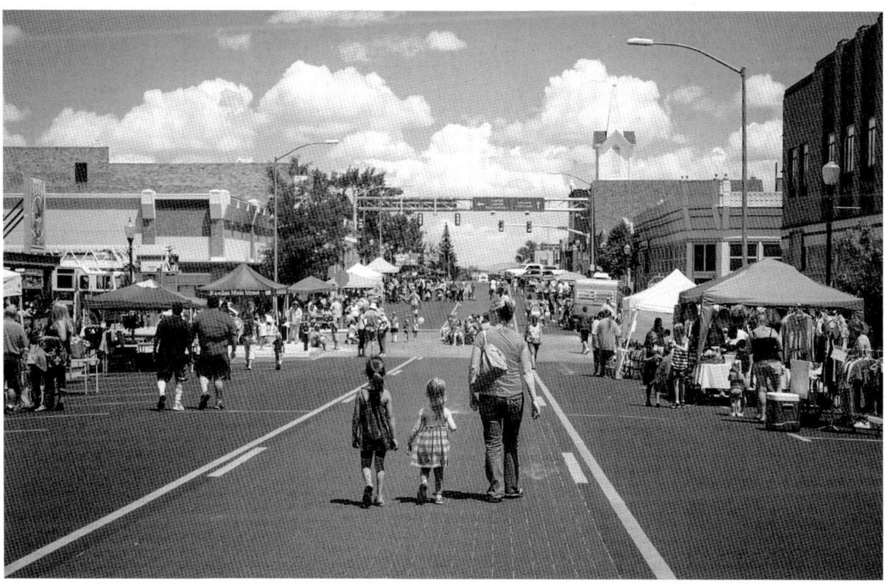

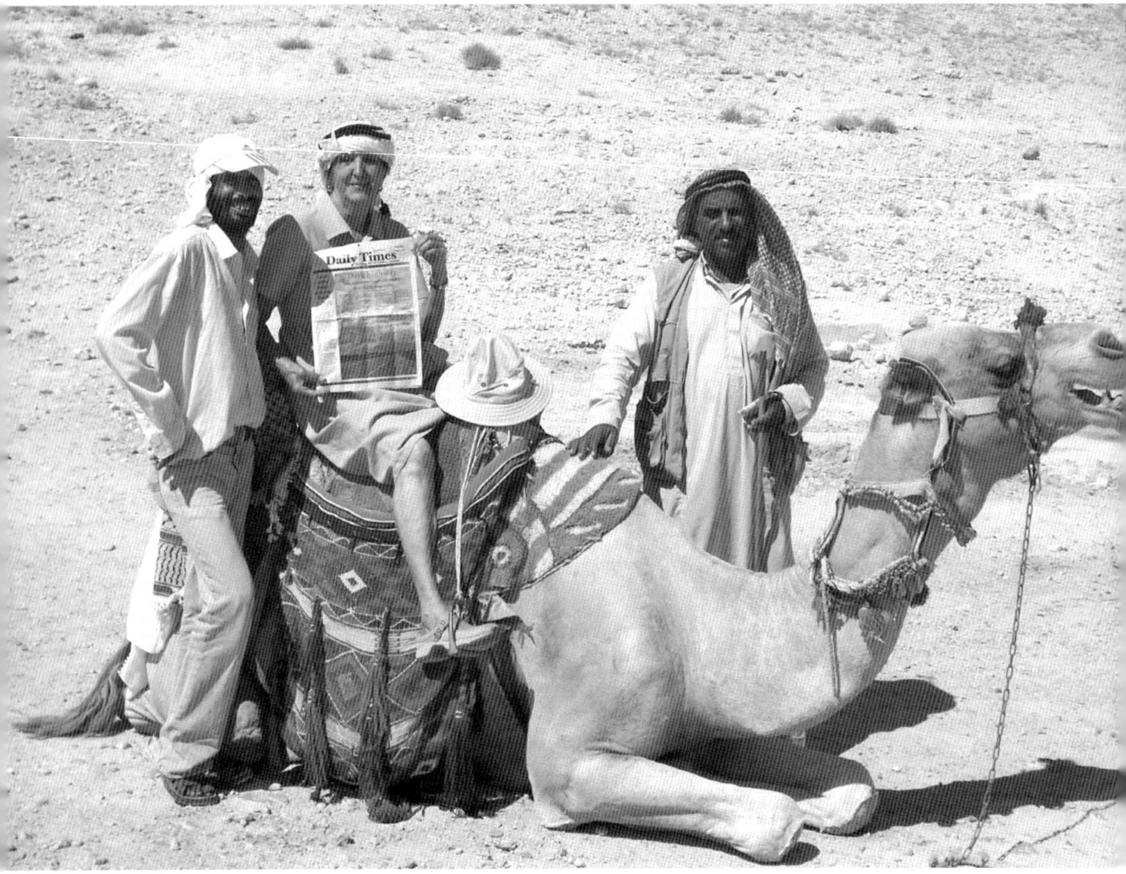

Delcy Moulder, World Traveler

After a stint as an elementary school teaching aide, Delcy Moulder decided to go back to waitressing, a job she had kept since she was 14 years old. "It made more money," she said. Moulder worked for all of the Wing family's restaurants throughout the years.

By saving $10 a day, Moulder was able to travel the world in her later years. Her first trip was to Israel in 1977, and she would return to the Holy Land four more times. Wherever she went, her pride for Rawlins was strong, and she would always have a photograph taken of herself reading the *Rawlins Daily Times* and mail it to the paper.

She personally met Pope John Paul II on her trip to Vatican City and presented him with a shirt with his name on the front and "Wyoming" on the back. This photograph was taken by her daughter, Babbette Mathill, on Moulder's fourth trip to Jerusalem. (Courtesy Delcy Moulder.)

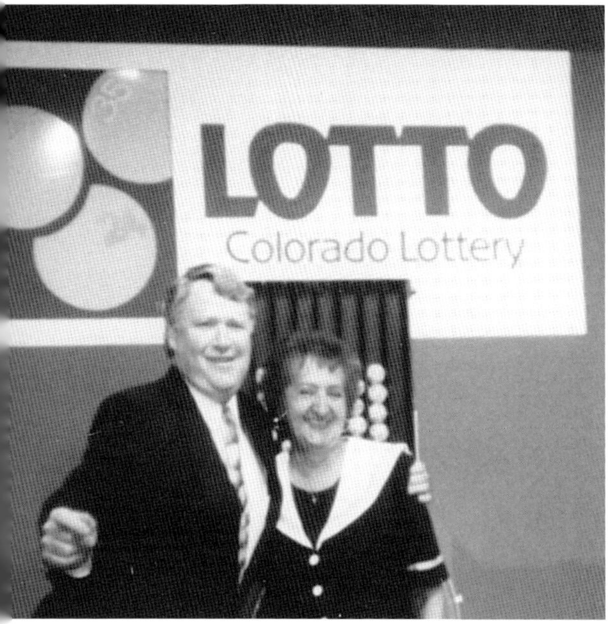

Delcy Moulder on TV
Moulder had her "minute of fame" when she appeared on Colorado's Channel 4 as a citizen witness for the Colorado lottery. "I wrote the station a letter asking why there were no Wyoming citizens featured." They wrote her back and invited her on the show. (Courtesy Delcy Moulder.)

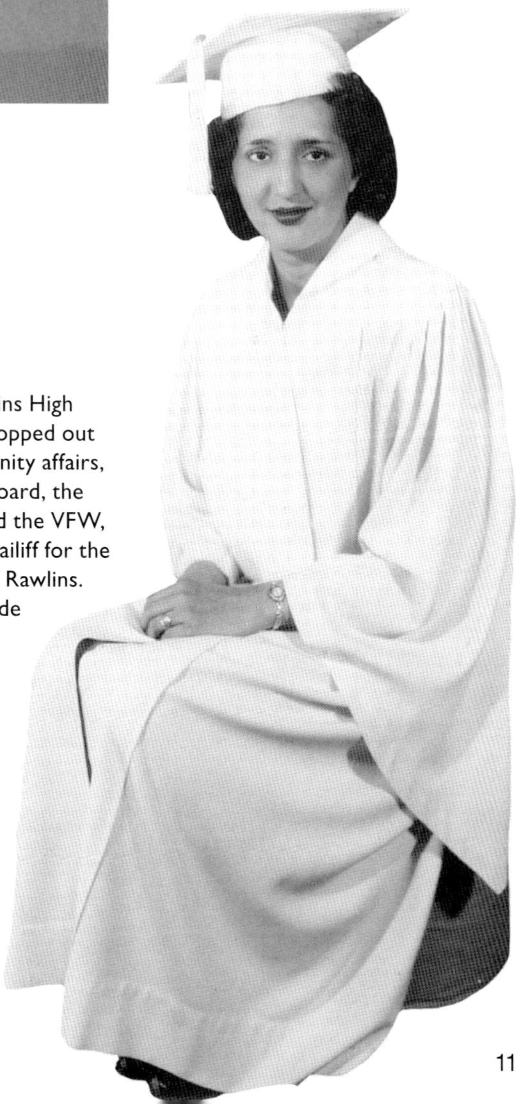

Delcy Moulder
Moulder is proud to have graduated from Rawlins High School in 1945 in a time when many women dropped out and got married. She was very active in community affairs, serving as a member of the St. Joseph School board, the president of the St. Vincent De Paul Society and the VFW, a den mother, a gray lady, an election judge, a bailiff for the circuit court, and an interpreter for the City of Rawlins. She also ran the Carbon County Cancer Crusade and the Rawlins Community Blood Drive for many years. "I've also been assistant for Babbette's school for 40 years," she laughed. (Courtesy Delcy Moulder.)

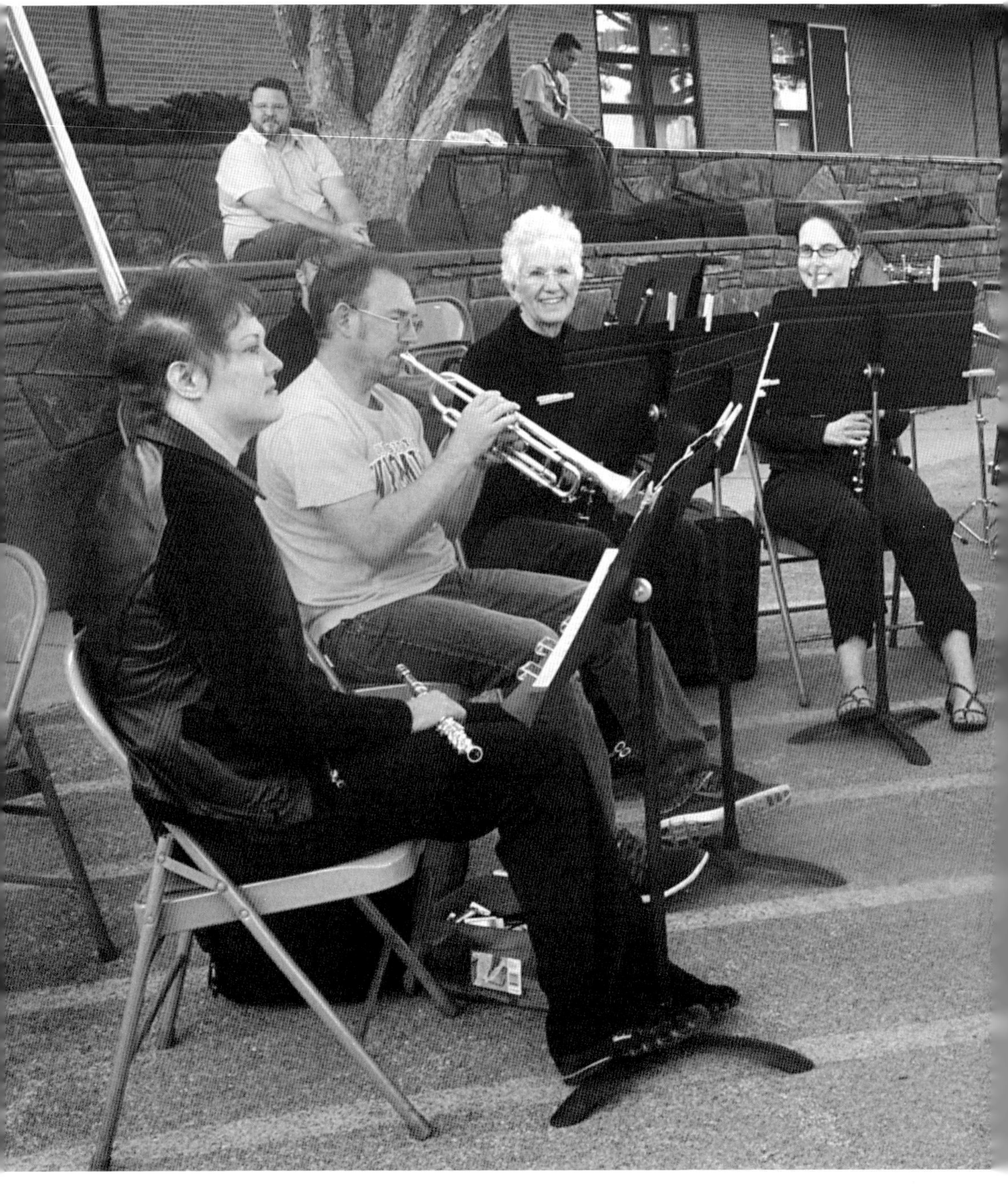

Jubilante Concert

Since 2006, Jubilante Ensembles of Carbon County has been making music accessible and providing a venue for community musicians to just have fun.

The group formed after seven musicians got together to play during the holiday season of 2005. They had so much fun that they decided to form a community music organization.

Three of these musicians are still in town: Della Smith, Judy Tigner, and Jenita Calton. The group grew over the years and has members who travel to Rawlins each week from towns as far away as Riverton.

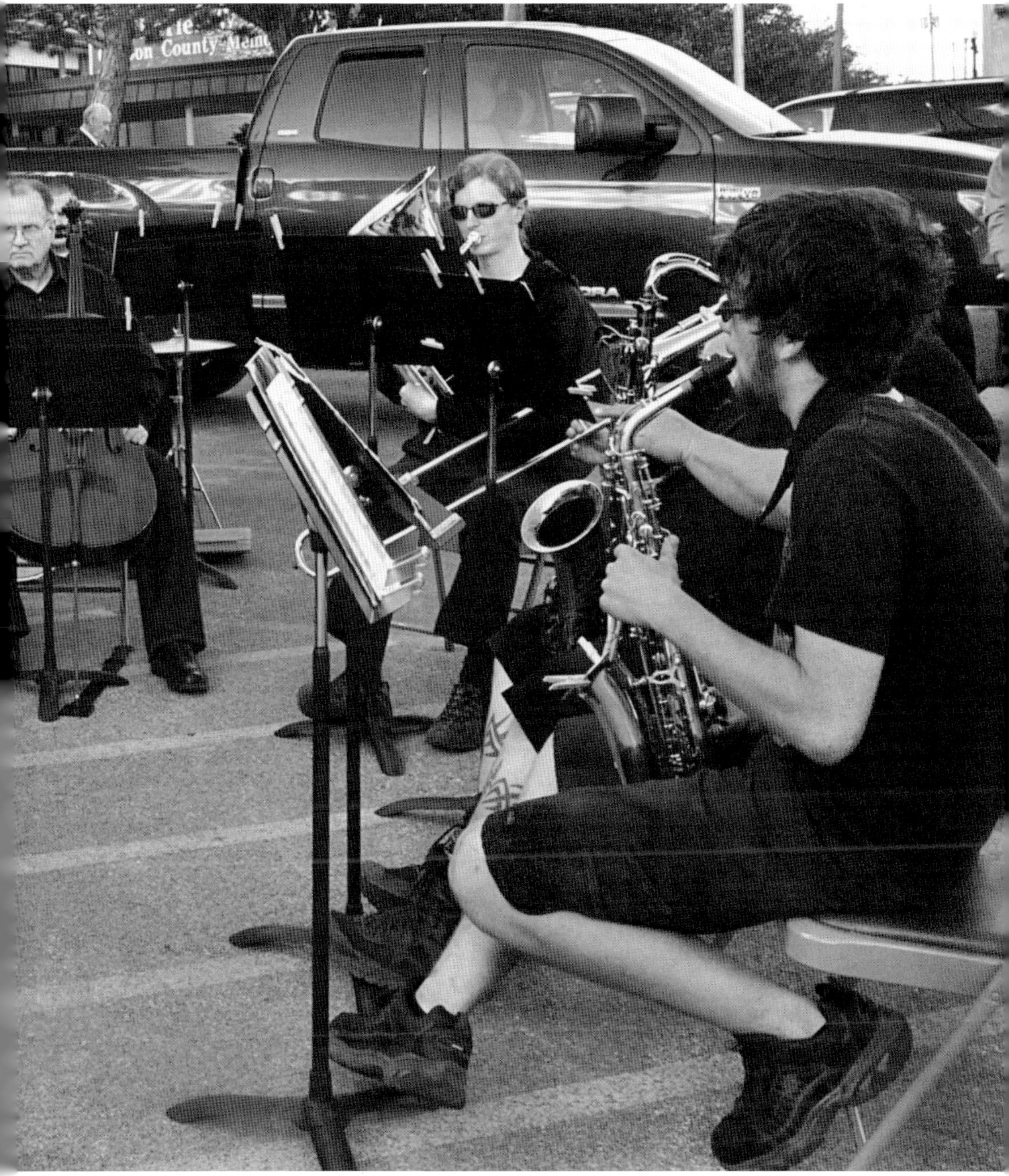

In 2007, the Jubilante Ensembles added handbells and handchimes to its repertoire and formed the Joyful Ringers and Happy Ringers. The group moved into the Rawlins Music Academy in 2008, and when the owner left town, the members took over the business and added it to their nonprofit. "We believed the negative impact on the community would be great," Tigner wrote. (Photograph by P.J. Cook, courtesy *Rawlins Daily Times*.)

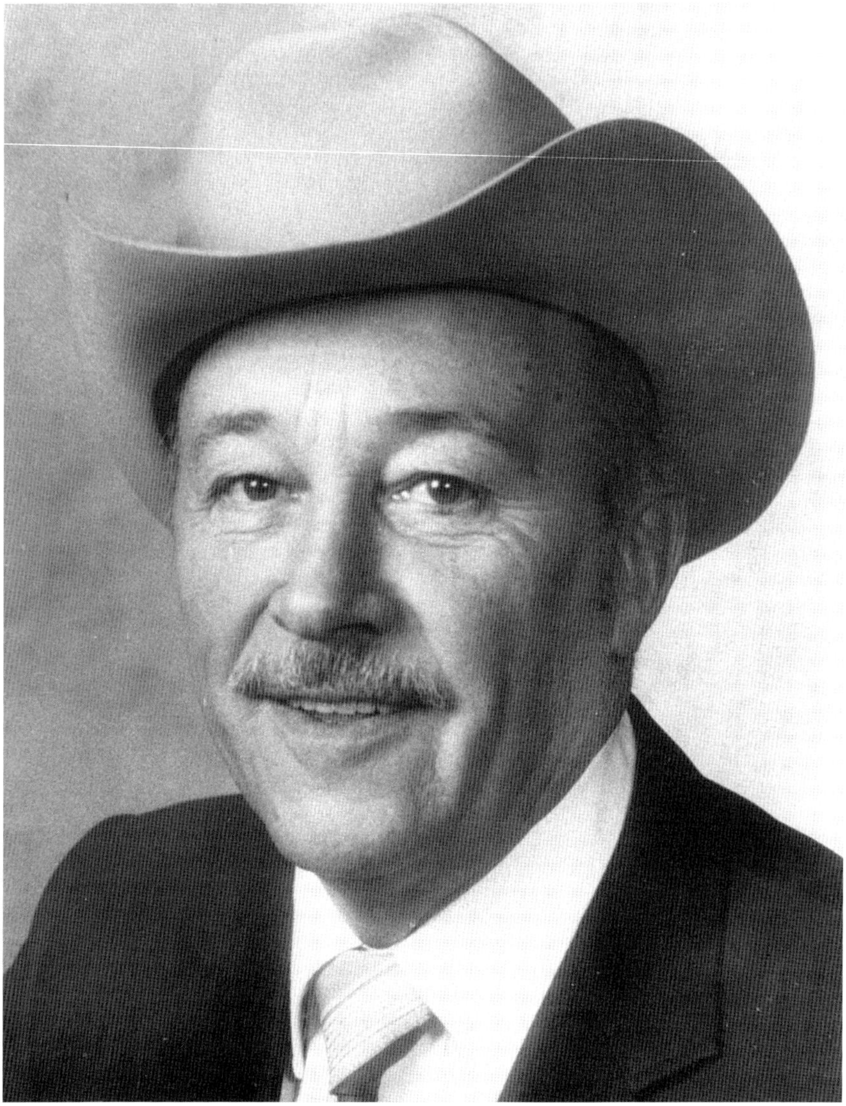

Everett Mann

After World War II, Everett Mann returned home to Wyoming and, in 1961, moved to Rawlins, where he eventually became mayor.

Mann's first term, from 1973 to 1980, was a prime example of the boom-and-bust cycle that played a significant part in Rawlins's recent history.

When Mann was first elected, Rawlins was facing a mineral boom of uranium and coal. "We had to hurry up and get ready to accommodate these people," he recalled. "The police force was beefed up, and the sewer and water system were worked on to handle the extra loads. There was a lot of activity at that time dealing with officials and different companies, and there wasn't an empty building or trailer spot for some time.

"This went on for two or three years and the bottom fell out. There [were] extra people and extra everything. Businesses dropped and shut their doors."

Mann's second stint, from 1991 to 1992, wasn't very memorable. "I kissed the babies and signed the proclamations," he laughed. (Courtesy City of Rawlins.)

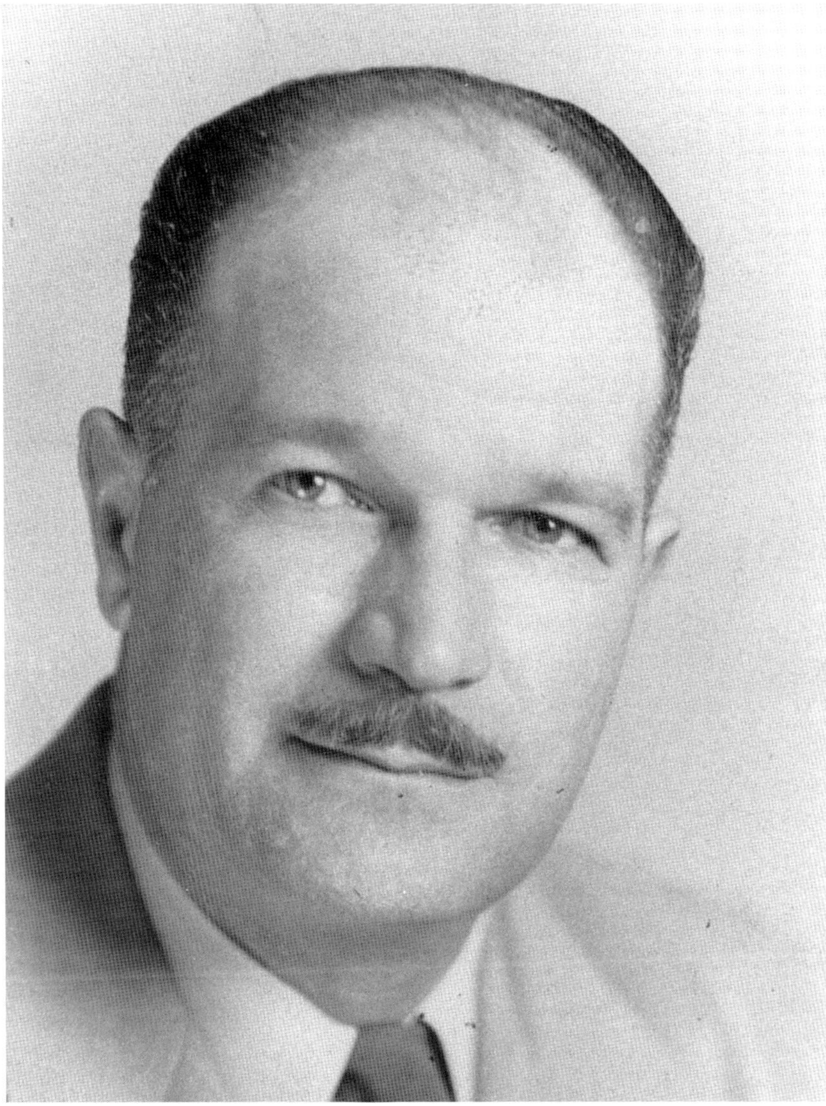

Sam Tully

Many old-timers remember seeing Mayor Sam Tully shirtless and on his knees, planting flowers in the median of Spruce Street.

Tully was a people's mayor, and it is reported that he would contribute his $5 pay for each council session to charity. The Great Blizzard of 1949 hit Rawlins just days into Tully's first term, and he personally assisted with the snow removal effort, driving a truck for 48 hours without sleep.

Another story tells of how he bought a dog license for two children so their dog would not have to be put down by the city pound.

In 1954, Tully marched to Washington, DC, "pounding the pavements, calling on bureaucrats and feeling pretty discouraged," according to a nationally syndicated column by Drew Pearson. He was protesting the Union Pacific closing down its coal mines in the area, causing 1,800 miners to lose their jobs.

"They've got kids who have got to eat, and that's why I'm in Washington," he told reporters. (Courtesy City of Rawlins.)

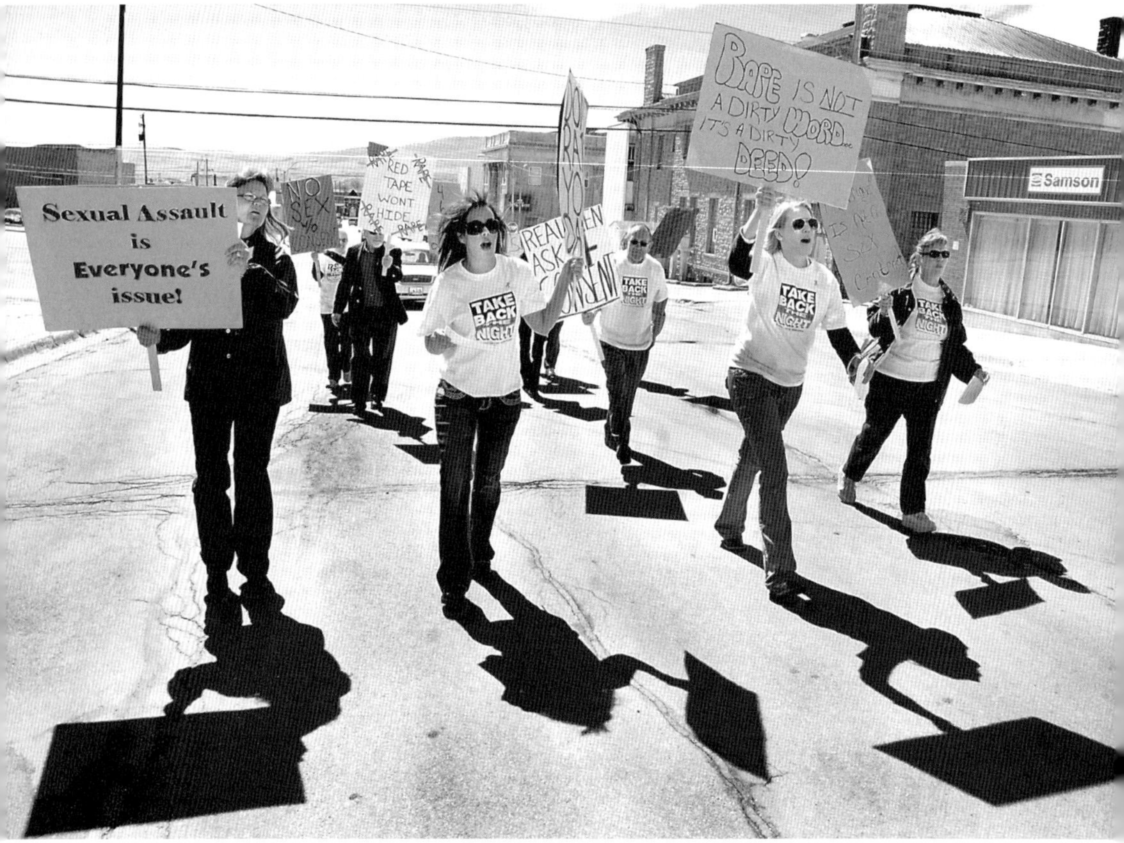

Carbon County COVE

Until the early 1980s, Rawlins didn't have many resources or a shelter for victims of domestic violence and sexual assault.

In 1981, twenty-three women volunteered to form the Victims Advocates Group with Becky Darbee as director. In its first year, the group sponsored the play *Goona Goona*, which dealt with family violence. That play was considered controversial and was banned in other cities, but was well received in Rawlins.

In 1982, the group established Rawlins's first permanent shelter for battered women and victims of sexual abuse. The first year, the shelter saw 57 women and 67 children and handled 104 crisis calls.

New director Andrea Hansen changed the name of the organization to COVE (Citizens Organized to see Violence Ended) to shift the focus away from the word *victim*.

The group continued to raise awareness, bringing the Wyoming State Coalition Against Family Violence meeting to Rawlins and starting a local March Against Fear. Each year, they would have the mayor sign a Domestic Violence Awareness proclamation.

Today, COVE's annual events include a Take Back the Night march and a Silent Witness ceremony to remember county residents who died as a result of domestic violence. (Courtesy *Rawlins Daily Times.*)

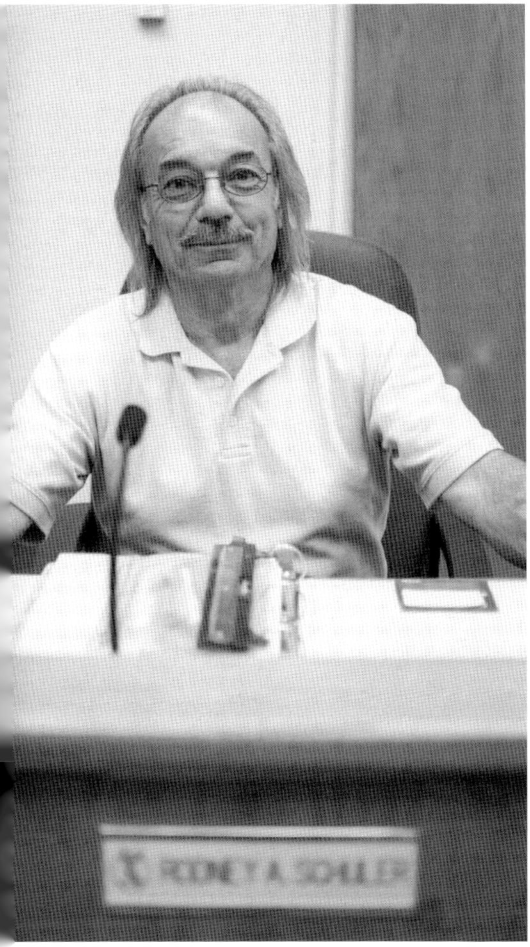

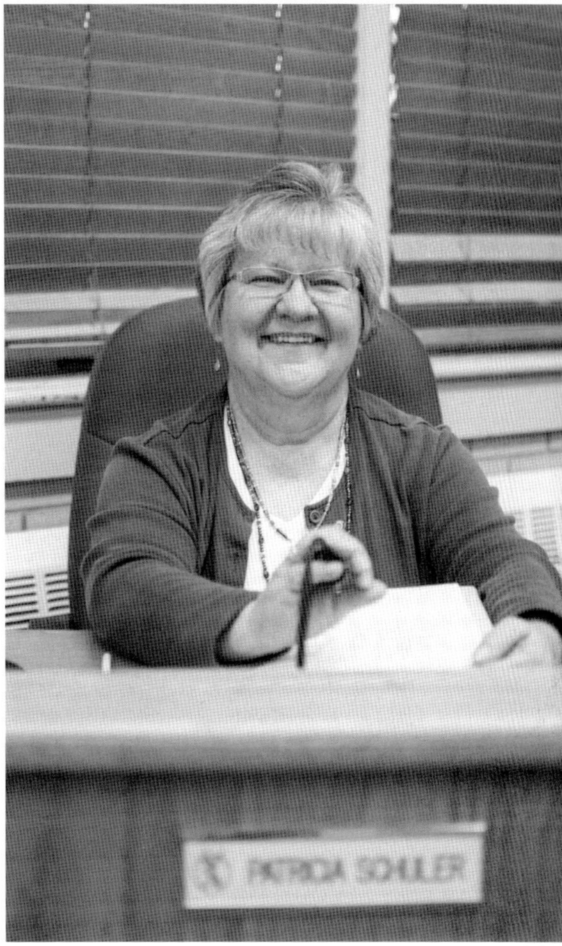

Patty and Rodney Schuler
Not only do the Schulers own the first tobacco- and alcohol-free bowling center in Wyoming, but they are also the first husband and wife to be city council members in Rawlins history.

"I was born, raised, and educated and now live, work, and play in Rawlins," Patty said. Rodney came to Rawlins later, as an engineer for the railroad, and they have been married for 36 years.

Patty was the one who first entered the political world, serving on the Rawlins City Council from 1991 to 1999, the last four years as mayor.

She served on the council again from 2007 to 2011, after which she decided her political career was over. Upon her departure, Rodney was elected to the council.

During the 2012 elections, Patty received enough write-in votes to run again. "I had no intentions of being back," she told the *Rawlins Daily Times*. "But when you're written in, you feel you're obligated for the people that wrote you in to run."

She won that election, and in January 2013, the Schulers made history when they took their council seats at the same time in city hall.

Having two Schulers on the city council was a bit confusing at first when calling roll. Fortunately, Patty was chosen as vice-mayor, and that resolved the issue. (Photographs by Han Cheung.)

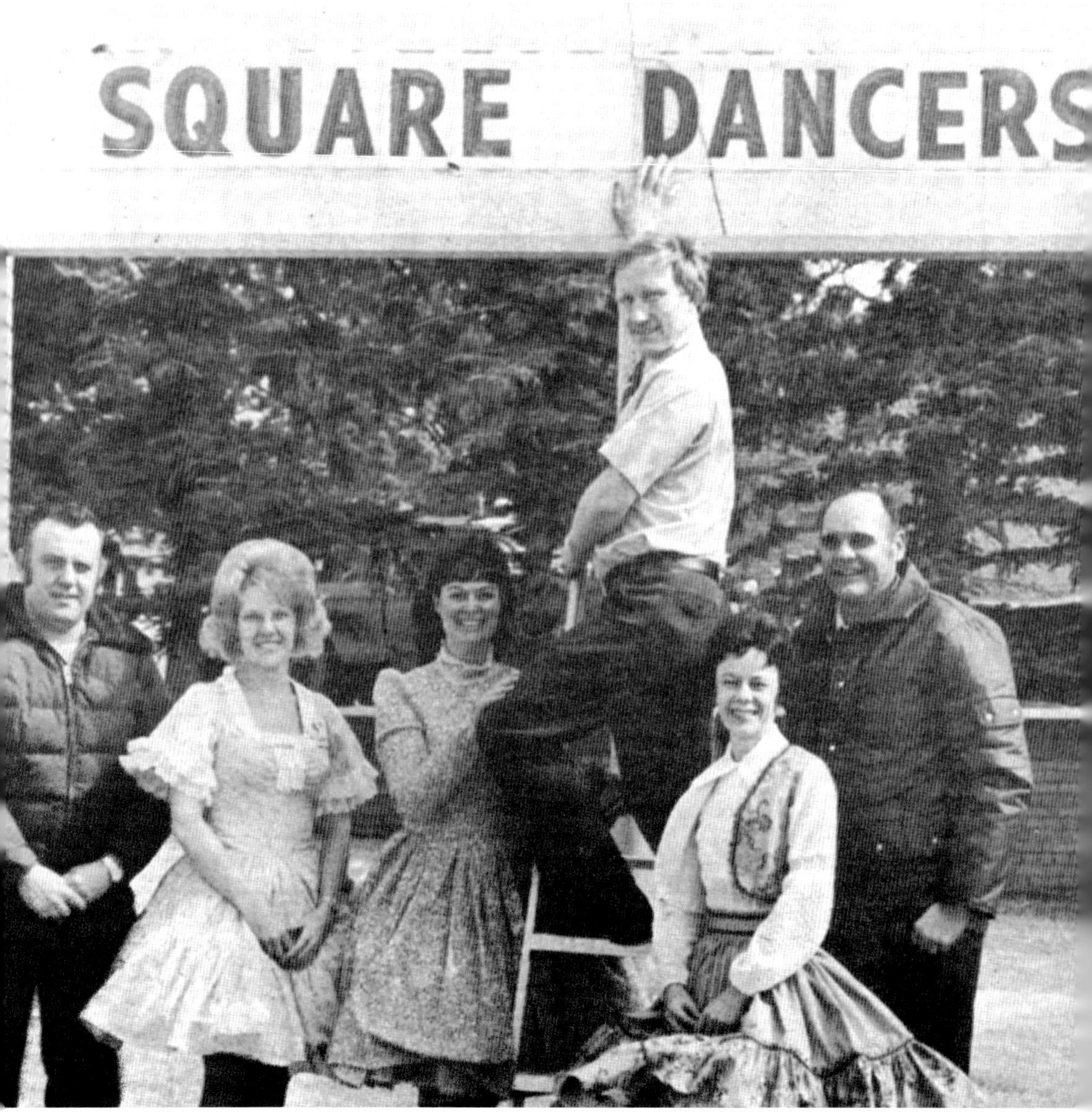

Rawlins Promenaders

The town's square dancing group started in Sinclair and had its first St. Patrick's Day dance in 1951. By 1970, the event had moved to the Jeffrey Center in Rawlins. At the time, these festivals would attract more than 300 promenaders. In 2013, about 70 dancers attended, but it was still a good time for all.

One unique event the group put on was the Buggy Stomp. It was held at a pavilion in Elk Mountain that had a floor made of springs from the wheels of a buggy, which added a little bounce to the dancers' movements. It has since been moved to Laramie. (Courtesy *Rawlins Daily Times*.)

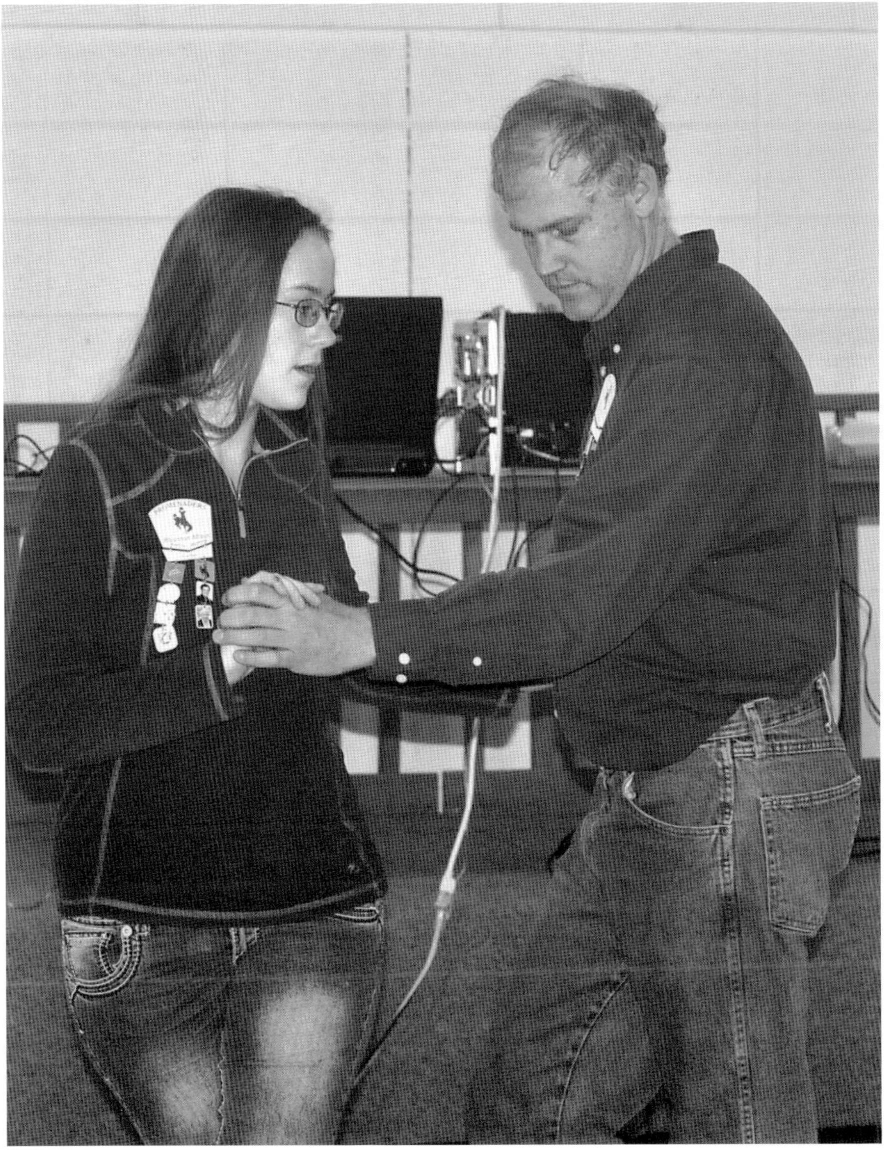

Allison Family

If you think only old people square dance, just look at the Allison family. Yancey Allison; his 16-year-old daughter, Rhiannon; and his 11-year-old son, D.J., are all avid dancers.

Yancey took over as caller for the Promenaders about three years ago. Rhiannon is following in his footsteps, taking her first caller class in June 2014. "I don't like calling as much as dancing, but someone has to do it," Yancey said while claiming that Rhiannon is much better than he is.

The truth is, however, that the club's membership is dwindling, and the Allisons have been trying hard to recruit new people. They are excited that another 16-year-old is planning on joining the club next season.

While part of Yancey's motivation is to preserve traditions, he mainly does it "because it's fun." He points out that square dancing has always come and gone in two to three generation cycles. "It almost died in the '20s," he said. And square dancing keeps evolving to keep up with the times. "What we do now is called 'Modern Square Dancing,' " he said. (Courtesy *Rawlins Daily Times.*)

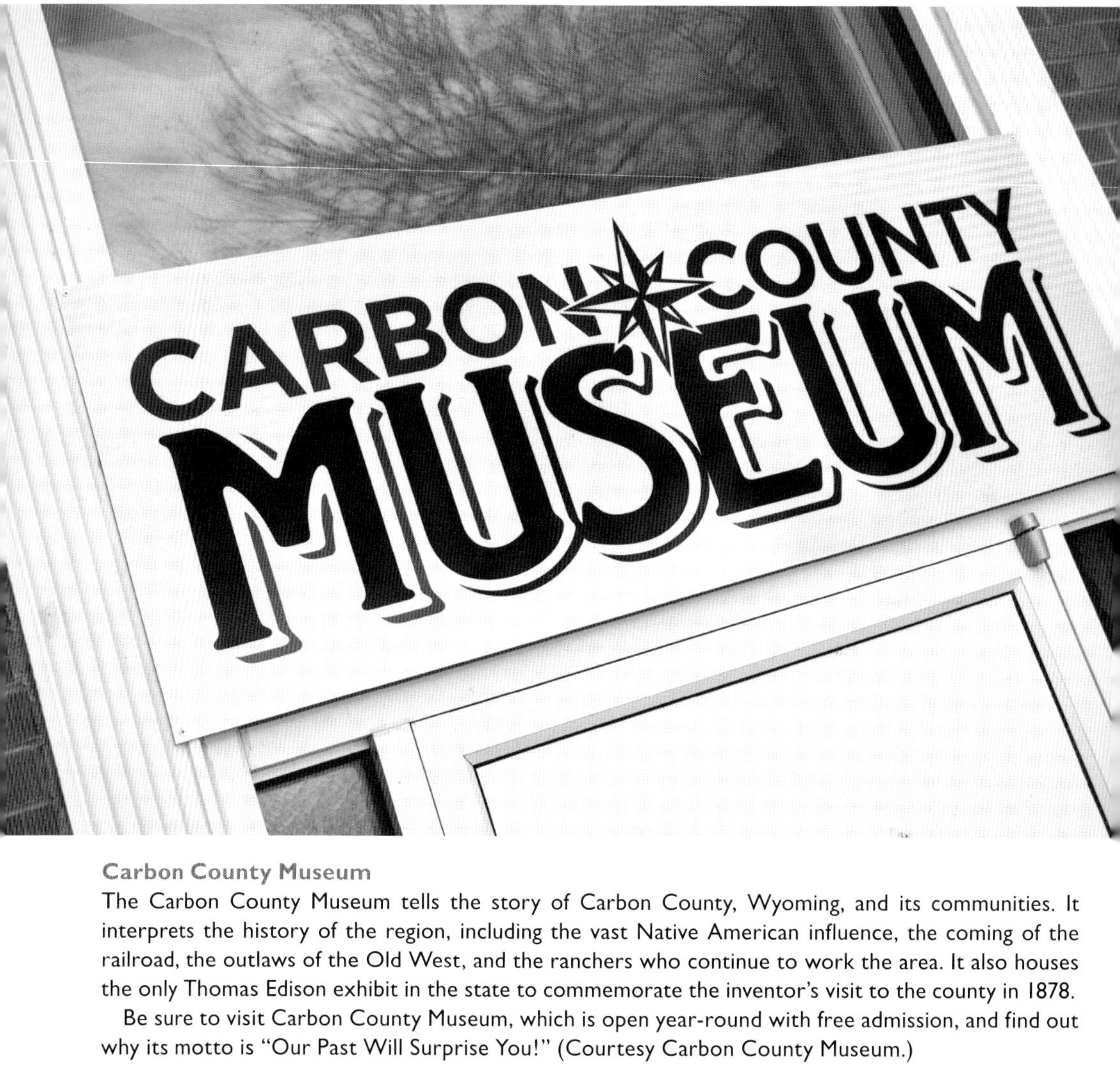

Carbon County Museum

The Carbon County Museum tells the story of Carbon County, Wyoming, and its communities. It interprets the history of the region, including the vast Native American influence, the coming of the railroad, the outlaws of the Old West, and the ranchers who continue to work the area. It also houses the only Thomas Edison exhibit in the state to commemorate the inventor's visit to the county in 1878.

Be sure to visit Carbon County Museum, which is open year-round with free admission, and find out why its motto is "Our Past Will Surprise You!" (Courtesy Carbon County Museum.)

904 West Walnut Street
Rawlins, WY 82301
307-328-2740
carboncountymuseum.org

INDEX

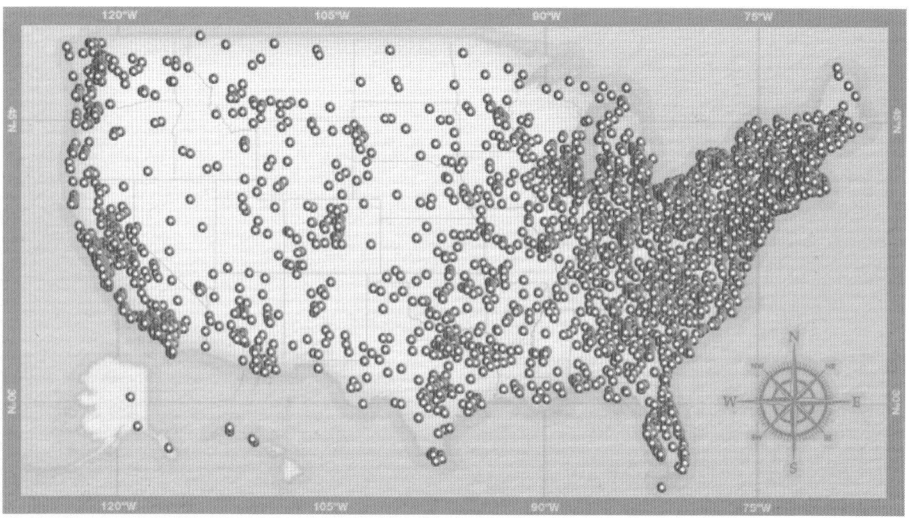